Contents

Resources for Reaching All Learners

Use with *United States History*

CHALLENGE ACTIVITIES

SUPPORT FOR LANGUAGE DEVELOPMENT

To the Teacher

If your classroom is typical of many in schools throughout the country, you have a variety of students with their own unique strengths and instructional needs. Some of your students may be struggling readers, recipients of special services, or in need of extra support to access social studies content and skills. You may have students who need to be challenged regularly. Your classroom may also have many of the increasing number of English Language Learners (ELL) who require language development and specialized teaching. *Houghton Mifflin Social Studies* addresses these subgroups of the student population and provides the resources necessary to differentiate your instruction.

Student Book includes:

- Reading Skills with Graphic Organizers that help organize information for English Language Learners and students who need extra support.

- Review questions after sections of the text that help students check their understanding.

- Hands-on and Writing Activities in Lesson Reviews to address a variety of learning styles or modalities.

- Extend Lessons for additional ways to teach important concepts through a variety of learning modalities.

- Leveled Extend Activities for extra support and challenge opportunities.

Teacher's Edition includes:

- Unit activities for Extra Support or Challenge students and English Language Learners.

- Core Lesson support for leveled instruction and strategies for teaching English Language Learners.

- Support for every Extend Lesson that includes teaching activities for all levels of learners, as well as ELL instruction.

Resources for Reaching All Learners

This booklet has three sections for meeting the needs of different types of learners:

- **Lesson Summaries** are used with Extra Support students, advanced English Language Learners, and for students who may have missed critical lessons.

- **Challenge Activities** are intended for students who can work independently on more advanced material.

- **Support for Language Development** activities address the needs of intermediate English Language Learners and other struggling learners, who might benefit from special instruction to develop their language skills.

iv

Lesson Summaries

One-page summaries highlight important concepts and details from the lessons. Each summary is written below grade level for universal access to critical social studies content. The summaries also help develop students' ability to understand the content. Before and After Reading activities direct students to circle, underline, and interact with the content as they answer review questions and identify critical vocabulary. The comprehension activities listed below can also be assigned as students read the summaries. These strategies will prompt students to interact with the summary text and foster comprehension skills.

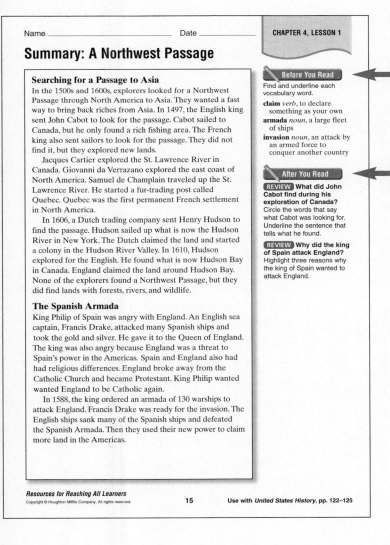

Name _____ Date _____

CHAPTER 4, LESSON 1

Summary: A Northwest Passage

Searching for a Passage to Asia

In the 1500s and 1600s, explorers looked for a Northwest Passage through North America to Asia. They wanted a fast way to bring back riches from Asia. In 1497, the English king sent John Cabot to look for the passage. Cabot sailed to Canada, but he only found a rich fishing area. The French king also sent sailors to look for the passage. They did not find it, but they explored new lands.

Jacques Cartier explored the St. Lawrence River in Canada. Giovanni da Verrazano explored the east coast of North America. Samuel de Champlain traveled up the St. Lawrence River. He started a fur-trading post called Quebec. Quebec was the first permanent French settlement in North America.

In 1606, a Dutch trading company sent Henry Hudson to find the passage. Hudson sailed up what is now the Hudson River in New York. The Dutch claimed the land and started a colony in the Hudson River Valley. In 1610, Hudson explored for the English. He found what is now Hudson Bay in Canada. England claimed the land around Hudson Bay. None of the explorers found a Northwest Passage, but they did find lands with forests, rivers, and wildlife.

The Spanish Armada

King Philip of Spain was angry with England. An English sea captain, Francis Drake, attacked many Spanish ships and took the gold and silver. He gave it to the Queen of England. The king was also angry because England was a threat to Spain's power in the Americas. Spain and England also had had religious differences. England broke away from the Catholic Church and became Protestant. King Philip wanted wanted England to be Catholic again.

In 1588, the king ordered an armada of 130 warships to attack England. Francis Drake was ready for the invasion. The English ships sank many of the Spanish ships and defeated the Spanish Armada. Then they used their new power to claim more land in the Americas.

Before You Read

Find and underline each vocabulary word.

claim *verb*, to declare something as your own

armada *noun*, a large fleet of ships

invasion *noun*, an attack by an armed force to conquer another country

After You Read

REVIEW What did John Cabot find during his exploration of Canada? Circle the words that say what Cabot was looking for. Underline the sentence that tells what he found.

REVIEW Why did the king of Spain attack England? Highlight three reasons why the king of Spain wanted to attack England.

Resources for Reaching All Learners
Copyright © Houghton Mifflin Company. All rights reserved.

15

Use with *United States History*, pp. 122–125

These sections pre-teach lesson vocabulary and prompt students to identify the terms in the context of the summaries.

Students answer the same Review questions that are in the textbook, but identify the answer by interacting with the summaries in a variety of ways, such as circling or underlining text.

As You Read Comprehension Activities

The lesson summaries can also be used to reinforce students' comprehension skills. A variety of comprehension activities can be assigned to students as they read the summaries. Some of these activities include:

- **Main Idea/Details** As students read the summaries, encourage them to circle the Main Idea of each section. After they identify the Main Idea, prompt students to review the summary and locate and number the supporting details.

- **Cause and Effect** Direct students to read the summaries and analyze them for cause-and-effect statements. Once students find these statements, prompt them to organize the information in a graphic organizer.

- **Compare and Contrast** While students are reading the summaries, prompt them to locate comparing and contrasting statements. Have students record these statements in graphic organizers or on a separate sheet of paper.

- **Sequence** Begin by having students read the entire summary. Encourage students to review the summary a second time and focus on the order in which certain events are described. Then have them identify the sequence by numbering the events in the summary text. Students can also use the Sequence Chart in the Grade Level Resources to organize their answers.

Using the Lesson Summaries

- **Build background** You can give summaries to students before teaching the Core Lesson. Use the summaries as background with the whole class, as part of a reading group, with individualized instruction, or as homework in place of reading the Core Lesson itself. The summaries provide students with the critical lesson information (lesson content and structure) they need to participate in class discussions.

- **Reinforce concepts** After teaching the Core Lesson, you may distribute the summaries to students to ensure their thorough understanding and to offer lesson reinforcement.

- **Reteach the Core Lesson** After assessing students' understanding of the lesson content, you may find the need to reteach some or all of the content to students. The summaries provide a more interactive opportunity to absorb the concepts so that all students will be prepared for the Chapter-level assessment.

- **Assess Extra Support students in a real and fair way.** Each summary includes all the information needed to answer the Core Lesson Review questions, so the informal, continuous assessment of classroom comprehension checks can be applied to Extra Support students. Lesson Tests, provided in the *Assessment Options* booklet that comes with your program, have been written so that students who have only read the Lesson Summaries can answer them. They can therefore be used with the entire class.

Use with *United States History*

Challenge Activities

These activities—two or three per chapter—are intended for students who show their understanding of the material and are ready to be challenged with independent work that develops research, writing, and other skills. Assign Challenge activities to those students for whom a particular chapter or unit is more easily mastered. Additionally, some of these activities may also work well, perhaps with some support, with English Language Learners who demonstrate conceptual understanding.

Using the Challenge Activities

These activities are for independent work. You can copy the page and let students choose which activity they are interested in completing. You can also cut the page into smaller, individual activity sheets and assign them to students based on the skills that they need to develop.

Support for Language Development

English Language Learner Support

A growing number of English Language Learners no longer have the option of waiting to master the language prior to learning content area concepts and skills. The challenge in teaching social studies to these students is to deliver the content without diluting it. The goal of ELL support is to provide *universal access to the content through differentiated paths.*

- Much of the ELL student's need is to have the abstract made concrete.

- In working with ELL students in a mainstreamed classroom, begin with instruction to all students, and then provide scaffolding to those who require additional support.

- The ELL student progresses best with adult interaction. Therefore interactive teacher support suggestions are provided.

- Good teaching—interactive, multilayered, varied—is good for all students but is *essential* for students who are learning English.

English Language Learners and *Houghton Mifflin Social Studies*

If you have English Language Learners in your classroom, you are aware that ELL students are not a monolithic group with one set of skills. Students may be at Beginning, Intermediate, and Advanced levels of language acquisition. These levels can be described in a variety of ways. In *Houghton Mifflin Social Studies,* this simple system is used to describe the different levels:

- **Beginning** students are at the earliest stage of English language acquisition and may have a much greater ability to understand English than to speak it. This is sometimes called *preproduction* or *early production.* Many of the strategies suggested in the Teacher's Edition focus on Beginning students. Beginning students should be paired with an aide, or other more English-proficient students who speak their native language, if they are successfully to use the Support for Language Development materials in this booklet.

Use with *United States History*

- **Intermediate** students are more able to comprehend and express themselves in English. This group is called *speech emergent* for that reason. The Teacher's Edition includes strategies for the Intermediate group. The Support for Language Development materials in this booklet were designed so that students can use the pages independently or with limited help.

- **Advanced** students are in the final stages of becoming fluent speakers and can be considered *transitioning* or having acquired *intermediate fluency*. This group works more independently and might help beginning students with the Support for Language Development activities in this booklet. There are advanced ELL strategies in the Teacher's Edition, and many of the Extra Support strategies can be useful. In addition, Advanced ELL students have reached the level where the Lesson Summaries in this booklet would be excellent support.

For native English-speaking students with weak vocabulary and verbal skills, use the Support for Language Development activities. These activities employ non-verbal/visual instructional strategies (i.e., visual presentations and expressions) in a variety of formats that reinforce critical social studies content. ELL students may benefit from these strategies, along with the visual approach to vocabulary instruction.

Using the Support for Language Development

The Support for Language Development worksheets can be used in these ways: for independent work, to provide limited support for intermediate English language learners, and to provide more support for Beginning students. For each lesson, students are supported in two essential areas:

- **Vocabulary**
- **Tested Objectives**

Vocabulary The social studies vocabulary taught in each lesson of *Houghton Mifflin Social Studies* identifies key concepts in the areas of History, Geography, Economics, Citizenship, and Culture. Students, especially second language learners, may find some terms to be unfamiliar. Houghton Mifflin's approach to critical vocabulary is through the use of visual strategies. All vocabulary words are pictured on the pages, and students reinforce their understanding of them by connecting the words, the visuals, and their meanings in a variety of ways. You can use these worksheets to create an illustrated glossary that students may refer to as they develop their language skills.

Tested Objectives This section covers one or more of the lesson's tested objectives and enables students to focus on the most relevant factual matter and the most important ideas in the lesson. Students will complete a variety of activities that include fill-in-the-blanks, directed questions, and graphic organizers that help in the acquisition and connection of information.

Summary: Land and Climate

A Varied Land

To understand the United States, we must learn geography. Geographers ask where a place is and what it is like. They want to know how the land affects people, and how people affect the land. Geography helps us understand our past, present, and future.

There are many different landforms in the United States. The Sierra Nevada Mountains and the Coast Ranges are near the Pacific coast. The Basin and Range area is to the east of these mountains. This region has many high mountains and plateaus. A plateau is a high, steep-sided area rising above the land. Rivers running over plateaus have worn away rock to make canyons like those at Bryce Canyon National Park.

Further east are the Rocky Mountains. East of the Rockies are wide, flat plains that slope toward a valley in the middle of the country. The Mississippi River is in the center of this huge valley. East of the Mississippi, the Central Plains rise again to the Appalachian Mountains. These mountains go from Maine to Alabama. East of the Appalachians is the Atlantic Coastal Plain, which meets the Atlantic Ocean.

Climate

The United States has many climates. Climate is the type of weather a place has over a long period of time. It includes temperature and how much rain, snow, or sleet falls. The southern part of the country is usually warmer than the northern part. The closer a place is to the equator, the warmer it is.

Landforms affect climate. Lower places are usually warmer than places high in the mountains. Plants and trees also affect climate. Their leaves release water and make shade. A place with many plants or trees has a cooler temperature.

Before You Read

Find and underline each vocabulary word.

geography *noun,* the study of the world and the people and things that live there

landform *noun,* a feature on the surface of the land

plateau *noun,* a high, steep-sided area rising above the surrounding land

climate *noun,* the type of weather a place has over a long period of time

equator *noun,* the imaginary line around the middle of the Earth

After You Read

REVIEW **What questions do geographers ask?**
Underline two sentences that tell the answer.

REVIEW **What is climate?**
Circle the sentence that tells the answer.

Name _____ Date _____

Summary: Our Nation's Resources

Natural Resources

Many things we eat, wear, or use come from nature. Gasoline comes from oil found underground. Cars are made of iron ore from mines. Water to drink, air to breathe, and soil and sun for farming also come from nature. Without nature, humans could not survive.

Some resources are renewable. Trees are cut down for wood to make paper, furniture, or other things. New trees can be planted to replace the trees cut, so they are a renewable resource.

Oil and coal are mineral resources from the earth. They give us energy to heat our homes, cook our food, and run our cars. They cannot be replaced. They are nonrenewable.

Wind and water are flow resources. They can only be used at a certain time or place. For example, people can only use wind when it is blowing.

Other Important Resources

It takes many steps to turn natural resources into things we use. Capital resources are tools, such as tractors, computers, or other machines. Human resources are the skills and knowledge of the people doing the work. Without people, nothing would get done.

If many people want a product but there aren't enough for all of them, it is called scarcity. Sometimes people have to decide what they want most. If you can buy either a jacket or sneakers, but not both, you must choose one. The one you give up is the opportunity cost.

People need to be careful using resources so that there will be enough for the future. Everyone can practice conservation to use our natural resources wisely. Companies can use containers made from materials that can be recycled, such as metal or cardboard. People can recycle paper, cans, and bottles and not waste water, gas, and electricity.

Before You Read

Find and underline each vocabulary word.

capital resource *noun,* a tool, machine, or building people use to produce goods and services

human resource *noun,* a person and the skills and knowledge he or she brings to the job

scarcity *noun,* not having as much of something as people want

opportunity cost *noun,* the thing you give up when you decide to do or have something else

conservation *noun,* the protection and wise use of natural resources

After You Read

REVIEW What is the difference between renewable and nonrenewable resources? Highlight a sentence that describes each kind of resource.

REVIEW What is the difference between capital resources and human resources? Draw a box around the sentence that tells what capital resources are. Circle the sentence that tells what human resources are.

REVIEW Why do people practice conservation? Circle the sentences that tell the answer.

Summary: Regions of the United States

What Is a Region?

The United States can be divided into regions. States that are close to one another can be included in a region. The United States can be divided into four regions: Northeast, South, Midwest, and West. States in a region often share landforms. The Midwestern states have wide plains and few mountains. The West has many mountains.

The United States can also be divided into political regions, such as states. Regions can also be divided by climate. Another way to divide the country is by common activities, such as the work people do, or a common custom or language. For example, the Dairy Belt is a region that raises cows that produce a lot of milk. It includes parts of the Midwest and Northeast.

People's ideas about regions can change. The Great Plains region used to be called a desert, but today it has many farms.

Regions and Resources

Regions can also be grouped by the resources they have. For example, the Appalachian Mountain region has a lot of coal. Resources are important for a region's economy. The resources in a region help people decide what crops to grow and what goods to produce.

When a region makes a lot of one product, it is called specialization. In the South, the climate and soil are good for growing cotton. This can be made into clothing. In North Dakota, the climate is better for growing wheat.

Trade between regions lets consumers all over the country buy goods they want or need. Countries also specialize in producing goods. They trade for goods made in other countries. For example, the United States buys oil from Mexico and sells cars to Mexico. Trade connects businesses around the world.

Find and underline each vocabulary word.

region *noun,* an area that has one or more features in common

economy *noun,* the system people use to produce goods and services

specialization *noun,* the result of people making the goods they are best able to produce with the resources they have

consumer *noun,* someone who buys goods and services

trade *noun,* the buying and selling of goods

After You Read

REVIEW **What are the different ways the United States can be divided into regions?** Circle the sentences that tell different ways of dividing the country into regions.

REVIEW **Why do people in regions trade with each other?** Highlight the sentence that tells why there is trade between regions.

Summary: People and the Land

How Land Affects People

Geography affects how cities grow. San Diego, California, is one of the largest cities in the United States. It has a big harbor on the Pacific Ocean. Shipping and trade helped San Diego grow. It has the location and resources that allow many people to live there.

Denver, Colorado, began to grow when gold and silver were found nearby. Businesses opened when more people came to work in the mines. The city grew as its economy grew.

People live where they can find jobs. Others live in places because they like the environment. Geography affects what people do for fun. In mountainous places, people ski in the winter and hike in the summer. In warm places, people waterski.

Changing the Land

Natural forces, such as wind and water, change the land slowly over time. The Colorado River has carved the Grand Canyon through erosion. Water and wind can also form new land. Soil that is washed away or blown away can collect in another place. Much of Louisiana was formed by soil the Mississippi River carried there.

Humans also change the land. Some human activities make things easier for people. They can also hurt the environment or change how it is used. Highways make travel easier, but then the land can no longer be farmed. Mines provide jobs and mineral resources, but the chemicals used can cause pollution. This can make the environment unsafe for fish, wildlife, and people.

All parts of an ecosystem are connected. People can change an ecosystem without knowing it. Zebra mussels attached themselves to ships. The ships carried the mussels to the Great Lakes from a different ecosystem. Now, they have spread throughout the Great Lakes. The mussels clog pipes and eat food that local fish depend on. Today, people are more aware of the way their activities change the environment.

Before You Read

Find and underline each vocabulary word.

environment *noun,* the surroundings in which people, plants, and animals live

erosion *noun,* the process by which water and wind wear away the land

pollution *noun,* anything that makes the soil, air, or water dirty and unhealthy

ecosystem *noun,* a community of plants and animals along with the surrounding soil, air, and water

After You Read

REVIEW **In what ways did San Diego's location cause it to grow?** Which two industries helped San Diego grow? Which geographical feature made this possible? Circle the words that tell the answers.

REVIEW **What is one example of how natural forces can change the land?** Draw a box around the sentences that tell how the Grand Canyon and Louisiana were formed.

4
Use with *United States History,* pp. 28–31

Summary: Ancient Americans

People Arrive in the Americas

During the Ice Age much of the world's water was frozen in glaciers. The ocean floor between Alaska and Asia was a grassy land bridge. Many scientists think people followed migrating animal herds across it. Migration stopped about 10,000 years ago when the glaciers melted and the seas rose. People who had crossed from Asia, called Paleo-Indians, spread out over North and South America. They are the ancestors of modern American Indians.

Civilizations Develop

Early Paleo-Indians hunted big animals. About 11,000 years ago the big animals began to die out. People learned new ways to get food. They hunted smaller animals, fished, and gathered wild plants.

About 9,000 years ago some Paleo-Indians began to use agriculture. Scientists think people in present-day Mexico grew the first crops of corn, beans, and squash. People's lives changed as they stopped migrating to grow crops. More people survived because of the supply of food.

Paleo-Indians farmed and built villages and cities. The Adena, Hopewell, and Mississippians were Mound Builders. They built giant earth mounds and large villages in North America. Their civilization lasted for about 2,500 years.

The Ancient Pueblo civilization lived in the Southwest region for about 800 years. The Ancient Pueblo built big buildings made of stone with many rooms. The Ancient Pueblo also built underground rooms, called kivas, used for religious ceremonies. Around 1300, the Ancient Pueblo left their villages. No one knows why they left.

The Aztec civilization controlled Central Mexico around 1300 and was strong for 200 years. American Indian groups developed civilizations in almost every region of North America.

Before You Read

Find and underline each vocabulary word.

glacier *noun*, a huge, thick sheet of slowly moving ice

migration *noun*, movement from one region to another

agriculture *noun*, farming, or growing plants

civilization *noun*, a group of people living together with organized systems of government, religion, and culture

pueblo *noun*, the Spanish word for town

After You Read

REVIEW **According to scientists, how did people first come to North America?** Circle the sentences that tell how scientists think people came to North America.

REVIEW **Where did the mound building civilizations live?** Underline the sentence that tells you the answer.

REVIEW **What were kivas?** Highlight the sentence that tells how kivas were used.

Summary: Peoples of the Northwest

The Pacific Northwest

The Pacific Northwest region stretches from Alaska to northern California. It lies between the Pacific Ocean on the west and the mountains to the east. There are many islands and bays. Thick forests cover much of the land. American Indians who lived in the area around 1500 got everything they needed from the land and water. On land they gathered berries and fern roots. They hunted deer, geese, elks, and bears. One key resource was salmon. They caught so much salmon that the surplus was dried to eat during the year. They also ate seals, whales, and shellfish. The forests were another important resource. People made houses from wood and decorated them with carvings. They used cedar logs to make totem poles and placed them in front of their houses. The tall poles told the history of families who lived there. Canoes were also carved from cedar and used to carry goods. On important occasions, families held potlatches. Families demonstrated their wealth by giving gifts to the rest of the community.

The Tlingit

The Tlingit (KLINK-it) were one of the largest American Indian groups in the Pacific Northwest. They lived near the coast or on rivers. They shredded bark to make clothes. In cold weather they wore animal skins.

The Tlingit society is divided into clans. A clan is a group of related families. Strict rules told people how to act toward other clans. Several families from the same clan lived together in big houses. Each family had its own area. Families gathered by a central fire to talk and cook. During the winter, people stayed inside. They had time then to weave, carve, paint, and sew. They held ceremonies and potlatches.

About 17,000 Tlingit live in southeastern Alaska now. Their clans and traditions are strong. They still have potlatches for important occasions.

Before You Read

Find and underline each vocabulary word.

surplus *adjective*, extra

potlatch *noun*, large feast that lasts for days

clan *noun*, group of related families

After You Read

REVIEW What two important resources helped the Northwest Indians live? Underline the words that tell where the Indian people in the Northwest got the things they needed. Highlight two important resources.

REVIEW How were clans important to the Tlingit? Draw a box around the words that say what a clan is. Underline the sentence that tells how clans influenced how people lived.

Use with *United States History*, pp. 46–49

Summary: Peoples of the Southwest

The Southwest

The Southwest region includes New Mexico and Arizona, and parts of Utah, Nevada, Colorado, Texas, southern California, and northern Mexico. The Southwest is mostly low, flat desert or desert on high plateaus. There are some mountains and deep canyons. There is almost no rain and the land is very dry. Streams are fed by snow melting in the mountains. There are few trees.

Native Americans in the Southwest built houses of sticks, stones, and clay called adobe. They built their homes on top of steep mesas to keep them safe from attacks. They planted their corn deep in the ground so the roots could get moisture from the earth. They developed irrigation to water their crops in order to get good harvests. They also planted crops on land that was flooded in the spring.

The Hopi

The Hopi have lived in the Southwest for hundreds of years. They are Pueblo Indians. Early Hopi used irrigation to grow corn, beans, and squash. Corn was the staple food. Hopi grew red, blue, yellow, white, and purple corn. They grew enough to store so it would last all year. They also made clay pottery. They were among the first people to fire pottery. Firing pottery with coal makes the clay hard and strong.

Through their religion the Hopi acted as caretakers of the land. They believed that when the land is healthy, the harvest would be good. Throughout the year the Hopi prayed and held ceremonies as part of taking care of the land. For instance, at a ceremony called the Bean Dance, the Hopi danced and prayed for a good harvest.

Modern Hopi follow many traditions of their culture. They continue to take part in ceremonies. Visitors are sometimes allowed to watch. Many Hopi are skilled at traditional pottery, weaving, and jewelry making. Others hold jobs, are teachers, or run their own businesses.

Before You Read

Find and underline each vocabulary word.

irrigation *noun,* supplying water to crops using streams, ditches, or pipes

staple *noun*, main crop that is used for food

ceremony *noun*, special event at which people gather to express important beliefs

After You Read

REVIEW **Why was irrigation necessary for the Southwest Indians?** Highlight the sentence that describes the climate of the region.

REVIEW **What is the Bean Dance?** Underline the sentence that tells you the answer.

Use with *United States History*, pp. 54–57

Summary: Peoples of the Plains

The Great Plains

The Great Plains stretch from the Mississippi River to the Rocky Mountains, and from Texas into Canada. They used to be grassland. In the east, where there was more rain, the grass grew eight feet high. In the west, where the land was drier, the grasses were shorter.

American Indians have lived on the Plains for thousands of years. Their most important resource was the great herds of buffalo that used to roam the Plains. The Pawnee and Omaha farmed the Eastern Plains. They lived in villages near rivers and built earth lodges. In the spring and fall they worked their farms. In the winter and summer they hunted buffalo. American Indians used all parts of the buffalo. They ate the meat and used the skins for teepee covers, blankets, clothing, drums, and shields. Buffalo bones were carved to make tools. Buffalo hair was used for rope.

Plains Indians decorated their belongings with paint and porcupine quills. The dry Western Plains were not good farmland. The Western Plains Indians were nomads. They followed the herds of buffalo, carrying their belongings from place to place on travois. The Lakota once farmed the Eastern Plains, but they fought with the Ojibwa. The Lakota migrated west and became nomads.

The Comanche

Spanish explorers brought horses to North America in the 1500s. Horses made it easier to hunt, travel, and fight. The Comanche moved to the Great Plains in the 1600s. By the 1700s they had spread across what is now Texas and Oklahoma. They were nomads and fierce warriors. They controlled a large area of the Plains.

The Comanche nation was divided into smaller groups that lived and hunted together. Each group chose war and peace chiefs. The chiefs met to discuss issues that affected all Comanche. About 8,500 Comanche live in the United States now. They have their own government and continue to value their traditions.

Before You Read

Find and underline each vocabulary word.

lodge *noun,* a house made of bark, earth, and grass

nomad *noun,* a person who moves around and does not live in one place

travois *noun,* similar to a sled, used by nomads to carry their possessions

After You Read

REVIEW **In what ways were the lives of the Eastern and Western Plains Indians different?** Circle the names of the Indian nations that lived in the Eastern Plains. Highlight the sentences that describe how they lived. Then draw a box around the name of Indians who lived on the Western Plains. Highlight the words that describe how they lived.

REVIEW **Why were horses important to Western Plains Indians?** Circle the sentence that tells how horses helped the Plains Indians.

Resources for Reaching All Learners
8
Use with *United States History,* pp. 60–63

Summary: Peoples of the East

The Eastern Woodlands

The Eastern Woodlands stretched from the Atlantic coast to the Mississippi River and from the Gulf of Mexico to the Great Lakes. It had plenty of rain and was rich in natural resources. There were many sources of food. Forests covered the region. Many American Indian nations lived in the mountains, valleys, and plains. They hunted deer, bears, and rabbits. They made syrup from the sap of maple trees.

Near the Great Lakes American Indians gathered wild rice. Most were also farmers. Their staple crops, called the "three sisters," were corn, beans, and squash. Woodland Indians made houses appropriate to the climate. In the warm south, houses could have no walls, just roofs for shade and protection from rain. They wore light clothing woven from grasses. In the cold north, Woodland Indians built longhouses. Many families lived together in a longhouse. They wore warm deerskin clothing.

The Haudenosaunee

Five Haudenosaunee nations stopped warring and formed a confederation between 1100 and 1600. The confederation, known as the Haudenosaunee League, included Mohawks, Oneidas, Onondagas, Cayugas, and Senecas. Later, the Tuscarora joined. The Haudenosaunee, also called the Iroquois, lived in clans. Clan mothers, who were the oldest women in the clan, chose chiefs. The League was governed by chiefs from each nation. To make a decision, all of the chiefs had to agree. They discussed issues until they reached agreement.

The Haudenosaunee traded with other American Indians. They used wampum to symbolize agreements and show important events. When the Europeans came into the region they bartered furs for blankets and knives. More than 50,000 Haudenosaunee live in North America now. Some live in their homelands in Canada and New York State. Some live in cities. Many follow traditional customs and ceremonies. Some Mohawks are steelworkers. They helped build landmarks such as the Empire State Building and the Golden Gate Bridge.

Before You Read

Find and underline each vocabulary word.

longhouse *noun,* a large house made with wooden poles and bark

confederation *noun,* a type of government in which separate groups of people join together, but local leaders make most decisions for their group

wampum *noun,* carefully shaped and cut seashells strung like beads

barter *noun,* exchange of goods without using money

After You Read

REVIEW **What were the three sisters?** Circle the sentence that tells about the three sisters.

REVIEW **Why did the Haudenosaunee use wampum?** Circle the sentence that tells how the Haudenosaunee used wampum.

Summary: World Travel and Trade

Trade with China

Before 1500, there was almost no contact between the Eastern and Western hemispheres. Most people in Europe, Asia, and Africa did not know the Americas existed. Often, merchants were the first to travel to distant places looking for new goods to trade.

In 1271, Marco Polo traveled from Italy to China. He wrote a book about his adventures. He told about a trade route that connected Europe and China. It was called the Silk Road. He described inventions, such as paper, printing, and gunpowder. Merchants became rich by bringing silks, spices, and other goods to Europe.

In 1405, the Chinese began exploring and trading with people in distant places. Admiral Zheng He sailed with hundreds of ships throughout Southeast Asia to the east coast of Africa. In 1434, the new ruler of China stopped all Chinese exploration.

African Trading Kingdoms

People in Africa also traded. Some West African kingdoms became powerful through trade. In the 700s, Ghana was rich in gold but did not have enough salt. Salt was used to keep food from spoiling. Merchants from Arabia crossed the Sahara in big caravans to trade salt for gold.

Arab merchants taught people in Ghana about their religion, Islam. Many people in Ghana became followers of Islam. In 1234, the kingdom of Mali conquered Ghana. Mali's cities became new trade centers. One of its most important cities was Timbuktu. In 1324, Mali's ruler, Mansa Musa, traveled to Mecca. Mecca was the most holy city in Arabia. He set up trading agreements.

When he returned to Mali, he brought scholars and artists from Arabia with him. They made Timbuktu an important center for learning and art. In 1468, a new kingdom called Songhai took over most of Mali. The kingdom grew weaker after Mansa Musa's rule, but trade continued for over a hundred years.

Before You Read

Find and underline each vocabulary word.

merchant *noun,* someone who buys and sells goods to earn money

kingdom *noun,* a place ruled by a king or queen

caravan *noun,* a group of people and animals who travel together

After You Read

REVIEW What was the importance of the Silk Road? The Silk Road connected Europe to which country? Underline the sentence that tells you the answer.

REVIEW What effect did trade with North Africa have on Ghana's culture? What did Arab merchants teach the people of Ghana? What did the people of Ghana convert to? Highlight the sentences that tell the answer.

Summary: New Ideas in Europe

The Renaissance

Many changes took place in Europe in the 1300s and 1400s. This period was called the Renaissance, which means rebirth. People explored the ideas of ancient Greeks, Romans, and other peoples.

Learning led to new technology. The printing press was developed in 1454. Before then people copied books by hand. A printing press could print a page of type quickly. More books were made, and new ideas spread widely and rapidly.

New ideas also changed navigation. North Africans taught Europeans to use the astrolabe. It told them how far north or south they were. The Chinese taught Europeans to use a compass. It allowed sailors to steer without seeing stars or sun.

Gunpowder was another Chinese invention. Europeans used it in guns and cannons. They felt they could protect themselves if they were attacked when exploring new places.

A Sea Route to Asia

Europeans were eager to trade with Asia. Merchants could make big profits selling Asian goods, such as spices and silk. People in Europe loved spices like pepper.

Europeans knew a sea route would be faster than the Silk Road. In Portugal, Prince Henry started a navigation school to encourage explorers. Mapmakers, shipbuilders, and sea captains worked together to share their knowledge. They designed and built faster ships that were good for exploring.

Portuguese traders exploring the coast of West Africa captured Africans and forced them into slavery. Enslaved people were sold in Europe.

In 1487, Bartolomeu Dias was blown off course by a storm. His ship reached the eastern side of Africa. The Portuguese named the tip of Africa the Cape of Good Hope. They knew then that they could sail around Africa to get to Asia. In 1497, Vasco da Gama first took that route to India. Portuguese ships soon used the route to trade spices.

Before You Read

Find and underline each vocabulary word.

technology *noun*, the use of scientific knowledge and tools to do things better and more rapidly.

navigation *noun*, the science of planning and controlling the direction of a ship

astrolabe *noun*, a navigation tool that measures the height of the sun or a star against the horizon

profit *noun*, money left after all expenses have been paid

slavery *noun*, a cruel system in which people are bought and sold and made to work without pay

After You Read

REVIEW **What did new technology do to make exploration easier?** Underline the sentence that tells why a compass was useful. Highlight the sentence that tells why Europeans liked guns.

REVIEW **Why was sailing around the Cape of Good Hope important?** Underline the sentence that tells why Europeans wanted to find a sea route to Asia.

Summary: Europeans Arrive in the Americas

Christopher Columbus

Christopher Columbus believed he could reach Asia by sailing west across the Atlantic Ocean. He asked King Ferdinand and Queen Isabella of Spain to pay for the trip. They were at war with North African Muslims. These North Africans had ruled southern Spain for 700 years. The Spanish rulers needed the money to pay for the war. They hoped Columbus would find riches. They also wanted to tell people about Roman Catholicism. Columbus landed on an island in the present-day Bahamas. He thought it was close to India. He called the peaceful Taíno people who lived there Indians.

The Columbian Exchange

The Spanish rulers wanted Columbus to start a settlement and look for gold. His ships carried horses, cows, pigs, wheat, barley, and sugar cane. These animals and plants were new to the Americas. The Spanish also carried new diseases. People died in epidemics. Most of the Taíno died. The settlement destroyed many plants and animals. Columbus took home new foods, including potatoes, corn, beans, peanuts, and cacao. This movement of plants and animals between Europe, Asia, Africa, and the Americas is called the Columbian Exchange. Potatoes became an important food in Europe.

Exploration Continues

Other European rulers soon sent their own explorers to the Americas to claim lands and find riches. Pedro Alvares Cabral claimed eastern South America for Portugal in 1500. In 1513, de Balboa saw the Pacific Ocean from Panama. Ferdinand Magellan tried to circumnavigate the Earth. He named the ocean Pacific, which means peaceful, because it looked so calm. Magellan was killed, but his crew was the first to sail around the world.

Before You Read

Find and underline each vocabulary word.

settlement *noun,* a small community of people living in a new place

epidemic *noun,* an outbreak of a disease that spreads quickly and affects many people

circumnavigate *verb,* to sail completely around something

After You Read

REVIEW **Why did Ferdinand and Isabella finally agree to give Columbus money for his voyage in 1492?** Highlight the sentences that tell two reasons Ferdinand and Isabella wanted to pay for Columbus's explorations.

REVIEW **How did the Columbian Exchange change the diet of Europeans?** Underline the words that tell which food became important in Europe.

REVIEW **Who named the Pacific Ocean and why?** Circle the name of the explorer. Highlight the sentence that tells the answer.

Summary: Conquest of the Americas

Cortés Conquers the Aztecs

European rulers wanted explorers to find riches to bring back to Europe. Hernán Cortés led an expedition to Mexico in 1519. His ships carried 600 conquistadors with horses and weapons. They wanted fame and riches. Cortés had heard about the Aztecs. The Aztecs ruled an empire that covered much of present-day Mexico. Its capital city, Tenochtitlán, was beautiful and huge. It was twice as big as any European city. The Aztec ruler, Moctezuma, welcomed Cortés, but Moctezuma soon sent the Spaniards away. The conquistadors were greedy for gold. Cortés got help from neighboring Indian nations that had been conquered by the Aztecs. His soldiers had horses, guns, and armor, and the Aztecs did not. Smallpox made the Aztecs weak. Cortés defeated them. In 1535, Spain controlled the Aztec empire and named it New Spain. After Cortés, conquistadors explored Central and South America to find gold and treasure. Pizarro conquered the Inca empire in South America in the 1530s.

Exploring North America

Conquistadors went north looking for gold. Juan Ponce de León claimed present-day Florida for Spain in 1513. He was looking for a "fountain of youth." A legend said it would make an old person young again. Spain sent de Soto to search for gold in the area beyond Florida in 1539. He traveled as far as the Mississippi River. He found no gold. The conquistadors fought against and enslaved the American Indians they met. In 1540, Francisco Vásquez de Coronado and his men traveled 3,500 miles looking for gold. Spanish explorers were the first Europeans to see most of North America. They learned about the geography and peoples of the region.

Before You Read

Find and underline each vocabulary word.

expedition *noun,* a journey to achieve a goal

conquistador *noun,* Spanish word for conqueror

empire *noun,* many nations or territories ruled by a single group or leader

After You Read

REVIEW **Why did people inside the Aztec empire help Cortés defeat the Aztecs?** Highlight the sentence that tells why some Indian nations helped Cortés fight Moctezuma.

REVIEW **What did the Spanish hope to find in the lands north of Mexico?** Underline the words that tell why conquistadors made expeditions to the north. Circle the names of the leaders of the expeditions.

Use with *United States History,* **pp. 104–107**

Summary: New Spain

New Spain Grows

By the 1570s, Spain ruled Mexico as a colony. Spanish settlers farmed and built mines to find gold and silver. Soon more Spanish soldiers, government officials, and priests came. Over the next 200 years, the soldiers and priests traveled north and started missions. Priests wanted to convert American Indians to Roman Catholicism. Other European nations sent explorers and settlers to the Americas. The Spanish wanted to stop these nations from claiming land. They built forts called presidios to protect Spanish claims and guard against attacks. In 1565, Pedro Menéndez de Avilés started St. Augustine in Florida. It was the first town built in the present-day United States by Europeans. In 1598, Don Juan de Oñate started a settlement at Santa Fe, New Mexico. In 1769, a priest named Junípero Serra founded missions on the California coast.

Life in New Spain

The Spanish did not find much gold in North America. They started farms called haciendas to make money. They forced American Indians to work on farms and in mines. Many Indians died from overwork and bad treatment. A priest, Bartolomé de las Casas, spoke out against this bad treatment. Most settlers ignored him. Later, the Spanish imported enslaved Africans to replace the many American Indians who died. Most of the enslaved Africans worked on sugar cane plantations in the Caribbean colonies. By 1650, about 130,000 enslaved Africans and their descendants had been brought to New Spain. Some American Indians moved to missions, converted to the Spanish religion, and learned to speak Spanish. Others refused. In 1680, Pueblo Indian leader Popé led a revolt against the Spanish in New Mexico. They killed hundreds of Spanish and kept the Spanish out of the area until 1692. Then Spanish soldiers reconquered the area.

Before You Read

Find and underline each vocabulary word.

colony *noun,* a territory ruled by another country

mission *noun,* a religious community where priests teach Christianity

convert *verb,* to change a religion or a belief

hacienda *noun,* a large farm or ranch, often with its own church and village

revolt *noun,* a violent uprising against a ruler

After You Read

REVIEW **Why did the Spanish build presidios in New Spain?** Highlight the sentence that describes the Spanish forts.

REVIEW **What did some American Indians do when they moved to Spanish missions?** Highlight the sentence that gives the answer.

Summary: A Northwest Passage

Searching for a Passage to Asia

In the 1500s and 1600s, explorers looked for a Northwest Passage through North America to Asia. They wanted a fast way to bring back riches from Asia. In 1497, the English king sent John Cabot to look for the passage. Cabot sailed to Canada, but he only found a rich fishing area. The French king also sent sailors to look for the passage. They did not find it, but they explored new lands.

Jacques Cartier explored the St. Lawrence River in Canada. Giovanni da Verrazano explored the east coast of North America. Samuel de Champlain traveled up the St. Lawrence River. He started a fur-trading post called Quebec. Quebec was the first permanent French settlement in North America.

In 1606, a Dutch trading company sent Henry Hudson to find the passage. Hudson sailed up what is now the Hudson River in New York. The Dutch claimed the land and started a colony in the Hudson River Valley. In 1610, Hudson explored for the English. He found what is now Hudson Bay in Canada. England claimed the land around Hudson Bay. None of the explorers found a Northwest Passage, but they did find lands with forests, rivers, and wildlife.

Spain and England

King Philip of Spain was angry with England. An English sea captain, Francis Drake, attacked many Spanish ships and took the gold and silver. He gave it to the Queen of England. The king was also angry because England was a threat to Spain's power in the Americas. Spain and England also had had religious differences. England broke away from the Catholic Church and became Protestant. King Philip wanted wanted England to be Catholic again.

In 1588, the king ordered an armada of 130 warships to attack England. Francis Drake was ready for the invasion. The English ships sank many of the Spanish ships and defeated the Spanish Armada. Then they used their new power to claim more land in the Americas.

Before You Read

Find and underline each vocabulary word.

claim *verb*, to declare something as your own

armada *noun*, a large fleet of ships

invasion *noun*, an attack by an armed force to conquer another country

After You Read

REVIEW What did John Cabot find during his exploration of Canada? Circle the words that say what Cabot was looking for. Underline the sentence that tells what he found.

REVIEW Why did the king of Spain attack England? Highlight three reasons why the king of Spain wanted to attack England.

Summary: Roanoke and Jamestown

The Lost Colony

The English wanted a colony in North America. They wanted to find gold and silver there. In 1585, about 100 English men arrived in Roanoke Island, near North Carolina. In 1587, more settlers came to Roanoke. Their leader, John White, returned to England to buy supplies. When he returned to Roanoke, the colonists were gone. No one ever found them.

The Jamestown Colony

In 1606, English merchants started the Virginia Company. They wanted to build a settlement in North America. The king gave the company a charter for their colony. The merchants asked people to invest in the company. If the colonists found treasure, the people who bought stock would make money.

In 1607, more than 100 men and boys sailed to present-day Virginia. They named their colony Jamestown. The settlers looked for gold. They did not know how to farm. Jamestown was damp and hot. The insects carried diseases. The water wasn't good for drinking, and the settlers ran out of food. Many died from hunger and disease.

John Smith, a new leader, ordered the men to stop looking for gold and plant crops. Life was hard in Jamestown. In 1609, most of the colonists died in the winter. It was known as the "starving time."

In 1612, a settler named John Rolfe found that tobacco grew well in Jamestown. Soon tobacco became a cash crop. Settlers sold tobacco to England. They bought food and supplies from England. In 1619, the first women and Africans arrived. The first Africans probably came as indentured servants.

Powhatan Indians also lived in the area. The Powhatans saw that the English wanted their land. They fought. The two sides made peace when John Rolfe married Pocohantas, daughter of the Powhatan leader. The peace was short. The English tried to take more Powhatan land. They fought again. In 1646, the English killed many of the Powhatan and took control of most of their land.

Before You Read

Find and underline each vocabulary word.

charter *noun*, a document giving permission to a person or group to do something

invest *verb*, to put money into something to try to earn more money

stock *noun*, a piece of ownership of a company

cash crop *noun*, a crop that people grow and sell to earn money

indentured servant *noun*, someone who agreed to work for a number of years in exchange for the cost of the voyage to North America

After You Read

REVIEW **Why did the Jamestown colonists run out of food?** Underline the sentence that tells the answer.

REVIEW **Why did colonists in Jamestown fight the Powhatans?** Highlight the words that say what the English wanted.

Summary: New England Settlements

The Plymouth Colony

People called Separatists were unhappy with the Church of England. They decided to *separate* and start their own church. This was against English law. One Separatist group called Pilgrims went to the Netherlands for religious freedom. They practiced their religion freely in the Netherlands, but they wanted an entire community based on their religious beliefs. The Virginia Company of London agreed to let the Pilgrims build a community in the colony of Virginia.

In 1620, about 100 Pilgrims sailed across the Atlantic on the *Mayflower*. Bad weather blew the ship to Cape Cod, in Massachusetts. The Pilgrims built their settlement near there and named it Plymouth. The Virginia Company did not control Massachusetts, so the Pilgrims wrote a plan for their own government. They called it the Mayflower Compact. In it, the Pilgrims agreed to make laws for the good of the colony and to obey them.

Life was hard. The Pilgrims arrived in November. It was too late in the year to plant crops. They did not have enough food, and many colonists died in the winter. In the spring, a Wampanoag man named Squanto showed the Pilgrims how to plant crops, and how to hunt and fish. In the fall, the Pilgrims and Wampanoags celebrated to give thanks for the Pilgrims' first harvest. This feast is remembered during Thanksgiving.

Massachusetts Bay Colony

The Puritans were another religious group that did not agree with the Church of England. The Puritans wanted to build a community based on their religious beliefs. In 1630, the Puritans landed in Salem, Massachusetts. They decided to settle in present-day Boston. They named their colony the Massachusetts Bay Colony, after the Massachuset Indians.

The Puritans were better prepared than the Pilgrims. They arrived in June and planted crops. By the 1640s, 20,000 Puritans settled in the area. The area was called New England because so many people from England lived there.

Before You Read

Find and underline each vocabulary word.

pilgrim *noun*, a person who makes a long journey for religious reasons

compact *noun*, an agreement

cape *noun*, a strip of land that stretches into a body of water

After You Read

REVIEW **Why did the Pilgrims leave the Netherlands for North America?** Underline the sentence that tells the answer.

REVIEW **How did Squanto help the Plymouth Colony succeed?** Highlight the sentence that tells what Squanto taught the Pilgrims.

Use with *United States History*, pp. 136–139

Summary: A Nation at War

North Against South

Eleven southern states left the Union and formed the Confederacy. Four border states stayed in the Union. The North wanted to keep the Union together. They planned to stop the Confederacy from trading with other nations. They would attack the South from the East and West at the same time. The North had more people, more factories, and more railroads. The South planned to fight off northern attacks until the Confederacy could survive as a nation. The South had good military leaders. They hoped France and Britain would help because these countries needed southern cotton. Most of the war was in the South, so Confederate soldiers knew the land. Both sides thought they could win quickly. In July 1861, at the Battle of Bull Run they learned the war might last a long time.

The War's Leaders

Robert E. Lee led the Confederate army. He stopped the Union army from capturing Richmond. He invaded the North. The Union army stopped him at Antietam in September 1862. There were at least 23,000 casualties in one day. Union General Ulysses S. Grant captured Confederate forts in the West and defeated the Confederates at Shiloh. Because the ports were blocked, the South was low on food, weapons, and money. The Confederacy had to draft soldiers. In the North, rich people could pay to get out of the draft. People who were too poor to pay protested. So did people who opposed the whole war.

Turning Points

In 1863, Lincoln made the Emancipation Proclamation, freeing the enslaved people. The Union captured Vicksburg and won control of the Mississippi River. Lee attacked the North, and the Union beat him at Gettysburg.

Before You Read

Find and underline each vocabulary word.

border states *noun*, slave states that stayed in the Union

casualties *noun*, soldiers who are killed or wounded in war

draft *noun*, the way a government forces people to become soldiers

emancipation *noun*, the freeing of enslaved people

After You Read

REVIEW **What was the Confederacy's plan for winning the war?** Highlight the sentence that tells what the South planned to do.

REVIEW **Why did people in the North oppose the draft?** Underline the sentences that tell you the answer.

REVIEW **Why was the victory at Vicksburg important to the Union?** Circle the sentence that tells you the answer.

Use with *United States History*, pp. 176–181

Summary: Geography of the Colonies

The Thirteen Colonies

The English colonies in North America were located between the Atlantic Ocean and the Appalachian Mountains. France had colonies to the north. Spain had colonies to the south. The thirteen colonies can be separated into three parts, or regions, by geography and climate: New England, the Middle Colonies, and the Southern Colonies.

The land in New England was shaped by glaciers. During the Ice Age, thick sheets of ice cut through the mountains. Glaciers pushed rocks and rich soil south. A thin layer of rocky dirt was left. Crops did not grow well in the rocky, sandy soil. Forests and hills made it hard to farm. In New England the summers were warm, but winters were long and cold. The growing season was only about five months long.

Colonists in New England used other natural resources to make a living. They cut down trees to make buildings and boats. They caught fish and whales for food and other products.

Glaciers pushed the soil from New England into the Middle Colonies. The soil was rich and deep. It was good for farming. The growing season was longer than in New England. There was more sun and lots of rain. Colonists used riverboats on long, wide rivers such as the Hudson and Delaware. They sent crops to sell in nearby towns. Colonists also hunted deer and beaver for food and fur.

The Southern Colonies had the best climate and land for farming. The climate was warm almost all year long. The soil was rich. The growing season lasted for seven or eight months. The many waterways along the southern coast formed the tidewater region. Ocean tides made rivers rise and fall as much as 150 miles inland. The fall line was along the Appalachian Mountain range. There, rivers flowed from higher lands to lower lands. The backcountry was the land in back of the area where most colonists settled. It was steep and covered with forests. Farms were small. Colonists hunted and fished for food.

Before You Read

Find and underline each vocabulary word.

growing season *noun*, the time of year when it is warm enough for plants to grow

tidewater *noun*, the water in rivers and streams that rises and falls every day with the ocean's tides

fall line *noun*, the area in which rivers flowing from higher land to lower lands often form waterfalls

backcountry *noun*, the land "in back of" the area along the coast where most colonists settled

After You Read

REVIEW Why was farming difficult for New England colonists? Draw a box around the sentence that tells why crops did not grow well. Circle the sentence that tells why it was hard to farm. Underline the sentence that tells about the climate.

REVIEW Why was farming in the Middle and Southern colonies better than in New England? Draw a box around the sentences that describe the soils in these colonies. Underline the sentences that tell about the climates.

Summary: New England

Massachusetts

In the 1600s, English Puritans settled in New England. People in their communities obeyed the rules of the Bible. Puritan religion shaped the government of the Massachusetts Bay Colony. All settlers had to go to church.

A town meeting was held once a year. Only men with property could vote on laws for their town. Puritan towns had more self-government than most colonies.

Some colonists thought Puritans should not tell them what to believe or how to act. Roger Williams was a dissenter. He did not believe the government should make laws about religion. Williams wanted religious freedom. The Puritans banished him from Massachusetts Bay.

In 1636, Williams started a new colony that became Rhode Island. Rhode Island's government was separate from the church. Anne Hutchinson also disagreed with Puritan ministers. She held meetings that allowed men and women to discuss religion. Puritans did not think women should teach men about religion. Hutchinson was banished and went to Rhode Island.

Thomas Hooker also disagreed with the Puritans. He wanted to start a place where men who did not belong to the church could vote. He started the colony of Connecticut. Other colonists settled the area that became New Hampshire and Maine.

Conflicts over Land

The Puritans lived on American Indian land. Colonists bought the land from the Indians and expected them to leave. Indians believed land could be shared, but not owned. Colonists and the Pequot Indians fought over the land. Colonists killed most of the Pequot Indians and took their land. More colonists arrived. The Wampanoag Indian leader Metacomet, called King Philip, felt his people had to defend their land. In 1675, another war began. A year later the colonists won King Philip's War. They enslaved some Wampanoags and forced the rest to leave. Few American Indians remained in eastern New England after the war.

Before You Read

Find and underline each vocabulary word.

town meeting *noun*, a gathering where colonists held elections and voted on the laws for their towns

self-government *noun*, a system of government that lets people make laws for themselves

dissenter *noun*, a person who does not agree with the beliefs of his or her leaders

banish *verb*, to force someone to leave

After You Read

REVIEW In what ways were Roger Williams and Anne Hutchinson alike? Circle the words that tell what Roger Williams did not believe. Circle the words that tell what Anne Hutchinson did.

REVIEW What caused the Pequot War? Draw a box around the sentence that tells why the colonists and Pequot Indians fought.

Summary: Life in New England

Using the Sea

Most colonists in New England grew just enough crops to feed their families. The rocky coast had good harbors. The thick forests provided wood to build ships. Boston became the center for the shipbuilding industry. The fishing industry grew rapidly in the 1600s. Cod and whales were key resources. By the 1700s, whaling was an important industry.

Merchants shipped exports of fish and lumber to Europe, the West Indies, and Africa. They traded for imports of tea, spices, and manufactured goods. These shipping routes were called the triangular trade. The slave trade was part of the triangular trade. Merchants forced captured people from Africa to travel the Middle Passage from Africa to the West Indies. They were packed in crowded ships. Many died on the way. During the 1600s and 1700s, hundreds of thousands of Africans were forced to work as slaves in the colonies.

Home and Community Life

Most New England families lived in small houses with one main room. They cooked on the fireplace and slept on mattresses on the floor. Colonial homes were like busy workshops. Almost everything people wore, ate, or used was made by hand at home. Men and boys worked the farm, cared for animals, and fixed buildings. Women and girls cooked and preserved food. They made soap, candles, and the family's clothing. They also helped at planting and harvest time.

Some Puritans taught their children to read the Bible at home. Many New England towns had schools. In the early 1700s, colonists no longer had strong religious beliefs. In the 1730s, new ministers convinced people to return to religion. This movement was called the Great Awakening. It caused people to join new churches and to see religion in new ways.

Before You Read

Find and underline each vocabulary word.

industry *noun*, all the businesses that make one kind of product or provide one kind of service

export *noun*, a product sent to another country and sold

import *noun*, a product brought into one country from another country

Middle Passage *noun*, the voyage from Africa to the West Indies

slave trade *noun*, the business of buying and selling human beings

After You Read

REVIEW **What was triangular trade?** Highlight three sentences that tell what the merchants traded in the triangular trade.

REVIEW **How did boys and girls help their families?** Draw a box around the sentence that tells what work the boys did. Underline the sentences that tell what work the girls did.

REVIEW **Why did many New England colonists return to religion in the 1730s?** Circle the name given to the renewed interest in religion.

Summary: The Middle Colonies

New York and New Jersey

In 1664, England captured the colony of New Netherland. King Charles II gave the colony to his brother, James the Duke of York. James kept some of the land and named it New York. He gave the rest of the land to two friends. They divided the land into East Jersey and West Jersey. In 1702, the two colonies joined to form New Jersey.

The proprietors of New York and New Jersey picked governors to rule the colonies. The proprietors allowed the colonists to be part of the government in two ways. First, the governors chose a council that helped make decisions. Second, colonists elected representatives to an assembly. The assembly did not have much power, but it was a step toward self-government.

Pennsylvania and Delaware

William Penn belonged to a religious group called the Quakers. In England, people who did not belong to the Church of England were punished. Penn wanted a colony where all Christians could live in peace.

In 1681, King Charles gave Penn land in the Middle Colonies. This land was named Pennsylvania. The Duke of York gave Penn more land, which later became Delaware.

In Pennsylvania, colonists worshiped freely. They also had a more powerful elected assembly that could approve or reject laws. Penn bought land and made treaties with the Lenni Lenape Indians. His fairness helped everyone live together peacefully.

Penn planned the colony's first city, Philadelphia. This city became a big trade center because it had a good harbor. Ships brought goods from other colonies and from Europe.

Benjamin Franklin was Philadelphia's most famous citizen. He published a newspaper. He also helped to start Philadelphia's first fire company, hospital, and library. Franklin became famous for his inventions.

Before You Read

Find and underline each vocabulary word.

proprietor *noun,* a person who owned and controlled all the land in a colony

representative *noun,* someone who is chosen to speak and act for others

treaty *noun,* an official agreement between nations or groups

After You Read

REVIEW **How did colonists in New York and New Jersey take part in government?** Highlight two sentences that tell how the proprietors allowed the colonists to take part in the government.

REVIEW **How did the government of Pennsylvania differ from those of New York and New Jersey?** Circle the sentence that describes the government of Pennsylvania.

Summary: Life in the Middle Colonies

A Mix of People

In the 1600s, the Middle Colonies accepted people of different religions and cultures. The colonists were German, Dutch, Scots-Irish, Scandinavian, English, and enslaved Africans. Some were Catholic or Jewish. Proprietors allowed them to practice different religions. Proprietors allowed this religious tolerance for two reasons. First, leaders like William Penn believed that people of all religions should live together in peace. Second, some proprietors did not care about the colonists' religious beliefs. They just wanted colonists to buy or rent land.

Making a Living

Many families in the Middle Colonies were farmers. Men, women, and children all worked long hours in the fields and in the home. Boys helped plant and harvest crops. Girls did housework, cooking, and sewing.

The climate and soil of the Middle Colonies were very good for farming. Many farmers grew more than they needed for their families. They sold extra grain and livestock in the cities. Farmers used the long, wide rivers to ship their goods to Philadelphia and New York. Merchants there sold the farmers' goods to other cities and nations.

As in the other English colonies, the Middle Colonies had a free market economy. Proprietors did not tell the colonists what to do. Colonists could make what they thought would earn them the most money. This is called free enterprise.

Philadelphia and New York became busy ports and trade centers. Many artisans and laborers found work in these cities. Some of the laborers were enslaved Africans.

Many colonial children became apprentices to learn useful skills. Boys learned things like shoemaking and printing. Girls learned to spin thread and weave cloth.

Before You Read

Find and underline each vocabulary word.

free market economy *noun,* an economy in which the people, not the government, decide what will be produced

free enterprise *noun,* a system in which people may start any business that they believe will succeed

artisan *noun,* someone who is skilled at making something by hand

laborer *noun,* a person who does hard physical work

apprentice *noun,* someone who studies with a master to learn a skill or business

After You Read

REVIEW **Why did proprietors allow religious tolerance?** Highlight two reasons that proprietors allowed religious tolerance.

REVIEW **Why did colonial children become apprentices?** Highlight the sentence that tells the answer.

Summary: The Southern Colonies

Virginia

In 1607, Virginia became the first permanent English colony. Early settlers started plantations. Plantation owners grew rich by growing and selling tobacco and rice. Many workers were enslaved Africans. Early settlers built their plantations on the best farmland near the ocean. Later, settlers moved inland.

In 1619, Virginia became the first colony to have an elected legislature. This assembly was called the House of Burgesses. Colonists elected the burgesses. Only white men who owned land could vote or be elected. Most of them belonged to the Anglican Church. In 1632, the legislature made this church the official church of Virginia. People who were not Anglican had to leave the colony.

New Colonies in the South

England settled four more colonies in the South: Maryland, North Carolina, South Carolina, and Georgia. Maryland began in 1632 when King Charles I gave land to a Catholic named Cecilius Calvert. Calvert wanted Maryland to be a refuge for Catholics. In 1649, Maryland passed the Toleration Act. This law promised that all Christians could worship freely.

In 1663, King Charles II formed a colony south of Virginia. France and Spain claimed this area. The king hoped that an English settlement would keep the French and Spanish away. The settlement was called Carolina. Later it was divided into North Carolina and South Carolina. South Carolina had good farmland and harbors. North Carolina did not.

In 1732, King George II gave land to James Oglethorpe. Oglethorpe formed Georgia as a place for English debtors. Oglethorpe made strict rules for the colonists. Later, these rules changed. In time, Georgia became a rich plantation colony.

Before You Read

Find and underline each vocabulary word.

plantation *noun,* a large farm on which crops are raised by workers who live on the farm

legislature *noun,* a group of people with the power to make and change laws

refuge *noun,* a safe place

debtor *noun,* a person who owes money

After You Read

REVIEW **Who were burgesses?** Underline the sentence that says who could be elected as burgesses.

REVIEW **What were differences between North Carolina and South Carolina?** Circle two things that South Carolina had that North Carolina did not have.

Summary: Life in the South

Southern Agriculture

The Southern Colonies had an agricultural economy. The climate was good for growing crops. Planters used enslaved Africans to do the hard work needed to grow tobacco and rice.

In Virginia and Maryland, tobacco was the most important crop. In North Carolina, colonists used sticky pine sap to make pitch. Pitch was used to seal the boards of a ship to keep out water. In South Carolina and Georgia, the main crops were rice and indigo.

The Southern Colonies had fewer towns and cities than other colonies. Charles Town was the capital of South Carolina. It was the biggest southern city and a busy trade center.

Plantations and Small Farms

Plantations were huge, with many buildings and workers. Planters' children had private teachers. They learned reading, writing, and dancing. Later, parents taught their children how to manage a large plantation.

However, most colonists lived on small farms in the backcountry, away from schools and towns. Farmers' children only learned to read and write if their parents taught them.

Southern Slavery

Slaves lived in all the colonies by 1750. Most lived in the Southern Colonies. Enslaved Africans were treated as if they were property, not people. Plantation owners used cruel laws and punishments to make slaves work hard. Some overseers whipped and even killed workers. Many slaves died young because of this bad treatment. Some ran away. Others created a new culture that blended African traditions to help them survive. They formed close communities. Many adopted Christianity. They combined African music with their religious beliefs to make powerful spirituals.

Before You Read

Find and underline each vocabulary word.

indigo *noun,* a plant that can be made into a dark blue dye

overseer *noun,* a person who watches and directs the work of other people

spiritual *noun,* an African American religious folk song

After You Read

REVIEW **Why was Charles Town an important city?** Highlight the sentences that describe Charles Town.

REVIEW **How did the children of planters and the children of backcountry farmers learn how to read and write?** Who taught planters' children? Who taught farmers' children? Find two sentences that tell the answers and underline them.

REVIEW **What did slaves do to survive the hardships of slavery?** Draw a box around the sentences that tell the answer.

Summary: The French and Indian War

War Between France and Britain

In the 1750s, Britain and France had colonies in North America. The British wanted to settle in the Ohio River Valley and to trade with the Native Americans who lived there. The French built forts to protect their trade with the Indians. In 1754, George Washington led an army against the French. He was defeated.

Britain declared war on France. The war for control of the valley was called the French and Indian War. Most American Indians in the region were allies of the French. The American Indians liked the French because they traded but did not settle on the land.

In 1754, a congress of the British colonies met in Albany, New York. Benjamin Franklin thought the colonies should work together to defeat France. Each colony would still have its own government. They would also create one government together to decide important issues. His idea was called the Albany Plan of Union. The colonists rejected it. They did not want to join together under one government.

Victory for Britain

In 1757, Britain sent more soldiers to North America. This helped defeat the French in Canada. In 1763, Britain and France ended the war and signed the Treaty of Paris. France gave Britain control of Canada and most of the land east of the Mississippi River.

British soldiers stayed in the Ohio River Valley. The Indians wanted the soldiers to leave. An Ottawa chief named Pontiac led the Indians in a war against the British. This was called Pontiac's Rebellion. The British defeated the Indians in less than a year.

To avoid more conflict with American Indians, Britain made the Proclamation of 1763. It recognized the Indians' right to the land. It did not allow colonists west of the Appalachian Mountains. The colonists were angry. They wanted to settle on the land. They did not want the British soldiers to live among them.

Before You Read

Find and underline each vocabulary word.

ally *noun,* a person or group that joins with another to work toward a goal

congress *noun,* a group of representatives who meet to discuss a subject

rebellion *noun,* a fight against a government

proclamation *noun,* an official public statement

After You Read

REVIEW **What was the Albany Plan?** Underline the sentence that describes what Franklin thought the British colonies should do in order to defeat France.

REVIEW **Why were colonists upset with Britain after the French and Indian War?** Highlight two reasons the colonists were angry.

Summary: Early Conflicts with Britain

Britain Needs Money

Britain spent a lot of money to defeat the French. The British government said that the colonies should pay for the War. The government raised money by taxing goods brought into the colonies. The Sugar Act of 1764 taxed goods like sugar, coffee, and cloth. When a colonist bought cloth, part of the money went to the government as a tax. Some merchants avoided the tax by smuggling goods into the country.

In 1765, Britain passed the Stamp Act. This act taxed anything printed on paper. Many colonists said the new taxes were unfair. Colonists had no say in making tax laws because they did not have representatives in Parliament. Men like Samuel Adams in Boston formed groups to protest the Stamp Act. Adams was the leader of a group called the Sons of Liberty. Sometimes this group and others used violence to resist new taxes.

Conflict over Taxes

In 1765, the nine colonies met to discuss the taxes at the Stamp Act Congress. They decided that only colonial governments should tax the colonies. Merchants in ports like New York and Philadelphia held a boycott of British goods. The protests and boycott worked. Britain repealed the Stamp Act.

In 1767, Britain needed money to pay for the services of colonial governors and soldiers. Parliament created the Townshend Act. This Act made colonists pay taxes on tea, glass, paper, and other items. Colonists boycotted British goods again. They threatened to use violence against tax officials. British troops were sent to protect the officials. A group of women called the Daughters of Liberty made their own cloth instead of buying British cloth.

By 1770, the protests worked. The British repealed most of the taxes, but left the tax on tea. They wanted to show that they still had the power to tax the colonies. Anger grew toward the British government.

Before You Read

Find and underline each vocabulary word.

tax *noun,* money people pay their government in return for services

smuggling *noun,* to import goods illegally

liberty *noun,* freedom from being controlled by another government

protest *noun,* an event at which people complain about an issue

boycott *noun,* a refusal to buy, sell, or use goods

repeal *verb,* to cancel a law

After You Read

REVIEW **What was the goal of Samuel Adams and other Sons of Liberty?** Underline the sentence that explains why Samuel Adams formed the Sons of Liberty.

REVIEW **Why did the British Parliament pass the Townshend Acts?** Circle two services the government needed to pay for.

Resources for Reaching All Learners
27
Use with *United States History,* pp. 234–237

Summary: Conflicts Grow

Trouble in Boston

Britain sent soldiers to Boston when colonists resisted taxes. Colonists did not want soldiers in their city. On March 5, 1770, a crowd yelled and threw snowballs at some of the soldiers. The soldiers started to shoot. Five colonists were killed. Colonists called the fight a massacre.

News traveled slowly. Samuel Adams started the Committees of Correspondence to share news and ideas with people in other colonies. Members wrote letters that told what the British were doing. Members suggested action colonists could take.

The Boston Tea Party

In 1773, the Tea Act allowed the East India Company of Britain to sell tea for a very low price. But if colonists bought the cheap tea, they also paid a tax to Britain. Many colonists did not want to pay taxes to Britain at all. They also didn't want one company to control the tea trade. Merchants refused to sell the tea or unload it from the ships. On December 16, 1773, some Sons of Liberty illegally boarded the ships. They threw the tea into the harbor. This protest was called the Boston Tea Party.

The British government was angry. It passed laws called the Coercive Acts. These laws stopped all trade between Boston and Britain, did not allow town meetings, and gave Britain control of the colony. Britain sent soldiers back to Boston. Colonists were forced to quarter them. Colonists called the laws the "Intolerable Acts" and said they were too harsh.

On September 5, 1774, delegates from most colonies met in the First Continental Congress. Delegates discussed the Intolerable Acts. They asked King George III to stop taxing the colonies without their agreement. They stopped trade with Britain. Colonists gathered weapons in case they needed to fight. King George sent more soldiers. He said the colonists had started a rebellion.

Before You Read

Find and underline each vocabulary word.

massacre *noun*, the killing of many people
correspondence *noun*, written communication
quarter *verb*, to give people food and shelter
delegate *noun*, someone chosen to speak and act for others

After You Read

REVIEW **What was the importance of the Committees of Correspondence?** Circle the sentence that tells why Samuel Adams started the Committees of Correspondence.

REVIEW **Why did the First Continental Congress meet?** Draw a box around the sentence that tells what the delegates wanted King George III to do.

Resources for Reaching All Learners
28
Use with *United States History*, pp. 240–243

Summary: War Begins

Moving Toward War

Colonists who opposed British rule called themselves Patriots. They were angry about the Intolerable Acts. Throughout the colonies, militias prepared for war against Britain.

General Thomas Gage was the British official in Massachusetts. He learned that Patriots were storing cannons and gunpowder in Concord. He sent soldiers to destroy the supplies. Patriots Paul Revere and William Dawes learned of the plan. They rode through the night to warn the minutemen that the British were coming.

The First Battles

On April 19, 1775, British soldiers and minutemen in Lexington began shooting. Colonists were killed and wounded. Hundreds of minutemen gathered in Concord. They forced the British soldiers back to Boston. Along the way, colonists killed or wounded more than 250 British soldiers.

Colonists heard of the battles. Militias trapped British soldiers in Boston. Patriots planned to build a fort on Bunker Hill. They built it on Breed's Hill instead. British soldiers marched up the hill. They fought until the Patriots ran out of gunpowder. The British captured the fort. This was called the Battle of Bunker Hill. Even though they lost the battle, the Patriots showed they could plan and fight well.

A Colonial Army

The Second Continental Congress met in 1775. It created an army to go to war against Britain. George Washington was commander of the Continental Army. Many delegates did not want a war. They sent the Olive Branch Petition to King George III. It asked him to help end the conflict peacefully. But the king sent more soldiers. The Continental Army captured Fort Ticonderoga. The army used cannons it found there to force the British to leave Boston.

Before You Read

Find and underline each vocabulary word.

Patriot *noun,* a colonist who opposed British rule

militia *noun,* a group of ordinary people who train for battle

minutemen *noun,* militia with special training

commander *noun,* an officer in charge of an army

petition *noun,* a written request from a number of people

After You Read

REVIEW **Why did General Gage send British soldiers to Concord?** Circle the words that tell what the colonists were storing near Boston.

REVIEW **Why was the Battle of Bunker Hill important for the colonists?** Underline the sentence that tells what the Patriots showed they could do.

REVIEW **What was the Olive Branch Petition?** Underline what the petition asked King George to do.

Summary: Declaring Independence

The Steps to Independence

After the battles of 1775, the American colonies and Britain were at war. Some colonists were Patriots. They wanted independence. Others still thought of King George as their king. One famous Patriot, Thomas Paine, wrote a pamphlet called *Common Sense*. He wrote that the king treated the colonists unfairly. He said the only way to stop this was to become independent. He also wrote that the colonists had nothing to gain and much to lose by staying tied to the king. Thousands of people read the pamphlet, and support for independence grew.

Declaration of Independence

Congress asked Thomas Jefferson and others to write a declaration of independence. Jefferson wrote about the rights of all people in the Declaration of Independence. Jefferson wrote that people have the right to live, the right to be free, and the right to seek happiness. He wrote that if a government does not protect these rights, people have the right to form a new government. He wrote that King George had tried to take away rights and force taxes on the colonies. The Declaration said the colonies should separate from Britain and that only free colonies could protect the colonists' rights.

Importance of the Declaration

On July 4, 1776, the Congress accepted the Declaration. The delegates knew it was dangerous to sign it. Britain would say it was treason. But delegates signed. The Declaration is still important because it says the American people believe in equal rights for all. Today we know that the words "all men are created equal" include everyone: women, men, children, and every race and group. But in 1776, people's ideas were different. Only white men who owned property had the right to vote. Laws that recognized equal rights of other groups were passed later.

Before You Read

Find and underline each vocabulary word.

independence *noun,* freedom from being ruled by someone else

declaration *noun,* a statement that declares or announces an idea

rights *noun,* freedoms that are protected by a government's laws

treason *noun,* the crime of fighting against one's own government

After You Read

REVIEW What were Thomas Paine's arguments for independence? Underline the sentences that tell you Paine's ideas.

REVIEW According to the Declaration, why did the colonies have the right to their own government? Underline the sentences that say why the colonies had a right to their own government.

REVIEW Why is the Declaration so important to Americans? Underline the sentence that says why the Declaration is still important.

30   Use with *United States History*, pp. 262–267

Summary: Life During the War

Taking Sides

On July 4, 1776, Congress declared independence. Not everyone thought this was a good idea. Many people thought Britain should rule America. When the Revolutionary War began, about half of the colonists were Patriots who supported independence. About one-fifth were Loyalists. The rest of the colonists were neutral.

Most Americans who worked for the British government were Loyalists because they wanted to keep their jobs. Many wealthy Americans were Loyalists because they thought war would hurt their businesses.

Some enslaved African Americans became Loyalists. The British offered them freedom if they helped the British in the war. A few fought in the army, and others built forts, drove carts, or worked as spies. Most American Indians stayed neutral. A few Indian nations fought for the Patriots, but more American Indians helped the British. They wanted the British to win and stop American settlers from taking their land.

Many enslaved African Americans were Patriots. Some were offered freedom if they became soldiers. Free African Americans also became soldiers. Some women Patriots worked as spies or messengers. Others helped at the soldiers' camps.

The Challenges of War

The War for Independence created many problems. People who lived near battlefields had to leave their homes. Both armies destroyed houses and robbed farms. Food, clothing, and supplies cost more. Inflation made it hard for people to buy things they needed. Some store and farm owners would not sell their goods. They wanted to wait for the prices to go higher so they could then sell their goods for more money. There were not enough supplies for soldiers and other people. Congress passed a law to stop store owners and farmers from waiting to sell their goods.

Before You Read

Find and underline each vocabulary word.

Loyalists *noun,* people still loyal to the king

neutral *noun,* not taking sides

inflation *noun,* a rise in the prices of most goods

After You Read

REVIEW **Why did enslaved African Americans fight on both sides in the war?** Circle the two sentences that tell the answer.

REVIEW **Why was inflation a problem for Americans?** Highlight the sentence that tells how inflation made it hard for people.

Summary: The War in the North

Washington's First Battles

The Continental Army was not as large or strong as the British army when the War for Independence started. British soldiers had better weapons and training. But the Americans had a great leader, George Washington. They were on their own land, which made it easier to plan attacks and defend themselves.

The Americans forced the British to leave Boston in the spring of 1776. In August, the British won the Battle of Long Island in New York. The Americans retreated and marched into Pennsylvania. George Washington planned an attack on the British in Trenton, New Jersey. He wanted to win a battle so his soldiers would not give up. On the night of December 25, the Americans rowed across the Delaware River. They attacked at dawn. The soldiers in Trenton were German mercenaries. They were still sleepy from celebrating Christmas, and the soldiers surprised them. The Americans won the battle and took almost 1,000 prisoners. The Patriots were very happy about this victory.

A Turning Point

The British marched into New York from Canada. They met the Americans at Saratoga. It was a hard battle, but the Americans won. After the Battle of Saratoga, France decided to help the Americans. They sent money, soldiers, and a navy. Later, Spain, the Netherlands, and Russia also helped the Americans.

The British captured Philadelphia and stayed there for the winter of 1777. The Americans stayed in tents at Valley Forge, about 20 miles away. Soldiers slept on the cold ground, and many men had no shoes. There was not enough food. Many soldiers died. Washington worked hard to get more food and uniforms. In the spring, Friedrich von Steuben, a German soldier, joined the army at Valley Forge. He trained the Americans to march and use their weapons better. They became better soldiers because of their training.

Before You Read

Find and underline each vocabulary word.

retreat *verb,* to move away from the enemy

mercenary *noun,* a soldier who is paid to fight for a foreign country

victory *noun,* the defeat of an enemy

After You Read

REVIEW **Why did Washington decide to attack Trenton?** Circle the sentence that tells why George Washington wanted to win in Trenton.

REVIEW **What happened at Valley Forge to make the Continental Army better soldiers?** Underline two sentences that tell who joined the soldiers at Valley Forge and how he helped them become better soldiers.

Summary: Winning the War

The War in the South and West

After more than three years of war, the British had not defeated the Patriots. They decided on a new strategy. They thought the South had more Loyalists than the North. They hoped these Loyalists could help them. The British invaded the South. At first, the new strategy worked. By the summer of 1780, the British had won Georgia and South Carolina. Many Loyalists helped them, including Benedict Arnold, a famous Patriot hero who secretly changed sides and became a British general. Today he is known as a traitor.

The British won many battles in the South, but the Patriots fought back. One officer used surprise attacks. His soldiers sneaked up on the British, attacked, and quickly retreated. Another Patriot, Nathanael Greene, forced the British to chase his small army. This tired the British and used up their supplies. Patriots in the West fought back too. They captured British forts in the Ohio River Valley. Spain also joined the war and captured British forts.

The War Ends

The Patriots fought the last big battle against the British in Yorktown, Virginia. Washington marched his army from New York to Virginia, where the British leader Cornwallis and his men were. French ships helped the Patriots. Washington's army and the French navy trapped the British army. Cornwallis hoped that British soldiers and ships in New York would help him. But the British could not defeat the French navy. Cornwallis's men fought for a week, but Cornwallis knew they could not win. On October 19, 1781, the British army at Yorktown surrendered. The war continued for two more years, but there was not much fighting. In September 1783, the United States and Britain signed the Treaty of Paris. The treaty said America was independent. Now Americans needed a government for their new country.

Before You Read

Find and underline each vocabulary word.

strategy *noun,* a plan of action

traitor *noun,* someone who is not loyal

surrender *verb,* to give up

After You Read

Check your understanding.

REVIEW **What was Greene's strategy to defeat the British?** Circle the two sentences that explained Greene's strategy.

REVIEW **What did the Treaty of Paris say?** Draw a box around the sentence that tells what the treaty said.

Summary: A New Nation

The Articles of Confederation

The 13 colonies had fought for self-government. Each new state had a constitution to protect its citizens. Americans did not want to give up their power to a strong, central government.

In 1781, the Articles of Confederation made Congress the national government. Each state had one vote in Congress. The states had more power than the national government. Congress could declare war, borrow and print money, and make treaties with other nations. It could not start an army, create taxes, or control trade.

People wanted to settle on land won in the Revolutionary War. Congress passed two ordinances to control what happened in the Northwest Territories. The Land Ordinance of 1785 explained how the land would be measured, divided, and sold. The Northwest Ordinance of 1787 described how a territory could become a state. It also outlawed slavery in the territories.

Problems for the New Nation

Congress owed money to banks and to other countries for the Revolutionary War. Congress could not raise money because it could not collect taxes. The states were not working together. They printed their own money. People could not agree on how much the money was worth.

In Massachusetts, many farmers did not earn enough money to pay their debts and high state taxes. If farmers did not pay, the state took their farms. In 1786, Daniel Shays led a rebellion of armed farmers. They demanded more time to pay debts. The state militia stopped them. Shays's Rebellion showed that a weak national government could not keep order. George Washington worried the government was not strong enough to protect people's rights. In February 1787, Congress invited state delegates to meet and change the Articles of Confederation to make the nation stronger.

Before You Read

Find and underline each vocabulary word.

constitution *noun,* a written plan for government

citizen *noun,* an official member of a city, state, or nation

territory *noun,* land ruled by a national government but which has no representatives in that government

ordinance *noun,* a law

After You Read

REVIEW **What did Congress do to organize the Northwest Territory?** Highlight the names of each ordinance. Underline what each ordinance said.

REVIEW **Why did farmers in western Massachusetts protest?** Circle the sentences that tell why the farmers had trouble paying taxes and what happened if they did not pay.

Summary: Constitutional Convention

Leaders of the Convention

The Constitutional Convention met in 1787. Delegates met to give Congress more power. Delegates included only white, male landowners. Some delegates wanted a republic. They thought a republic would protect citizens' rights. Others wanted a federal system. In a federal system, Congress could share power with the states.

Creating a New Government

James Madison suggested that the government should have three branches. One branch, the Congress, would make laws. A second branch would carry out laws. A third branch would settle legal arguments. States compromised in order to support the Constitution. Madison wanted the number of delegates from each state to be based on the state's population. Delegates from smaller states thought this would give bigger states more power.   Roger Sherman suggested dividing Congress into two parts. Each state would have the same number of representatives in one house, the Senate. In the other house, the House of Representatives, the number of representatives would depend on the state's population. Southern delegates wanted to count enslaved people in their populations. Northern delegates believed they should not be counted. The states compromised. Every five enslaved persons were counted as three free people. Some states wanted to end slavery. Southern states would not accept this. The states agreed to end the slave trade by 1808.

Ratifying the Constitution

Federalists supported the Constitution. Antifederalists wanted a Bill of Rights added to the Constitution. The Bill of Rights would protect people's liberties. Federalists agreed. Nine of thirteen states needed to ratify the Constitution for it to become law. In June 1788, nine states agreed to ratify the Constitution. The country had a new government.

Before You Read

Find and underline each vocabulary word.

federal *adjective,* a system of government in which the states share power with a central government

republic *noun,* a government in which the citizens elect leaders to represent them

compromise *noun,* both sides give up something they want to settle a disagreement

ratify *verb,* to officially accept

After You Read

REVIEW **What was the advantage of a federal system?** Circle the words that tell how the federal system was better.

REVIEW **Why did delegates argue over representation in Congress?** Highlight a sentence that tells why small states worried. Circle the sentence that tells about counting enslaved people.

REVIEW **Why did Antifederalists demand a Bill of Rights?** Circle the sentence that tells what a Bill of Rights would do.

Summary: The Constitution

A Plan for Government

The Constitution tells us that our government is a democracy. It divides the government into three branches. The legislative branch, or Congress, makes laws. Congress also collects taxes to pay for services. The executive branch carries out the laws. The President is the head of this branch. A new President is elected every four years. The judicial branch is made up of courts. They decide what laws mean and whether they have been followed. Everyone, including the government and its officials, must follow the laws.

Limits on Government

The Constitution includes checks and balances. They keep one branch from becoming stronger than the others. The President makes treaties and chooses judges. Congress can reject these treaties or judges. Congress makes laws. The President can veto these laws. The courts can decide if a law follows the Constitution. A law that is found unconstitutional is no longer in effect.

The Constitution creates a federal system. The national government has power over national issues. This includes defense, printing money, the postal service, and trade. State governments have power over local issues. States control education and elections. Both systems collect taxes and set up courts. Federal laws are stronger than state laws. The highest law is the Constitution itself.

Changing the Constitution

The Constitution was written so that it can be changed as the country changes. An amendment becomes law when two-thirds of the members of the House and Senate vote for it. Three-fourths of the states also have to ratify it. The first ten amendments are the Bill of Rights. They protect rights, such as freedom of speech. The tenth amendment limits the power of the federal government. In 1790, the Constitution did not protect the rights of all Americans. People have fought for their rights and won. Today the Constitution gives equal protection to more citizens.

 Before You Read

Find and underline each vocabulary word.

democracy *noun,* a government in which the people have the power to make political decisions

checks and balances *noun,* a system in which each branch of government can limit the power of the other branches

veto *verb,* to reject

unconstitutional *adjective,* does not agree with the Constitution

amendment *noun,* a change made to the Constitution

 After You Read

REVIEW **What are the jobs of each branch of the national government?** Circle the jobs of each branch.

REVIEW **Why did the authors of the Constitution create checks and balances and a federal system?** Circle the sentence that explains checks and balances.

REVIEW **Why does the Constitution include a way to make amendments?** Circle the sentence that tells what happens as the country changes.

Resources for Reaching All Learners
36
Use with *United States History,* pp. 312–317

Summary: President Washington

The First President

The Constitution set up the system for electing the President. Each state chose representatives for the Electoral College. They voted for the President. George Washington's inauguration as the first President was in 1789. He promised to "preserve, protect, and defend the Constitution of the United States." Every President makes the same promise.

Congress created departments to help the President run the executive branch. The leader of a department was called its Secretary. The Secretary of State decided how the United States would act toward other countries. The Secretary of the Treasury made decisions about the nation's money. The Secretary of War was in charge of protecting the country. The Attorney General made sure federal laws were obeyed. These men formed the President's Cabinet. They advised the President.

Arguments in the Cabinet

Jefferson and Hamilton often disagreed. Both had supporters who started political parties. Hamilton's supporters started the Federalist Party. It wanted a strong national government that would support manufacturing and trade. Jefferson's supporters started the Democratic-Republican Party. It wanted to limit the national government, and to support farming instead of trade.

Hamilton wanted to start a national bank. Jefferson said the government did not have the power to start a bank. Washington approved the national bank. People put money in bank accounts. The bank borrows money from people's savings to make loans. The borrower pays interest for the loan.

Hamilton and Jefferson agreed to locate the new nation's capital between Virginia and Maryland.

After eight years, Washington retired as President. He warned Americans to avoid forming political parties. He also did not want the nation to take sides in foreign wars.

Summary: People on the Move

Exploring the Frontier

When Europeans came to America, they settled between the Atlantic coast and the Appalachian Mountains. These mountains were difficult to cross. The British government also did not allow colonists to cross the mountains. Land on the western side of the mountains belonged to the Indians. As land in the East filled with farms and towns, colonists wanted more land. By the late 1700s, many settlers crossed the Appalachians. Daniel Boone was a pioneer. In 1769, he explored an Indian trail that led through the Cumberland Gap over the Appalachians. Boone helped build a road through the Gap, called the Wilderness Road. He helped settlers across the mountains to the frontier. They found land that was rich and beautiful.

Life on the Frontier

Going across the mountains was hard. Settlers traveled in large wagons with food and supplies. The wagons often broke on the rocky paths. Others traveled on flatboats. They floated down the Mississippi and Ohio rivers or through canals. When pioneers got to the frontier, they saw that American Indians had already built villages and farms.

Life on the frontier was hard and lonely. Settlers left behind their families to move to a new land. Pioneers did many kinds of work on the frontier. Settlers cut down trees and used the wood to build houses. They grew grain and vegetables for their families. They also raised farm animals. Men hunted for meat. Women worked at home and watched the children.

American Indians believed that the land belonged to everyone. They did not believe it could be bought or sold. The Indians signed treaties with the government. The treaties said colonists could hunt on the land, but they could not live on it. The colonists wanted to stay. They fought with the Indians. One American Indian chief, Chief Logan, was friendly to the colonists. Then settlers killed his family in 1774. After that he fought against the colonists for many years.

Before You Read

Find and underline each vocabulary word.

pioneer *noun,* one of the first people to enter or settle a region

frontier *noun,* the edge of a country or a settled region

flatboat *noun,* large, rectangular boat partly covered by a roof

canal *noun,* a waterway built for boat travel and shipping

After You Read

REVIEW In which river valleys did people look for farmland on the frontier? Circle the names of the rivers the settlers traveled and settled near.

REVIEW What kinds of transportation did settlers use to move west? Draw a box around the sentences that tell how settlers traveled west.

Summary: The Nation Grows

President Jefferson

John Adams was the second President of the United States.
He belonged to the Federalist party. This group believed the
national government should be stronger than the state
governments. The Federalists wanted to make laws to help
manufacturers. When Thomas Jefferson became President, the
Federalists gave up power. Jefferson belonged to the
Democratic-Republican party. This group believed state
governments should be stronger than the federal government.
They wanted to help farmers.

Farmers wanted to ship their products down the
Mississippi River to Louisiana. This land belonged to France.
President Jefferson sent representatives to meet with the
French ruler, Napoleon Bonaparte. They asked Napoleon if
Americans could keep trading on the river. Napoleon
needed money to go to war against Great Britain. He sold
Louisiana to the United States. The Louisiana Purchase
doubled the size of the country.

Exploring the West

Jefferson sent soldiers to explore Louisiana. Meriwether
Lewis and William Clark led the group. It was called the
Corps of Discovery. Jefferson wanted them to study the land,
plants, animals, and climates of the West. He also wanted the
corps to learn about the cultures of the western American
Indians and to look for a water route to the Pacific.
Sacagawea, the group's interpreter, was an American Indian
woman. She helped the corps speak to American Indians.
The corps left in 1804 and returned in September 1806.
They learned about the land and the people, but did not
find a water route to the Pacific.

In 1805 Zebulon Pike led a group to find the source of
the Mississippi River. They explored Missouri and went
north to Minnesota. They learned about the land, but did not
find the river's source. Later they explored the Arkansas and
Red rivers. The Corps of Discovery and Pike's explorers led
the way for traders and pioneers in the west.

Before You Read

Find and underline each
vocabulary word.

manufacturer *noun*, people
who use machines to
make goods

corps *noun*, a team of
people who work
together

interpreter *noun*, someone
who helps people who
speak different languages
understand each other

source *noun*, the place
where a river begins

After You Read

REVIEW **Why did
Jefferson send
representatives to France?**
Circle what the
representatives asked
Napoleon Bonaparte.

REVIEW **What tasks did
Lewis and Clark complete
on their expedition?**
Highlight the sentence that
tells what the Corps of
Discovery expedition learned.

Summary: The War of 1812

Trouble with Britain

In 1808, Britain and France were at war. The U.S. did not take either side, but Britain and the U.S. became enemies. British officers raided American ships to look for British sailors on the ships. American sailors were caught and forced to serve in the British Navy. This was called impressment. The government was angry about impressment. It was also angry that the British were helping Indians fight Western settlers. The Indian chief Tecumseh wanted Indians to unite to keep settlers away. In 1811, the Indians were defeated at their Tippecanoe settlement.

Fighting the War

In 1812, the U.S. declared war on Britain. Americans wanted to stop impressment. They also wanted Britain to stop arming the Indians.

In 1814, the British navy fired at Fort McHenry. Francis Scott Key watched the battle. He saw the American flag flying above the fort and wrote "The Star-Spangled Banner." This became the national anthem. Later that year, the U.S. and Britain signed a peace treaty. The Treaty of Ghent did not give either country any new land. Unaware of the treaty, British forces attacked Americans in New Orleans. The British were defeated.

A New Sense of Pride

After the war Americans had a time of prosperity. They developed a sense of nationalism and became interested in the American flag. In 1818, Congress passed a law that said the flag should have 13 stripes for the 13 original colonies. A star would be added for each state that joined the Union. Today there are 50 stars on the flag.

In 1816, President James Monroe worried that other European countries would invade America. He created a new foreign policy. The Monroe Doctrine warned European countries to stay out of North and South America. The United States would also stay out of Europe.

Before You Read

Find and underline each vocabulary word.

prosperity *noun,* economic success and security

nationalism *noun,* a devotion to one's country

foreign policy *noun,* a government's actions toward other nations

After You Read

REVIEW Why did Tecumseh want American Indian nations to unite? Circle the sentence that tells the answer.

REVIEW What inspired Francis Scott Key to write the poem that became "The Star-Spangled Banner"? Highlight the sentence that tells what Francis Scott Key saw.

REVIEW How did the law passed in 1818 change the appearance of the national flag? Circle the number of stripes on the flag. Underline the reason for that number. Underline what each star represents on the flag. Circle the number of stars the flag has today.

Summary: Age of Jackson

A New Kind of President

The first six Presidents of the United States were wealthy and well educated. In 1828, Andrew Jackson became President. He grew up poor in Carolina. Then he took the Wilderness Trail to Tennessee. He became a lawyer, politician, and business owner. He was the first President to come from a state west of the original 13 colonies.

Farmers, frontier settlers, and working men who lived on the territories were given suffrage when the territories became states. Women and African Americans could not vote. Only white men who had land or money could vote. Jackson supported the new voters. They liked his campaign. Their votes helped to elect him President.

As President, Jackson supported working people. He thought the bank only helped rich people and that the poor were not allowed to borrow money from the national bank. Jackson ordered the government to take its money out of the national bank and put it into state banks.

Indian Removal Act

As settlers came to the frontier, conflicts increased with American Indians there. Jackson believed the Indians slowed the growth of the United States. In 1830, Congress passed the Indian Removal Act. This law forced American Indians living east of the Mississippi River to leave their homes and businesses. The Indians had to move to Indian Territory in present-day Oklahoma. The Cherokee Indians objected. Cherokee Indian Chief John Ross took their case to the Supreme Court. Chief Justice John Marshall ruled that it was against the law to force the Cherokee to move. Jackson ignored the ruling. In 1838, the U.S. Army forced the Cherokee to travel 1,000 miles to Indian Territory. About one-fifth of the Cherokee died during this journey, called the Trail of Tears. The army also tried to force the Seminole Indians to leave Florida. Chief Osceola led their resistance. He was put in jail and died. Indians continued the struggle to keep their homes.

Before You Read

Find and underline each vocabulary word.

suffrage *noun*, the right to vote

campaign *noun*, a series of actions taken toward a goal

ruling *noun*, an official decision

After You Read

REVIEW **What types of people did Jackson want to help?** Circle words that describe the people who voted for Jackson.

REVIEW **What did the Cherokee do to fight against removal?** Underline the sentence that tells what Indian chief John Ross did to fight the Indian Removal Act.

Use with *United States History*, pp. 368–371

Summary: The Industrial Revolution

The Industrial Revolution Begins

The Industrial Revolution began with textile machines. These machines turned cotton into yarn. In 1793, Eli Whitney invented the cotton gin, a machine that cleaned cotton quickly. Cotton became America's biggest export. Then the government hired Whitney to make thousands of guns. At that time guns were made by hand. Whitney thought of a way to make them quickly and cheaply. He used interchangeable parts and mass production. Soon factories began using his ideas. The nation's productivity increased.

Machines Bring Change

Entrepreneurs used machines to change how people worked. Francis Lowell built a mill that turned cotton into cloth. Soon other factories opened. New inventions, like reapers and steel plows, made farm work easier and faster. Before the Industrial Revolution, people worked on farms or in workshops. Now many people worked in factories.

Changes in Transportation

In the 1800s, dirt roads could not be used in bad weather. The government built a paved road from Maryland to Ohio. People built towns and opened businesses to sell goods. Robert Fulton invented a steamboat that could travel without wind or currents. Soon there were many steamboats. In 1825, the Erie Canal opened. This canal made it easier to ship goods between Lake Erie and the Hudson River. Many canals were built. Rivers and canals became the fastest and cheapest way to ship goods.

Steam locomotive trains were even faster than steamboats. Trips that took 32 hours by steamboat took only 10 hours by train. Soon the United States had thousands of miles of railroad track. Factories and farmers sent their goods faster to places all over the country.

Before You Read

Find and underline each vocabulary word.

textile *noun,* cloth or fabric

interchangeable parts *noun,* parts made by a machine to be exactly the same size and shape

mass production *noun,* making many products at once

productivity *noun,* the amount of goods and services made by a worker in a certain amount of time

entrepreneur *noun,* a person who takes risks to start a new business

After You Read

REVIEW **What did Whitney do to manufacture guns more quickly and cheaply?** Circle the sentence that tells the answer.

REVIEW **In what ways did the workday change for many people during the Industrial Revolution?** Underline two sentences that tell the answer.

REVIEW **Why were steam locomotives better than other forms of transportation?** Underline 3 sentences that give reasons why.

Name _____ Date _____

Summary: Immigrants and Reformers

German and Irish Immigrants

Millions of Europeans came to the United States in the mid-1800s. Almost half were Irish and about one-third were German. Thousands of Germans left Europe because of crop failures and war. Many settled in the Midwest of the United States. Germans with money, education, and skills bought land to farm. Others worked in Chicago, St. Louis, and Milwaukee.

Many Irish people left Ireland because of the Irish Potato Famine. When a disease destroyed the potato crop in 1846, there was not enough food. Many people died. In the next 10 years, about 1.5 million Irish people came to the United States. Most of them didn't have enough money to leave the Northeast cities where they landed. They built canals and railroads or worked in factories or as servants.

Some people did not like immigrants because their customs seemed different. People also thought immigrants were taking their jobs. Many immigrants worked for little money because they needed jobs. Craftspeople who made goods by hand lost jobs because factories produced goods faster and cheaper. Many Americans left farms to look for jobs in cities.

Making a Better Society

In the 1820s, thousands of people joined Christian churches. This was the Second Great Awakening. During this time, many people tried to reform society. Antislavery and temperance were reform movements. The temperance movement wanted people to stop drinking alcohol.

Women who worked for reform, especially antislavery, saw that they were treated with injustice too. They could not vote, speak in public meetings, or have high-paying jobs. In 1848, women had a meeting in Seneca Falls to talk about their rights. This began the women's rights movement. Newspapers attacked the women's ideas, but many more women joined the movement.

Before You Read

Find and underline each vocabulary word.

famine *noun*, a widespread shortage of food

reform *noun*, an action that makes something better

temperance *noun*, controlling or cutting back the drinking of alcohol

injustice *noun*, unfair treatment that abuses a person's rights

After You Read

REVIEW Why did Irish immigrants usually stay in Northeastern cities, while most Germans moved to the Midwest? Circle the sentence that tells the answer.

REVIEW Why did women reformers decide to start a movement to protect their own rights? Draw a box around two sentences that tell the answer.

Summary: Texas and the Mexican War

The Texas Revolution

In 1821, Texas was part of Mexico. The land was cheap, so many Americans settled in Texas. Mexico tried to stop them, but they still came. Slavery was against Mexican law, but Americans brought slaves to Texas. Many American settlers and Tejanos, or Mexicans who lived in Texas, wanted to break away from Mexico. They did not like laws made by Santa Anna, Mexico's president. The Tejanos and Texans decided to fight for independence.

In 1836, Santa Anna took an army to San Antonio to take a fort called the Alamo. Fewer than 200 Texans and Tejanos met him. Most of them died in battle. After this, Texans declared independence and formed the Republic of Texas. Sam Houston led their army in a surprise attack at San Jacinto. They won, and captured Santa Anna. For his freedom, Santa Anna gave Texas its independence.

Texans elected Sam Houston president and voted to join the United States. They also made slavery legal. President Van Buren was against annexation. Mexico wanted to keep Texas, and Van Buren feared it would cause war. He also didn't want to add a new state to the Union that allowed slavery. People who wanted to annex Texas said it was the manifest destiny of the United States to spread from the Atlantic to the Pacific Ocean. In 1845, James Polk became President. Congress voted to annex Texas.

War with Mexico

The United States and Mexico disagreed on the border between Texas and Mexico. Congress declared war in 1846. Soldiers fought on three fronts. Americans captured Mexico City in 1847. In 1848, Mexico signed the Treaty of Guadalupe Hidalgo. Mexico agreed to the annexation of Texas and the Rio Grande as the border between Texas and Mexico. Mexico also gave a large area of land, the Mexican Cession, to the United States.

Before You Read

Find and underline each vocabulary word.

annexation *noun,* joining two countries or pieces of land together

manifest destiny *noun,* the belief that the United States should spread across North America

front *noun,* where the fighting takes place in a war

cession *noun,* something that is given up

After You Read

REVIEW **Why didn't President Van Buren want to annex Texas?** Underline the two sentences that tell the answer.

REVIEW **What did Mexico agree to under the Treaty of Guadalupe Hidalgo?** Circle the sentence that tells the answer.

Use with *United States History*, pp. 394–397

Summary: Moving West

Trails West

In 1843, about 1,000 people traveled west by wagon train. They wanted to find cheap land. They traveled on the Oregon Trail, which started in Missouri and went through the Rocky Mountains to what is now Oregon. The trip was hard, but by the end of the 1850s, thousands of pioneers had settled in Oregon. In 1846, Britain and the United States agreed on a border between the United States and Canada. The land south of this became the Oregon Territory.

A religious group, the Mormons, traveled west on the Mormon Trail. In 1847, the Mormons traveled to what is now Utah. They could settle and practice their religion freely there.

The California Gold Rush

Before the 1700s, American Indians lived in California. After Spain claimed California, the Spaniards forced Indians to live and work on their missions. In 1821, California became part of Mexico. The Californios, Mexicans who lived in California, forced Indians to work on their ranches.

In 1848, California became part of the United States. Gold was discovered, and more than 250,000 people, called forty-niners, rushed to California to find it. The gold rush changed California. People built boomtowns near the gold mines. Merchants sold goods to the miners. Bankers and innkeepers opened businesses. Lawyers found jobs settling arguments.

The gold rush ended about five years later. Most of the miners did not find gold, but thousands of people stayed in California. Miners and farmers killed Indians and took their land. Other Americans took the Californios' land, forcing them to leave. Cities such as San Francisco grew. By 1850, only two years after becoming a territory of the United States, California had enough people to become a state.

Before You Read

Find and underline each vocabulary word.

wagon train *noun,* a line of covered wagons that moved together

forty-niner *noun,* gold miner who went to California in 1849 during the gold rush

gold rush *noun,* many people hurrying to the same area to look for gold over a short time

boomtown *noun,* a town whose population grows very quickly

After You Read

REVIEW **Why did the first large group of people set out on the Oregon Trail?** Circle the sentence that tells the answer.

REVIEW **Who lived in the boomtowns around the gold mines?** Draw a box around four words that name people who lived in the boomtowns and did business with the miners.

Summary: Worlds Apart

Slavery in the United States

All 13 colonies allowed slavery, but it was more common in the South. Some northern states made slavery illegal after the Revolution. Some delegates to the Constitutional Convention tried to abolish slavery. They failed.

The cotton gin was invented in 1793. It made growing cotton easier. Southern planters bought more land and enslaved more people to do the work. By 1860, there were nearly 4 million enslaved African Americans in the South. Cotton became the South's most important crop. Textile mills in the North and Britain needed more cotton. The price for cotton went up.

Some enslaved people fought against slavery. In 1831, Nat Turner led a rebellion. New laws were passed to control all African Americans. By 1853, they had fewer rights than ever. In the South many people thought slavery was necessary. In the North some people thought slavery was wrong.

North and South

In the South, farming was the most important business. Huge plantations had many enslaved workers. Small farmers grew food and crops. The North also had farms, but many people moved to cities. They worked in factories, making textiles, shoes, tools, and other things. By 1860, more than half of Northerners lived in cities.

Congress passed tariffs on imported goods. These tariffs helped factories in the North. There were few factories in the South. Prices for manufactured goods were high. People blamed high prices on the tariffs and on the North.

Vice President John Calhoun said the tariffs were unfair. He argued for states' rights. He said the Constitution did not let the federal government set tariffs. People in the North and South continued to argue about tariffs and slavery. This increased sectionalism throughout the country.

 Before You Read

Find and underline each vocabulary word.

tariff *noun,* a tax on imported goods

states' rights *noun,* the idea that states, not the federal government, should make decisions about matters that affect them

sectionalism *noun,* loyalty to one part of the country

 After You Read

REVIEW **What led to the growth of slavery in the early 1800s?** Circle the new invention that changed the South. Then underline the sentence that tells the effect of this invention on slavery in the South. What was the most important crop in the South? Underline the sentence that tells the answer.

REVIEW **Why did southerners dislike tariffs?** Underline the sentence that tells who the tariffs helped. Circle the sentence that tells you what people blamed on the tariffs.

46

Summary: The Struggle for Freedom

The Antislavery Movement

Some Americans felt slavery was necessary. In the South, as cotton growing spread, many people also wanted slavery to spread. Other Americans felt slavery was wrong. Some thought that enslaving people went against their religious beliefs.

The Abolitionist movement to end slavery grew in the 1830s and 1840s. There were Abolitionists in the North and the South. Abolitionists were free blacks and whites, women and men. They wrote and spoke against slavery. William Lloyd Garrison started an Abolitionist newspaper called *The Liberator*. Free blacks gave most of the money to support the newspaper.

Frederick Douglass escaped slavery. He spoke to white people about what it was like to be enslaved. Sojourner Truth also escaped slavery. She spoke for abolition and women's rights. Sarah and Angelina Grimké grew up in a Southern slaveowning family. They traveled North and spoke out against slavery.

By 1860, about 500,000 free blacks lived in the United States. They faced discrimination in both the North and South. Free blacks joined whites in creating the American Anti-Slavery Society in 1833.

The Underground Railroad

Some Abolitionists worked in secret. Free blacks gave most of the money and did most of the work to support the Underground Railroad. The Underground Railroad was a series of escape routes and hiding places called "stations." Runaways could leave the United States and go north to Canada or south to Mexico, Florida, or the Caribbean. If they were caught, they were returned to slavery and punished. People who guided runaways were called "conductors." The most famous conductor was Harriet Tubman. She escaped slavery and then returned 19 times to the South to lead others to freedom.

Before You Read

Find and underline each vocabulary word.

abolitionist *noun,* someone who joined the movement to end slavery

discrimination *noun,* the unfair treatment of particular groups

Underground Railroad *noun,* a series of escape routes and hiding places to bring people out of slavery

After You Read

REVIEW **What did free blacks in the North do to convince people that slavery was wrong?** Circle the names of people who took an active part in the abolitionist movement. Underline the actions these people took to help enslaved people. Also underline sentences that tell what all free blacks did to fight slavery.

REVIEW **What was the purpose of the Underground Railroad?** Draw a box around two sentences that explain what the Underground Railroad was and what it was used for.

47
Use with *United States History*, pp. 424–427

Name _____ Date _____

Summary: Compromise and Conflict

Would Slavery Spread?

A territory became a state when it had enough people. New states could be slave states or free states. Northerners wanted free states. They tried to make slavery illegal. Southerners wanted slave states. In 1820, Missouri wanted to enter the Union as a slave state. To keep the number of free and slave states equal, Congress let Maine join as a free state. This was the Missouri Compromise.

Congress drew an imaginary line. Only those states south of the line could be slave states. The Compromise of 1850 let territories choose to be slave states or free states by popular sovereignty. In 1854, Congress gave popular sovereignty to the Kansas and Nebraska territories. Abolitionists objected because both territories were north of the line. Settlers for and against slavery traveled to Kansas to vote. In 1861, Kansas became a free state.

The Growing Crisis

The Fugitive Slave Law was part of the Compromise of 1850. It ordered people to return runaways to slavery. Many northerners would not obey the law. Harriet Beecher Stowe wrote the book *Uncle Tom's Cabin*. It was about the cruelty of slavery. The story convinced northerners to oppose slavery. Southerners said the book was false. The conflict over slavery pushed the North and South apart.

In 1857, the Supreme Court ruled on the Dred Scott case. It said that slaves were property. Living in a free state did not make them citizens. The court also said it could not ban slavery in any of the territories. Abolitionists feared slavery would spread.

Abolitionist John Brown thought that slavery was wrong. He tried to start a rebellion against slavery by attacking an Army post in Harpers Ferry, Virginia. Brown was captured, convicted, and hung. Many northerners said he was a hero. By 1860, some southerners wanted to leave the Union to defend their way of life.

Find and underline each vocabulary word.

slave state *noun*, a state that permitted slavery

free state *noun*, a state that did not permit slavery

Union *noun*, another name for the United States

popular sovereignty *noun*, the right of people to make political decisions for themselves

fugitive *noun*, a person who is running away

REVIEW **What compromises did Congress make as the nation grew?** Circle the date and name of each compromise.

REVIEW **Why did John Brown attack Harpers Ferry?** Draw a box around the sentence that tells what John Brown thought about slavery.

Summary: Civil War Begins

Abraham Lincoln

Conflict grew between the North and South. Southerners thought abolitionists would start slave rebellions. Some southerners wanted to leave the Union. Northerners were afraid slavery would spread. Americans who opposed slavery formed the Republican Party. Republicans opposed slavery in the territories.

Abraham Lincoln was a Republican. He was born in Kentucky, a slave state. He was raised on a farm in Illinois, a free state. His family was poor. He did not go to school, but he read a lot. Lincoln became a lawyer and a political leader.

Lincoln's Campaigns

In 1858, Lincoln ran for Senate in Illinois against Stephen Douglas. They debated so people could hear their ideas. Douglas wanted popular sovereignty for territories. He did not think slavery was wrong. Lincoln said slavery was evil, but he did not support abolition. Lincoln lost, but the debates made him famous. Many southerners thought he wanted to abolish slavery.

Lincoln ran for President in 1860. He was the only candidate against slavery. He won, but the election showed that the country was divided. No southern states voted for Lincoln. Some southerners said the federal government was too strong. They said tariffs and laws to limit slavery threatened states' rights. Some chose secession to protect their right to enslave people.

Secession Begins

In 1860, South Carolina left the union. In all, eleven southern states formed the Confederacy. Jefferson Davis was president. Lincoln wanted unity and peace but it was too late. Confederates attacked Fort Sumter on April 12, 1861. Lincoln called for men to fight the rebellion. The Civil War began.

Before You Read

Find and underline each vocabulary word.

secession *noun*, when part of a country leaves or breaks off from the rest

Confederacy *noun*, states that separated from the Union and formed a confederation

civil war *noun*, a war between two groups or regions within a nation

After You Read

REVIEW **Why did some southerners want their states to leave the Union?** Draw a box around three sentences that tell what southerners said about the federal government, what they thought threatened states' rights, and what right they wanted to protect.

REVIEW **Why did southerners see Lincoln as an enemy?** Circle what Lincoln said about slavery. Also circle what southerners thought he would do about slavery.

REVIEW **What event began the Civil War?** What happened on April 12, 1861? Draw a box around the answer.

Summary: Twenty-First Century Begins

The 2000 Election

On December 31, 1999, people all over the world celebrated the beginning of a new millenium. The new millenium really began on January 1, 2001. In a presidential election, the vote of individual citizens is called the popular vote. The The candidate who wins the popular vote in a state wins all of that state's Electoral College votes. To win the election you have to win the electoral vote.

The 2000 presidential election was an example of a close popular and electoral vote. The race was very close in Florida, where George W. Bush won the first count. Al Gore said the votes were not counted properly. Finally, the Supreme Court said that the Florida votes would not be recounted. Bush became President. In 2004, Bush ran again, and won both the electoral and popular votes.

Attack on the Nation

On September 11, 2001, nearly three thousand people were killed by acts of terrorism in the United States. Terrorists hijacked four airplanes. They crashed two airplanes into the World Trade Center in New York, and one into the Pentagon in Washington, D.C. A fourth plane crashed in Pennsylvania.

The terrorists were from a group called al-Qaeda. They were against the United States' involvement in the Middle East. After the attacks, Bush accused the country of Afghanistan of hiding the leader of al-Qaeda, Osama bin Laden, and his followers. In October, 2001, a coalition of nations led by the United States went to war in Afghanistan. They defeated the government, but they did not find bin Laden.

In 2003, Bush said Saddam Hussein, the leader in Iraq, was a danger to his neighbors and to the United States. In March, 2003, the United States went to war in Iraq. After defeating Hussein's army and arresting Hussein, the military stayed in Iraq while a new Iraqi government formed.

Before You Read

Find and underline each vocabulary word.

millenium *noun,* a period of 10 centuries, or 1,000 years

popular vote *noun,* the vote of individual citizens

Electoral College *noun,* representatives, called electors, from each state

terrorism *noun,* the use of violence against ordinary people to achieve a political goal

After You Read

REVIEW **What is the difference between the popular vote and the electoral vote?** Circle the words that tell what a popular vote is. Highlight the words that tell what the votes in the Electoral College are. Underline the words that explain how a presidential election is won.

REVIEW **How did the United States respond to the terrorist attacks of September 11, 2001?** Circle the sentences that tell you the answer.

Summary: Neighbors in North America

Canada

Canada is the United States' neighbor to the north. It has three territories and ten provinces. Its history is similar to American history. American Indians lived first in both countries. Europeans colonized both countries. In Canada, the colonists were mostly French. After a French-British war in 1754, Canada became a British colony. Many people in Canada speak both French and English. Both languages are now official languages there. In 1867, Canada gained its independence from Britain. Canada is a democracy. Like the United States, Canada is multicultural.

In 1992, Canada signed the North American Free Trade Agreement (NAFTA) with the United States and Mexico. NAFTA increased trade among the three nations. Canada is the United States' biggest trade partner. The two countries also work together to solve environmental problems that affect both countries.

Mexico

Mexico is the United States' neighbor to the south. It has 31 states and one federal district. The Maya and Aztecs lived in Mexico first, and they built large, beautiful cities. Spain began to colonize Mexico in the 1520s. In 1821, Mexico fought Spain for its independence and won. Mexico has a representative government that gives a lot of power to the President. Most Mexicans have a mixture of Spanish and Mexican Indian heritage. Spanish is the official language, but many people speak Indian languages. Mexican art, building styles, and food are common in the Southwest United States, which was once part of Mexico.

Many Mexicans work in maquiladoras, and many Mexicans come to the United States to work. This helps the U.S. economy. In 1992, Mexico signed NAFTA with the United States and Canada. Mexico's most important trading partner is the United States. After Canada, Mexico is the United States' second most important trading partner.

Before You Read

Find and underline each vocabulary word.

province *noun*, a political region of a country that is similar to a state

multicultural *adjective*, having many cultural traditions

maquiladora *noun*, a factory in Mexico near the U.S. border

After You Read

REVIEW Why is French one of the two official languages in Canada? Circle the sentence that tells the answer.

REVIEW How and when did Mexico gain its independence? Draw a box around the sentence that tells how and when Mexico gained its independence.

REVIEW What are some of Mexico's connections with the United States? Circle the sentences that tell about connections with Mexican culture, work, and trade.

Summary: United States Today

A Nation of Immigrants

Millions of immigrants come to the United States. Some come for a better life, and some come for religious or political freedom. Until 1965, most immigrants came from Europe or Mexico. In 1965, Congress changed the immigration laws. Now immigrants come from many nations. Spanish-speaking immigrants come from Central and South America and the Caribbean. Refugees from wars in El Salvador and Nicaragua came during the 1980s.

People also come from Africa and the West Indies. Today almost one-third of America's immigrants are Asians from India, China, the Philippines, and other countries. Immigrants often live in communities where other people from their country live. They influence the culture and government of the places where they live.

Many People, One Nation

Many immigrants to the United States find the freedom they need to start successful careers. The United States has a diverse population, with many different ethnic groups. People bring music, food, language, art, and customs from their countries. Each person brings knowledge, skills, and talents. These things improve the United States. Ethnic diversity is one of the greatest strengths of the United States.

All people in the United States share a heritage of democracy. All United States citizens share the Constitution and the Bill of Rights. The Constitution and the Bill of Rights explain the rights of U.S. citizens. Our democratic heritage unites us into one nation. You can see the Latin motto "E Pluribus Unum" on American money. These Latin words mean "out of many, one." These words remind us that the United States became one nation by joining together 13 colonies. Today 50 states and many ethnic groups are joined together into one nation.

Before You Read

Find and underline each vocabulary word.

refugee *noun*, a person who escapes war or other danger and seeks safety in another country

heritage *noun*, something that is passed down from one generation to the next

motto *noun*, a short statement that explains an ideal or goal

After You Read

REVIEW **Why did immigration to the United States change after 1965?** Circle the sentence that tells the answer.

REVIEW **What do all United States citizens share?** Draw a box around the sentence that tells the answer.

52   Use with *United States History*, pp. 484–487

Summary: Reconstruction

Plans for Reconstruction

After the war, the country had to be reunited. This period was called Reconstruction. Some northerners wanted to punish the South. Lincoln asked people to forget their anger. He wanted the defeated states to set up state governments and rejoin the Union quickly. Radical Republicans in Congress wanted to change the South and protect the rights of African Americans. Lincoln was shot on April 14, 1865 by John Wilkes Booth. His assassination shocked the country.

Reconstruction

Vice President Andrew Johnson became president. He put Lincoln's plan into action. Southern states had to abolish slavery. Most passed Black Codes to limit the rights of African Americans. Congress set up the Freedmen's Bureau to provide support for poor blacks and whites. In 1867, Congress put the South under military rule. Soldiers forced states to obey Congress and pass laws letting all men vote. In 1868, Congress impeached Johnson. They said he broke laws. Some southerners supported Congress. They were called scalawags. Some northerners went to the South just to make money. They were called carpetbaggers.

The Constitution Changes

During Reconstruction, Congress created three amendments to the Constitution. They gave the national government more power over the states. The Thirteenth Amendment ended slavery. Black Codes still limited the rights of African Americans. To protect those rights Congress passed the Fourteenth Amendment. It gave blacks full citizenship. Southern states had to ratify this amendment to rejoin the Union. The Fifteenth Amendment recognized the right of African American men to vote. But African Americans faced a long struggle for equality.

Before You Read

Find and underline each vocabulary word.

Reconstruction *noun*, period when the South rejoined the Union

assassination *noun*, the murder of an important leader

Freedmen's Bureau *noun*, an agency set up to provide food, clothing, medical care, and legal advice to poor blacks and whites

impeach *verb*, to charge a government official with a crime

After You Read

REVIEW What was Lincoln's plan for Reconstruction? Underline the sentence that tells you the answer.

REVIEW Why were soldiers sent to the South? Circle the sentence that tells the answer.

REVIEW Why did Congress pass the Fourteenth Amendment? Highlight the sentences that tell you the answer.

Summary: The Challenge of Freedom

Freedom and Hardship

Reconstruction was a time of hope for African Americans. Slavery was over. New laws protected their rights. The plantation system was over. African Americans knew how to farm, but they could not afford to buy land. Some landowners let freed African Americans farm on their land. This system was called sharecropping. Landowners loaned sharecroppers tools and seeds. Sharecroppers gave the landowners a share of the crop. Often sharecroppers did not make enough money to pay their debts.

Some southerners opposed Reconstruction. They did not like federal troops in their states. They did not support laws that gave rights to African Americans. People formed secret organizations, like the Ku Klux Klan, to stop African Americans from taking part in government. They threatened, beat, and killed African Americans to stop them from voting.

The End of Reconstruction

By 1877 many people thought Reconstruction had not reunited the nation. President Rutherford B. Hayes told the federal troops to leave the South. Without soldiers to protect them, many African Americans could not vote. They lost their political power. Southern states passed Jim Crow laws to keep African Americans separate. Segregation was enforced in schools, hospitals, even cemeteries. The states usually spent less money on schools and hospitals for African Americans. Many African Americans believed education was important. In 1881, a former slave named Booker T. Washington opened the Tuskegee Institute where students studied and learned useful skills. The teachers and students were African Americans. Washington believed that educated African Americans would get equal treatment. Churches became important centers in African American communities.

Before You Read

Find and underline each vocabulary word.

sharecropping *noun,* system where farmers used land and gave landowners a share of the crop

Jim Crow *noun,* laws that kept African Americans separate from other Americans

segregation *noun,* forced separation of races of people

After You Read

REVIEW **Why did many freed African Americans become sharecroppers?** Underline the sentence that tells the answer.

REVIEW **What was the purpose of the Tuskegee Institute?** Circle the name of the man who started the Tuskegee Institute. Then highlight the words that tell what people did at the Institute.

Use with *United States History,* pp. 482–485

Summary: Linking East and West

The Telegraph Helps Communication

In the early 1800s the only way to get a message or news from one place to another was to travel there. Sometimes news from one part of the country didn't reach another part for several weeks. In 1844, a new kind of communication was introduced. The new telegraph machine sent electric signals through wires to a distant location. Samuel Morse invented a code for sending messages. People could send and get messages in just a few minutes. By 1861, telegraph wires stretched from coast to coast. Reporters sent news stories to their newspapers, and people sent personal messages and business information. During the Civil War, battle plans were made using the telegraph.

A Transcontinental Railroad

Many Americans began moving west by the 1840s. They were looking for gold and for farmland. There were only two good ways to travel. One way was to sail around the tip of South America. The other way was to travel to the end of the railroad line and take a rough trail on land in wagons pulled by horses, mule, or oxen. Both ways were long, difficult, and expensive. In 1862, railroad companies got money and land from Congress to build a transcontinental railroad to connect the coasts. The Union Pacific hired former Civil War soldiers, formerly enslaved African Americans, and Irish immigrants to build track from east to west. They started in Nebraska with existing railroad lines from the east coast. The Central Pacific hired many Chinese immigrants to lay tracks from California toward the east. Because of prejudice, these workers were paid less than other workers and given the most dangerous jobs.

The two tracks met at Promontory Point, Utah on May 10, 1869, to make a 1,800 mile long transcontinental railroad. It was the first of several railroads. It was easier to cross the continent by train. Western farmers made money by shipping cattle and wheat to the east.

Before You Read

Find and underline each vocabulary word.

transcontinental *adjective,* from one edge of a continent to the other

prejudice *noun,* an unfair negative opinion that can lead to unjust treatment

After You Read

REVIEW How did people travel west in the 1840s? Circle the two sentences that tell how people traveled.

REVIEW What kinds of goods were shipped on transcontinental railroads? Circle the words that describe what Western farmers sold to the east in order to make money.

Use with *United States History,* pp. 498–501

Summary: Life on the Great Plains

Settling the Great Plains

In the early 1800s, few people lived on the Great Plains. The Great Plains are in the middle of the United States. People did not think the land was good for farming. It was very dry and flat.

In 1862 the Homestead Act was passed. The government helped people to settle on the Great Plains. The government sold adults 160 acres of land for a small amount of money. If they could farm the land for five years, they could own it. A settler's home and land was called a homestead. Many homesteaders came from the east coast, where farmland cost a lot. In the Great Plains, land was cheaper. Settlers also came from Europe, where there was not much land to buy. There was a lot of land to buy in the Great Plains. African Americans also wanted to start farms. Many African Americans were poor. They faced prejudice and violence after the Civil War. They started their own towns in Kansas. African Americans were called Exodusters, after a book in the Bible that tells the story of how people escaped slavery.

Settlers Face Hardships

Settlers had to learn how to farm on the Great Plains. The soil was held together by grass roots. It was called sod. Settlers were called sodbusters because they had to break through the sod to plant crops. There was not a lot of wood, so settlers used sod to build homes. Winters were long and cold. Summers were hot and dry. There were many droughts. There were grass fires because it was so dry. Farmers had to grow crops that did not need much water. They carried water from streams. Some farmers used windmills to pump water from underground. In the 1870s millions of grasshoppers ate the crops. There weren't many people in the area to do farm work, so farmers made new and better farm machines. New machines made it faster and easier to grow more crops.

Before You Read

Find and underline each vocabulary word.

homestead *noun*, a settler's home and land

Exodusters *noun*, African Americans who moved to the Great Plains

drought *noun*, a long period with little or no rain

sodbusters *noun*, name given to settlers who had to break through sod to build houses and plant crops

After You Read

REVIEW Why did settlers from Europe and the East move to the Great Plains? Circle two reasons why these settlers moved.

REVIEW Why was life on the Great Plains so difficult? Underline sentences that describe the land.

REVIEW How did settlers adapt to the lack of extra workers on the Great Plains? Underline what the settlers did to make growing crops easier and faster.

Summary: Cattle Ranchers

Texas Cattle

In the 1860s, millions of longhorn cattle lived in Texas. They were strong animals. They ate grass and they did not need a lot of water. Cowhands made sure the cows did not run away. They herded the cattle. Cowhands burned brands into the cattles' skin. The cowhands knew which cattle they owned by looking at these marks.

Cattle ranchers could not make much money selling their cattle in Texas. There was a big supply, or lots, of cattle. There were not many people to buy them. There was not a big demand. The price of cattle was low. The cattle ranchers herded their cattle onto trains. They sent the cattle to cities in the North and East. There were many people in the cities who wanted to buy beef and leather. The demand was high. The supply was low. This meant the cattle were worth more in the cities.

The Cattle Drives

Cattle ranchers needed to get their cattle to railheads. They were often hundreds of miles from the cattle ranches. Ranchers hired cowhands to take their cattle on cattle drives to the railheads. In a cattle drive, cowhands rode on horseback next to the herd of cattle to make them move. The cattle drives had to stay near rivers. This way the cattle had water to drink. The work was dirty, hard, and dangerous.

The cattle drives ended in the late 1880s for three reasons. First, there was the invention of barbed wire. This wire had sharp points on it. Settlers used barbed wire to make fences on their property. The fences blocked the cattle trails. Second, more railroads were built. Railheads were closer to the ranches. Ranchers did not need to send the cattle on long cattle drives. Third, by the mid-1880s, there was not enough grass to feed all the cattle. Sheep ranchers wanted the land for their flocks.

Before You Read

Find and underline each vocabulary word.

demand *noun,* the amount of something that people want to buy at a certain price

supply *noun,* the amount of something that people want to sell at a certain price

railhead *noun,* a town where railroad tracks begin or end

barbed wire *noun,* wire with sharp points on it

After You Read

REVIEW **Why did Texas cattle ranchers want to sell their animals in the East and North?** Highlight the sentence that tells about selling cattle in cities.

REVIEW **What led to the end of the big cattle drives?** Circle three reasons why cattle drives ended.

Use with *United States History,* **pp. 514–517**

Summary: Conflicts on the Plains

War on the Plains

In the 1840s, settlers moved west to the Great Plains. They were looking for land and gold. The government built roads and railroads for the settlers. Many Indians lived on the Great Plains. The government tried to get them to sell their land. The government wanted the Indians to move to reservations.

The Plains Indians did not want to live and farm on the reservations. The reservations were small. The land was poor. Most of the Indians were not farmers. They were hunters. For years millions of buffalo lived on the Great Plains. The Indians hunted them for their meat and fur. The settlers killed many buffalo. New railroads, roads, and settlements hurt the buffalo habitat. By 1889, the buffalo were nearly extinct.

U.S. soldiers tried to make the Plains Indians give up their land. The Indians fought against the soldiers. Some famous battles were the Battle of the Little Bighorn, the Battle of Wounded Knee, and the Sand Creek Massacre. Finally the Indians were defeated and forced to move to the reservations.

Government Policy

Government officials wanted to make the Indians live like white settlers. Lawmakers wanted the Indians to assimilate. They tried to force the Indians to give up their culture and traditions. Indians were not allowed to have religious ceremonies. Indian children had to go to special schools. They were not allowed to speak Indian languages. They could not wear Indian clothing.

The government wanted the Indians to become farmers. In 1887, Congress passed the Dawes Act. This law broke reservation land into small pieces. The government gave some pieces to Indians who promised to farm them. It sold the rest of the land to settlers.

Before You Read

Find and underline each vocabulary word.

reservation *noun,* land the government reserved for Indians

habitat *noun,* the area where an animal or plant normally lives or grows

extinct *adjective,* when a certain type of plant or animal no longer exists

assimilate *verb,* to change a group's culture and traditions so that it blends with a larger group

After You Read

REVIEW **Why did Plains Indians need large areas of land?** Circle reasons why Indians did not want to live on reservations.

REVIEW **Why did the buffalo herds shrink?** Highlight the sentence that tells how settlers changed the habitat.

REVIEW **What did the Dawes Act do to reservation land?** Circle the sentence that tells what happened to reservation land.

Resources for Reaching All Learners
58   Use with *United States History*, pp. 522–527

Summary: The Rise of Big Business

A Time of Invention

In the late 1800s, inventions changed people's lives. They could do more work in less time. E. Remington and Sons made the first typewriter. It saved office workers time. Elijah McCoy invented the oil cup. It dripped oil on machine parts. This helped the parts run longer. Alexander Graham Bell invented the telephone. People in different places could talk to each other. Thomas Edison invented light bulbs. Electric lights kept streets bright at night. Factories and shops could stay open longer.

Big Business

New machines and technologies helped businesses grow. Andrew Carnegie used a new invention to start his steel company. John D. Rockefeller started Standard Oil. The company became a corporation. It bought small companies. This got rid of competition. Standard Oil became a monopoly. It owned 90 percent of America's oil. No competition meant consumers had fewer choices. Monopolies could provide poor service or charge higher prices. After making large fortunes, Carnegie and Rockefeller gave millions of dollars to schools, libraries, churches, and hospitals.

Workers' Lives Change

Factories hired many people to run machines. Factory work was boring and dangerous. Workers did the same thing for ten or twelve hours a day. They often worked in unsafe conditions. Factory workers did not make much money. Some families needed more money to survive. They sent their children to work.

Factory workers formed labor unions. They had more power as a group. They wanted businesses to change. Unions wanted safer work. They wanted an eight-hour day and better pay. They did not want children to work. Unions used strikes. Businesses fought back. Some strikers were hurt or killed, but labor unions kept fighting for their rights.

Before You Read

Find and underline each vocabulary word.

corporation *noun*, a business in which many people own shares, or parts, of the business.

competition *noun*, occurs when more than one business sells the same goods or service to customers.

monopoly *noun*, a company that has no competition.

labor union *noun*, an organization of workers that tries to improve pay and working conditions for its members.

strike *noun*, when workers refuse to work in order to force business owners to make changes

After You Read

REVIEW **In what ways did inventions of the late 1800s save time?** Underline the sentences that tell how inventions helped people.

REVIEW **What is a monopoly?** Circle the sentences that tell what no competition meant for consumers.

REVIEW **Why did workers form labor unions?** Highlight changes the unions wanted.

Summary: Immigrants in America

Arriving in America

Before 1880, most immigrants living in America came from countries in northern or western Europe. Between 1880 and 1924, about 25 million new immigrants came to the United States. Many came from countries in southern or eastern Europe such as Italy, Russia, Hungary, Greece, and Poland. Some immigrants came looking for jobs. Others were escaping persecution. Most immigrants found greater political freedom in the United States. Arriving immigrants had to pass through immigration stations, such as Ellis Island in New York Harbor and Angel Island in San Francisco Bay. Government officials asked immigrants about their plans. They were checked for diseases. Many immigrants from China came to the west coast. Asian immigrants faced more more prejudice than European immigrants. More Chinese immigrants were turned away and sent back to China.

Living in a New Country

Immigrants often lived in large cities. Immigrants had their own languages, religions, and customs. They lived in neighborhoods with family or friends that belonged to their ethnic group. Life was hard for immigrants. Many lived in tenements. Many immigrants worked in dangerous factories. Businesses liked to hire immigrants because they worked many hours and were not paid a lot of money. Some Americans worried that immigrants would take their jobs. They did not want immigrants to speak other languages or follow other customs. Immigrants faced prejudice from some Americans. In 1921 and 1924, Congress limited the number of immigrants that could come to the United States.

   Immigrants helped to make the United States one of the richest, fastest-growing countries in the world. Immigrants built railroads, dug mines, and worked in factories.

Before You Read

Find and underline each vocabulary word.

persecution *noun*, unfair treatment or punishment

ethnic group *noun*, a group of people who share a culture or language

tenement *noun*, a poorly built apartment building

After You Read

REVIEW In what ways were Asian immigrants treated differently than immigrants from Europe? Underline two sentences that tell how immigrants from Asia were treated.

REVIEW What did immigrants do to help the United States grow? Highlight the sentence that tells how immigrants helped build the United States.

Resources for Reaching All Learners
60
Use with *United States History*, pp. 542–545

Summary: Growing Cities

Moving to Cities

Many people moved to cities in the late 1800s and early 1900s. Many immigrants lived in cities. People who lived on farms also moved to the city. Machines were used on many farms. Fewer workers were needed. People moved to cities to find jobs. Cities grew very fast. By 1910, almost half of all Americans lived in a city.

Chicago was a city that grew quickly. It was in a good place. Chicago is near Lake Michigan. Canals linked Chicago to the Mississippi and Illinois rivers. Railroads and boats brought natural resources to the city. Logs were shipped to factories. Machines cut the logs into lumber. Wheat and corn were also shipped to Chicago. Mills turned them into food. Cows and pigs were sent to stockyards. One stockyard could hold thousands of animals. Factories turned the animals into meat.

Changes in Cities

Cities changed as they got bigger. Thomas Edison and Nikola Tesla were inventors. They invented new ways to make electricity and send it through wires. New inventions needed electricity for power. Electric elevators were used in skyscrapers to carry people to different floors. Theater stages were lit with electric lights. Stores used electric signs to attract shoppers. Electricity powered the rapid transit system. Streetcars and subways moved people around the city quickly.

Growing cities had problems. Cities became crowded and noisy. There was not enough housing. People lived in slums. City people, especially immigrants, helped each other find housing and jobs. Reformers wanted city life to be better. In 1889, Jane Addams and Ellen Gates Starr started Hull House. This was a new settlement house in Chicago. People came to Hull House to learn English. They got medical care and looked for jobs. There were clubs for children. Reformers in other cities built settlement houses.

Before You Read

Find and underline each vocabulary word.

stockyard *noun*, a fenced area where large numbers of animals are kept until they are used for food or moved

skyscraper *noun*, a very tall building

rapid transit *noun*, a system of trains that people use to travel around cities

slum *noun*, a poor, crowded part of a city

settlement house *noun*, a community center for people in cities

After You Read

REVIEW **Why did so many people move to cities in the late 1800s and early 1900s?** Circle the sentence that tells what people were looking for in cities.

REVIEW **What kinds of help did immigrants find in settlement houses?** Underline the sentences that say why people went to Hull House.

Summary: Time of Reform

The Progressives

In the early 1900s, adults and children worked in unsafe factories. Factories polluted cities. Dirty air and water made people sick. Progressives wanted to make factories and cities safer. They fought for laws to end child labor and protect factory workers.

Upton Sinclair was a muckraker. He wrote a book about the dangers of meat factories. In 1906, Congress passed two laws. One law was The Pure Food and Drug Act. It stopped factories from using harmful chemicals in food. The second law was The Meat Inspection Act. It said factories had to be cleaner and safer. President Theodore Roosevelt also wanted to protect the environment. He saved land for national parks and wilderness areas.

Working for Equal Rights

Women fought for the right to vote for many years. In 1920, Congress passed the Nineteenth Amendment. It gave women suffrage.

In the early 1900s, African Americans faced prejudice when they tried to get jobs or a places to live. Some states did not allow African Americans to vote. Some laws made African American children go to different schools. W.E.B. Du Bois wrote about African American life. He helped people see why laws should be changed. Booker T. Washington started a school to educate African Americans.

In 1909, the National Association for the Advancement of Colored People (NAACP) was founded. "Colored People" was a term then used for African Americans. The NAACP worked for equality. It wanted African Americans to be treated fairly. Between 1910 and 1930, about 1.5 million African Americans moved to northern cities. This was called the Great Migration. African Americans wanted better lives. They found jobs in factories and businesses in the North.

Before You Read

Find and underline each vocabulary word.

progressives *noun*, reformers who believe the government should make laws to protect citizens' rights

muckraker *noun*, someone who "rakes up," or points out unpleasant truths

After You Read

REVIEW **What did the Pure Food and Drug Act and the Meat Inspection Act do to make food safer?** What did the Pure Food and Drug Act stop factories from doing? Circle the sentence that tells you the answer. What did the Meat Inspection Act make factories do? Circle the sentence that tells you the answer.

REVIEW **What is the NAACP and what is its purpose?** Circle the words that tell what NAACP means. Underline two sentences that say what the NAACP worked for.

Summary: New Territories

The Nation Expands

In 1867, the United States was recovering from the Civil War. Russia offered to sell its colony of Alaska to the United States. William Seward was the Secretary of State. He convinced Congress to buy Alaska from Russia. Most Americans thought the idea was foolish. They changed their minds when gold was found near Alaska in 1896. Not many people found gold, but they found other valuable resources. Buying Alaska no longer seemed foolish.

In the late 1700s, Americans sailed to Hawaii. They grew pineapple and sugar cane on large plantations. By the late 1800s, Americans owned most of the land and businesses. Hawaiians were unhappy about the Americans' power. Queen Liliuokalani wanted her people to have the land. Americans in Hawaii revolted against her. They asked to join the United States. In 1898, Hawaii became a territory of the United States. Some people thought the United States had started a policy of imperialism.

The Spanish-American War

In the 1890s, Spain had colonies in Cuba and Puerto Rico. It also controlled Guam and the Philippine Islands. In 1895, Cubans revolted against Spain. American newspapers wrote shocking stories about Spain's cruelty to Cuba. The stories were not all true, but people believed them. In 1898, newspapers blamed Spain for blowing up an American ship in Cuba. The United States declared war on Spain.

Theodore Roosevelt led volunteers called the Rough Riders. With African American soldiers called Buffalo Soldiers, they won the battle of San Juan Hill. The U.S. Navy destroyed Spanish ships in Cuba. Spain gave Puerto Rico, the Philippines, and Guam to the United States. After the war, Theodore Roosevelt became President. He wanted to cut a canal across the isthmus of Panama. Panama was part of the nation of Colombia. Roosevelt helped Panama gain its independence. It took 10 years to build the Panama canal. It opened in 1914. Trade increased and shipping was faster between the east and west coasts.

Before You Read

Find and underline each vocabulary word.

imperialism *noun,* when nations gain colonies to build empires

isthmus *noun,* a narrow strip of land with water on two sides

After You Read

REVIEW **How did Alaska and Hawaii become United States territories?** Circle the words that tell the answer.

REVIEW **Where did most of the fighting take place in the Spanish-American War?** Underline the name of the battle Roosevelt won.

Summary: World War I

War in Europe

In the early 1900s, nationalism was strong. Britain, France, Germany, and Italy wanted to be world powers. They raced to claim colonies. They made big armies. Countries formed alliances. Britain, France, and Russia made one alliance. They were called the Allies. Germany and Austria-Hungary made another alliance. They were called the Central Powers.

In 1914, Austria-Hungary declared war on Serbia. Other countries joined in. The Allies and Central Powers declared war on each other. World War I began.

America Enters the War

Most Americans wanted the United States to stay out of the war. In 1917, Germany attacked American ships. Congress declared war on the Central Powers. The United States joined the Allies.

Many American men left to fight in the war. America's factories lost many workers. Many African Americans left the South to work in northern factories. Women also worked in factories.

Soldiers fought from long trenches.   They tried to capture the enemy. Thousands of men were killed in trench warfare. This fighting lasted for four years. Soldiers used many new weapons. Machine guns, cannons, and tanks were used on the ground. Submarines sank ships. Airplanes were used in war for the first time.

America helped the Allies win the war. On November 11, 1918, the Allies and Central Powers signed an armistice. Leaders from each alliance met in Versailles, France. They signed a peace treaty. President Wilson wanted the treaty to include a new organization. It was called the League of Nations. The organization would work for peace. Many Americans felt they had done enough for other countries. There was a growing feeling of isolationism. The United States did not join the League of Nations.

Before You Read

Find and underline each vocabulary word.

alliance *noun,* an agreement between nations to work together and to defend each other

trench warfare *noun,* a type of fighting in which soldiers fought from long ditches

armistice *noun,* an agreement to stop fighting

isolationism *noun,* when a country stays out of other countries' affairs

After You Read

REVIEW **What were two major causes of World War I?** Highlight words that tell about things that led to the war.

REVIEW **What was trench warfare?** Highlight the sentence that tells about trench warfare.

REVIEW **What caused the shortage of workers in the United States during World War I?** Underline the words that say why factories lost workers.

Summary: The 1920s

A Growing Economy

During the 1920s, the United States became one of the richest nations in history. The automobile industry grew very fast. Henry Ford changed the way factories made cars. He used assembly lines and division of labor. Ford's ideas made it faster and cheaper to make cars. As the auto industry grew, the steel, rubber, and oil industries also grew. Its success helped the nation's economy grow.

Americans believed the economy would keep growing. This changed the way they bought goods. Many people used credit to buy items. They made small payments. This was easier than making one big payment with cash. Credit allowed many people to own homes for the first time. Using credit also meant people owed money.

A Changing Society

The 1920s was an exciting time. In 1920, women won the right to vote. Women changed the way they lived. They wore modern clothes. They took jobs in business. They played sports.

Many African Americans moved north to work in industrial cities. In New York City, African Americans formed new communities. One community was called Harlem. Many writers and artists lived in Harlem. Some African American musicians played jazz. This was a new kind of music. Millions of people heard jazz on the radio. They danced to jazz. The 1920s were called the Jazz Age.

During this time, many Mexicans came to the United States. They worked on large farms. Some worked in Texas. Other Mexicans worked in California.

Movies, like radio, became popular in the 1920s. People heard about new heroes on the radio. In 1927, they heard about Charles Lindbergh. He flew over the Atlantic Ocean alone. People from different parts of the country had more in common.

Before You Read

Find and underline each vocabulary word.

assembly line *noun,* a line of workers or machines that puts a product together piece by piece

division of labor *noun,* a system in which workers perform different parts of a large task

credit *noun,* getting an item today, but paying for it later with small payments

After You Read

REVIEW **How did credit change the way people paid for goods?** How did people make payments? Underline the sentence that tells you.

REVIEW **In what way did the lives of American women change in the 1920s?** Circle the sentences that answer the question.

Summary: The Great Depression

Hard Times for Americans

During most of the 1920s, the United States economy grew. Many people invested their money. They bought stocks in companies. A stock is a small part of a company. The value of stock goes up when a company does well. The value of stock goes down when a company does poorly. Then stockowners lose money.

By the end of the 1920s, the economy had started to slow down. In 1929, the value of many stocks quickly dropped. The American stock market crashed. Stockowners were frightened. Many stocks became worthless. Thousands of people lost all of their money.

The economy became even weaker. Factories did not need many workers. Businesses closed. Many people lost their jobs, so unemployment went up. Some families had to give up their homes. Each day, hungry people waited for free food at community kitchens.

Many farmers did not make enough money, so they went out of business. In the early 1930s, almost no rain fell in the Great Plains. Farmers' lives became even harder. The soil turned to dust. This area was called the Dust Bowl. This time of hardship is known as the Great Depression. It was the worst depression in United States history.

The New Deal

In 1932, Franklin D. Roosevelt became President. He wanted to stop the Depression. Roosevelt started new programs to help Americans. He called these programs the New Deal. Congress quickly passed the programs into law. Some programs gave food and shelter to people. The Public Works Administration (PWA) hired people to build dams and improve roads and parks. The New Deal did not end the depression, but it gave people new hope.

Before You Read

Find and underline each vocabulary word.

stock market *noun,* a place where people can buy and sell shares of a company's stock

unemployment *noun,* the number of people without a job

depression *noun,* a period when many people can't find work, and many others have no money to keep businesses going

After You Read

REVIEW **What made unemployment go up during the Great Depression?** Underline two sentences that tell why many people lost their jobs.

REVIEW **What kinds of projects did the PWA hire people to work on?** Highlight the projects done by the PWA.

Summary: World War II

The Road to War

After the Great Depression, millions of people were unemployed all around the world. They wanted strong leaders. In 1933, Adolf Hitler became the dictator of Germany. Hitler blamed Jews for Germany's problems. Nazi soldiers arrested many Jews and sent them to prison.

Mussolini was Italy's dictator. Italy was Germany's ally. They were the Axis Powers. Poland, Britain, and France formed the Allied Powers. In 1939, Hitler invaded Poland. The Allies declared war on Germany. World War II began. At the beginning of the war most Americans did not want to fight in Europe again.

America Goes to War

In 1940, Japan joined the Axis. Japan wanted to expand its empire in Asia. In 1941, Japan destroyed U.S. Navy ships at Pearl Harbor. Thousands of Americans died. The United States declared war on Japan.

The United States joined the Allied Powers. The Axis Powers declared war on the United States. Many Americans joined the military. Americans supported the war. They bought war bonds. Women worked in factories. Americans collected metal to make war supplies.

Some Americans feared Japanese Americans would help Japan. The government forced thousands of Japanese Americans to live in internment camps.

Fighting the War

The war was fought in Europe, North Africa, and the Pacific. In May 1945, Germany surrendered. In August, Americans dropped atomic bombs on two Japanese cities, Hiroshima and Nagasaki. The bomb dropped on Hiroshima killed 100,000 people. Japan surrendered. World War II ended.

As the war ended, Allied troops found out that Nazis had forced millions of Jews and other people into concentration camps. Over 12 million people died in the camps. About six million of those people were Jews. This mass murder is known as the Holocaust.

Before You Read

Find and underline each vocabulary word.

dictator *noun,* a ruler who has total power over a country and its people

war bonds *noun,* a loan from the American people to the federal government

internment camp *noun,* a place where prisoners are held during wartime

atomic bomb *noun,* a powerful bomb that can destroy an entire city

concentration camp *noun,* a place where large numbers of people are held prisoner and forced to work

---

After You Read

REVIEW **Why didn't the United States join the Allies in 1939?** Circle the sentence that tells the answer.

REVIEW **What action did the United States take after the attack on Pearl Harbor?** Highlight the sentence about the United States going to war.

REVIEW **What did the United States military do to force Japan to surrender?** Highlight the names of the Japanese cities bombed by the United States.

Resources for Reaching All Learners

67

Use with *United States History,* pp. 600–605

Summary: The Cold War

Superpowers at War

After World War II, the United States and the Soviet Union were the world's strongest nations. They were called superpowers. They had different ideas about economics and government. They fought a war of ideas called the Cold War. The Soviet Union was a communist country. In communism, the government controls production and resources. It decides where people live and work. The United States is a capitalist country. In capitalism, people and businesses control the production of goods. People decide where they live and work.

The Cold War began in Europe after World War II. The Soviet Union won control of Eastern Europe. It controlled half of Germany and half of Germany's capital, Berlin. The United States, Britain, and France controlled western Germany and West Berlin. In June 1948, the Soviet Union blocked roads and railroads that led to West Berlin. The United States, Great Britain, and France flew in supplies. This was called the Berlin Airlift.

Cold War Conflicts

After World War II, Korea was divided into North and South Korea. North Korea became communist. South Korea was a capitalist country. North Korean army invaded South Korea. The United Nations sent soldiers to help South Korea. China sent soldiers to help North Korea. The war ended in 1953. Neither side won. Korea is still divided.

The United States and the Soviet Union were in a nuclear arms race. In 1959, Cuba became a communist country and the Soviets secretly put missiles there. President Kennedy was afraid the Soviet Union would attack the United States. He sent warships to surround Cuba. He hoped a blockade would force the Soviet Union to remove its missiles. This conflict was called the Cuban Missile Crisis. For six days, nuclear war seemed possible. Then the Soviet Union removed the missiles.

Before You Read

Find and underline each vocabulary word.

communism *noun*, a system in which the government controls production and owns the nation's natural and capital resources

capitalism *noun*, a system in which ordinary people and businesses control the production of goods and services

arms race *noun*, a contest between nations to build bigger and more powerful weapons

After You Read

REVIEW What was the Berlin Airlift just before the Cold War began? Circle the paragraph that tells how the United States, Britain, and France helped people in West Berlin.

REVIEW What did Kennedy do to end the Cuban Missile Crisis? Underline the sentences that tell why President Kennedy sent warships to Cuba.

Resources for Reaching All Learners
68
Use with *United States History*, pp. 612–615

Name _____ Date _____

Summary: Life in the 1950s

Post-War Prosperity

In 1952, General Dwight D. Eisenhower was elected President. He was a war hero who had led the Allied troops in Europe during World War II. Americans trusted him to bring peace and prosperity to the country. The United States economy grew quickly under Eisenhower. Many veterans returned home after the war. They wanted to have families and buy houses. So many new families were started that the United States had a baby boom.

Because of the baby boom, there were not enough houses for everyone. Builders started building huge housing developments. The government gave veterans loans to buy new houses. New families also bought cars and household items, such as washing machines and clothes driers.

Businesses grew and produced more products. So workers had more income. Families had more things to buy. They made budgets to plan for saving and spending.

Cultural Changes

In the 1950s, cars became very important. People living in the suburbs needed a car to drive everywhere. They drove to work, to shop, and to have fun. People drove to national parks. They drove to drive-in theaters to watch movies. They ate at drive-in burger restaurants and ice cream shops. Shopping centers outside of cities became very popular.

Cars made it easy for people to go to new places. Now television made it easy for people to see places without leaving their homes. On television, people could see faraway events as they happened. They watched soap operas and comedy shows.

In the 1950s, television and radio helped rock 'n' roll become popular. Teenagers loved rock 'n' roll and huge crowds cheered for singers like Chuck Berry and Elvis Presley. Some people said rock 'n' roll would not last. But rock 'n' roll continued to grow and changed into new kinds of music that people listen to today.

Before You Read

Find and underline each vocabulary word.

veteran *noun*, a person who has served in the military

baby boom *noun*, increase of babies born after World War II

budget *noun*, a plan for saving and spending income

After You Read

REVIEW **What did families use budgets for?** Highlight the sentence that tells what people planned.

REVIEW **In what new ways did people use their cars during the 1950s?** Draw a box around the paragraph that tells you places people drove to.

Summary: Civil Rights

The Movement Begins

Nearly 100 years after the Civil War, the civil rights of African Americans were limited by state laws and discrimination. Some civil rights are the right to vote, the right to equal treatment, and the right to speak out.

In the early 1950s, segregation was legal. Many Americans believed it should not be. African Americans went to court to end segregation. In 1954, the Supreme Court ordered the desegregation of public schools.

An Alabama law said that African Americans had to sit at the back of the bus. In 1955 in Montgomery, Alabama, Rosa Parks refused to move to the back of a bus. She was arrested. Her church organized a protest. African Americans boycotted the buses until buses were desegregated. This was the Montgomery Bus Boycott. Martin Luther King Jr. helped lead the boycott. He believed in nonviolent protest. He wanted people to fight back using peaceful actions. In 1956, the Supreme Court said that segregation on buses was illegal.

Civil Rights Victories

In 1960, African Americans held sit-ins in 54 cities. They sat at lunch counters that only served food to white people. They would not leave until they were served. In 1963, Congress was discussing a bill to end segregation. Martin Luther King Jr. and other leaders organized a protest march in Washington, D.C., to show support for the bill. The march on Washington got Americans to pay attention to the civil rights movement.

President Lyndon Johnson worked with Congress to pass the Civil Rights Act of 1964. It banned segregation in schools, at work, and in public places. The Voting Rights Act of 1965 guaranteed citizens of all races and ethnic backgrounds the right to vote.

In 1968, Martin Luther King Jr. was shot. People from all backgrounds continued the struggle for civil rights.

Before You Read

Find and underline each vocabulary word.

civil rights *noun,* the rights and freedoms that countries guarantee their citizens

desegregation *noun,* ending the separation of people by racial or ethnic group

nonviolent protest *noun,* a way of bringing change without using violence

After You Read

REVIEW **What was the goal of the Montgomery Bus Boycott?** Underline the sentence that tells about the boycott.

REVIEW **What did the march on Washington do to help the civil rights movement?** Draw a box around the sentence that tells how the march on Washington affected people in America.

Summary: Life in the 1960s

Presidents Kennedy and Johnson

In 1960, John F. Kennedy was elected President. Kennedy wanted Americans to serve their country. He began the Peace Corps to send volunteers to countries that needed help.

While Kennedy was President, the United States got into the space race. The Soviet Union won the race. In 1957, a Soviet rocket sent Sputnik I into space. It was the first human-made object to circle Earth. In April 1961, a Soviet cosmonaut named Yuri Gagarin circled Earth in a space capsule. The next month, Alan Shepard became the first American to go into space. In February 1962, John Glenn circled Earth. In 1969, Neil Armstrong and Buzz Aldrin were the first humans to land on the moon.

Kennedy was assassinated in 1963. Vice President Lyndon Johnson became President. He created the Great Society programs to help Americans in need.

The Vietnam War

Vietnam was split in two. North Vietnam was Communist. South Vietnam was capitalist. North Vietnam supported communists who wanted to overthrow the South Vietnamese government. The United States sent military advisors and supplies to help South Vietnam. Then they sent soldiers to fight.

Some Americans thought the United States should fight to stop communism. Many other Americans disagreed. They thought the United States should not interfere in a civil war. They held demonstrations to protest the war.

In 1969, Richard Nixon became President. He brought some soldiers home, but U.S. planes increased bombing in North Vietnam. They began bombing Cambodia. In 1973, North Vietnam, South Vietnam, and the United States agreed to a cease-fire. The American soldiers returned home. The North Vietnamese defeated the South Vietnamese in 1975. More than 55,000 U.S. soldiers and millions of Vietnamese people died in the war.

Before You Read

Find and underline each vocabulary word.

space race *noun*, a struggle between the United States and the Soviet Union to be the first country to send people into space

demonstration *noun*, a large gathering of people who want to tell the public and the government their opinion

cease-fire *noun*, an agreement to stop all fighting

After You Read

REVIEW **Who won the race to send a person into space?** Underline the sentence that tells you about the first person to circle Earth.

REVIEW **Why did many people in the United States protest against the war in Vietnam?** Draw a box around the sentence that tells you the answer.

Resources for Reaching All Learners
71
Use with *United States History*, pp. 632–635

Summary: Challenges of the 1970s

The Nixon Years

Richard Nixon was elected President in 1968. He helped build better relations between the United States and the two largest Communist countries: China and the Soviet Union.

In 1973, Israel was attacked by Egypt and Syria . Oil-producing countries that supported Egypt and Syria wanted to punish the United States for helping Israel. They produced less oil, so oil prices went up. High oil prices made costs rise for making and shipping goods, so prices rose. This is called inflation.

In 1972, Nixon's campaign workers broke into the Democratic Party headquarters in the Watergate building to steal information. They were caught. Nixon said he did not know about the break-in. An investigation proved that he had lied and was trying to cover up the crime. Nixon had to resign in 1974. Vice President Gerald Ford became President.

A Time of Change

In the 1970s many people struggled for equal rights. Women were paid less than men for doing the same job. They wanted equality. By the late 1980s, more women were legislators, and 40 states had equal pay laws.

American Indians on reservations did not have good health care or education. Unemployment was high. They wanted more control of reservations. They wanted the government to honor treaties. Migrant workers formed unions and forced employers to improve conditions. Consumers pushed for product safety laws.

The Carter Years

In 1976, Jimmy Carter was elected President. Carter brought leaders from Israel and Egypt together to sign the Camp David Peace Accord. Carter tried to control inflation by raising taxes and lowering government spending. But oil prices continued to rise. In 1980, Carter lost the election to Ronald Reagan. Carter won the Nobel Peace Prize in 2002.

Before You Read

Find and underline each vocabulary word.

resign *verb,* to give up your job

migrant worker *noun,* a person who moves from place to place to find work, mostly on farms

accord *noun,* an agreement.

After You Read

REVIEW **Which events caused inflation during the 1970s?** Highlight the sentence that tells what started the war in the Middle East in 1973. Then circle the sentences that tell what action oil-producing countries took.

REVIEW **What were two goals of the Indian rights movement?** Circle two sentences that tell you the answer.

REVIEW **What were President Jimmy Carter's successes?** Highlight the sentence that tells what President Carter did to solve the problems in the Middle East.

Use with *United States History,* **pp. 648–653**

Summary: The 1980s

Reagan Becomes President

Ronald Reagan was elected President in 1980. Many Presidents before Reagan used government money to pay for programs to provide people with services such as health care, job training, and housing. Reagan spent less money on government programs.

Reagan believed a strong economy would help people more than government programs. He used deregulation to help businesses. At the end of his term, about 20 million more people had jobs than when he took office. Reagan spent a lot more government money on the military. He thought a strong military would keep America safe and end the Cold War. Increased spending caused the highest deficit America ever had.

International Events

In the 1980s the Soviet Union was having serious trouble. Its economy could not provide enough goods, jobs, and housing for its people. Too much money was spent on the arms race with the United States.

Soviet leader Mikhail Gorbachev worked to end the Cold War. He wanted a better relationship with the United States. Reagan and Gorbachev first met in 1985 to talk about the arms race. In 1987, they signed a treaty that lowered the number of nuclear weapons each country had.

In 1988, George Bush was elected President. The Soviet Union was growing weaker. The Cold War was over. Many nations split from the Soviet Union to form independent countries.

In 1990, there was more trouble in the Middle East. Saddam Hussein, the leader of Iraq, invaded a neighboring country, Kuwait, to take over its oil fields. President Bush asked other countries in the United Nations to form a coalition to fight Iraq. The Persian Gulf War lasted about seven weeks. In 1991, the coalition forces won because they had better technology and highly trained soldiers. Iraq left Kuwait, but Hussein stayed in power.

Before You Read

Find and underline each vocabulary word.

deregulation *noun*, the process of removing rules about what businesses can and cannot do

deficit *noun*, shortage caused by a government spending more money than it collects in taxes

coalition *noun*, a group of allies that work together to achieve a goal

After You Read

REVIEW **Why did President Reagan spend government money on the military?** Underline the sentence that tells the answer.

REVIEW **How did President Reagan help end the Cold War?** Highlight the sentence that tells who Reagan met with to talk about the arms race. Then circle the sentence that tells what the two leaders did.

Summary: Life in the 1990s

Clinton's Presidency

In 1992, Bill Clinton was elected President. He believed government money should be used to help people. There was not enough money because of the budget deficit from the Reagan years. The economy grew and more taxes were collected. Clinton put more money into social programs. By 1998, the United States had a budget surplus. The government had more money than it spent.

Clinton helped start peace processes in Northern Ireland and the Middle East. In the former country of Yugoslavia, different groups fought to form separate nations. The United States and other countries sent troops to stop the fighting there in 1999.

Clinton's second term was hurt by a scandal. He was impeached by the House of Representatives. The Senate found him not guilty.

A Changing Economy

During the 1990s, the United States had the longest period of economic growth in its history. Many people had more income to save, spend, or invest. Changes in computers and the development of high-tech businesses helped the economy grow. Computer programs were invented that people could use at home, at school, and at work. The Internet made it possible for people to get information, shop, and communicate quickly and easily.

New technology made the U.S. economy more productive. Jobs changed with the economy. More people did service jobs. Some companies moved factories overseas where they could make products at a lower cost. People with more education did better in the 1990s than people with less education.

A Connected World

Improved communication and transportation made trade between countries easier and less expensive. Nations are now more interdependent. Mexico, Canada, and the United States signed free-trade agreements in the 1990s.

Before You Read

Find and underline each vocabulary word.

Internet *noun,* network that links computers around the world with each other

high-tech *adjective,* high-technology, uses the most recent knowledge and equipment

free-trade agreement *noun,* treaties among countries that trade with one another

After You Read

REVIEW In which places did President Clinton help settle conflicts? Circle the names of three places where President Clinton helped settle conflicts.

REVIEW What effect did computers have on the economy in the 1990s? Circle the sentence that answers the question.

REVIEW In what ways did better communication change life for people during the 1990s? Highlight the sentence that tells you the answer.

Summary: Twenty-First Century Begins

The 2000 Election

On December 31, 1999, people all over the world celebrated the beginning of a new millennium. The new millennium really began on January 1, 2001. In a presidential election, the vote of individual citizens is called the popular vote. The candidate who wins the popular vote in a state wins all of that state's Electoral College votes. To win the election you have to win the electoral vote.

The 2000 presidential election was unusual because no one knew who won for weeks. The race was very close. Whoever won the vote in Florida would win the election. In Florida, Bush won the first count. Gore said the votes were not counted properly. Finally, the Supreme Court said that the Florida votes would not be recounted. Bush became President.

Attack on the Nation

On September 11, 2001, nearly three thousand people were killed by acts of terrorism in the United States. Terrorists hijacked four airplanes. They crashed two airplanes into the World Trade Center in New York, and one into the Pentagon in Washington, D.C. A fourth plane crashed in Pennsylvania.

The terrorists were from a group called al-Qaeda. They were against the United States' involvement in the Middle East. After the attacks, Bush accused the country of Afghanistan of hiding the leader of al-Qaeda, Osama bin Laden, and his followers. In October, 2001, a coalition of nations led by the United States went to war in Afghanistan. They defeated the government but they did not find bin Laden.

In 2003, Bush said Saddam Hussein, the leader in Iraq, was a danger to his neighbors and to the United States. In March 2003, the United States went to war in Iraq. After defeating Hussein's army and capturing Hussein, the military stayed in Iraq while a new Iraqi government formed.

Before You Read

Find and underline each vocabulary word.

millennium *noun,* a period of 10 centuries, or 1,000 years

popular vote *noun*, the vote of individual citizens

Electoral College *noun*, representatives, called electors, from each state

terrorism *noun*, the use of violence against ordinary people to achieve a political goal

After You Read

REVIEW **What is the difference between the popular vote and the electoral vote?** Circle the words that tell what a popular vote is. Highlight the words that tell what the votes in the Electoral College are. Underline the words that explain how a presidential election is won.

REVIEW **How did the United States respond to the terrorist attacks of September 11, 2001?** Circle the sentences that tell you the answer.

Use with *United States History*, pp. 672–675

Summary: Neighbors in North America

Canada

Canada is the United States' neighbor to the north. It has three territories and ten provinces. Its history is similar to American history. American Indians lived first in both countries. Europeans colonized both countries. In Canada, the colonists were mostly French. After a French-British war in 1754, Canada became a British colony. Many people in Canada speak both French and English. Both languages are now official languages there. In 1867, Canada gained its independence from Britain. Canada is a democracy. Like the United States, Canada is multicultural.

In 1992, Canada signed the North American Free Trade Agreement (NAFTA) with the United States and Mexico. NAFTA increased trade among the three nations. Canada is the United States' biggest trade partner. The two countries also work together to solve environmental problems that affect both countries.

Mexico

Mexico is the United States' neighbor to the south. It has 31 states and one federal district. The Maya and Aztecs lived in Mexico first, and they built large, beautiful cities. Spain colonized Mexico in 1521. In 1821, Mexico fought Spain for its independence and won. Mexico has a representative government that gives a lot of power to the President. Most Mexicans have a mixture of Spanish and Mexican Indian heritage. Spanish is the official language, but many people speak Indian languages. Mexican art, building styles, and food are common in the Southwest United States, which was once part of Mexico.

Many Mexicans work in maquiladoras, and many Mexicans come to the United States to work. This helps the U.S. economy. In 1992, Mexico signed NAFTA with the United States and Canada. Trade between the three countries increased. Today, Mexico's most important trading partner is the United States. After Canada, Mexico is the United States' second most important trading partner.

Before You Read

Find and underline each vocabulary word.

province *noun*, a political region of a country that is similar to a state

multicultural *adjective*, having many cultural traditions

maquiladora *noun*, a factory in Mexico near the U.S. border

After You Read

REVIEW **Why is French one of the two official languages in Canada?** Circle the sentence that tells the answer.

REVIEW **How and when did Mexico gain its independence?** Draw a box around the sentence that tells how and when Mexico gained its independence.

REVIEW **What are some of Mexico's connections with the United States?** Circle the sentences that tell about connections with Mexican culture, work, and trade.

Summary: United States Today

A Nation of Immigrants

Millions of immigrants come to the United States. Some come for a better life, and some come for religious or political freedom. Until 1965, most immigrants came from Europe or Mexico. In 1965, Congress changed the immigration laws. Now immigrants come from many nations. Spanish-speaking immigrants come from Central and South America and the Caribbean. Refugees from wars in El Salvador and Nicaragua came.

People also come from Africa and the West Indies. Today about one-fourth of America's immigrants are Asians from India, China, the Philippines, and other countries. Immigrants often live in communities where other people from their country live. They influence the culture and government of the places where they live.

Many People, One Nation

Many immigrants to the United States find the freedom they need to start successful careers. The United States has a diverse population, with many different ethnic groups. People bring music, food, language, art, and customs from their countries. Each person brings knowledge, skills, and talents. These things improve the United States. Ethnic diversity is one of the greatest strengths of the United States.

All people in the United States share a heritage of democracy. All United States citizens share the Constitution and the Bill of Rights. The Constitution and the Bill of Rights explain the rights of U.S. citizens. Our democratic heritage unites us into one nation. You can see the Latin motto "E Pluribus Unum" on American money. These Latin words mean "out of many, one." These words remind us that the United States became one nation by joining together 13 colonies. Today 50 states and many ethnic groups are joined together into one nation.

Before You Read

Find and underline each vocabulary word.

refugee *noun*, a person who escapes war or other danger and seeks safety in another country

heritage *noun*, something that is passed down from one generation to the next

motto *noun*, a short statement that explains an ideal or goal

After You Read

REVIEW **Why did immigration to the United States change after 1965?** Circle the sentence that tells the answer.

REVIEW **What do all U.S. citizens share?** Draw a box around the sentence that tells the answer.

Summary: Citizenship and Democracy

Citizenship

In many countries throughout history, most people have had no say in their government. In a democracy, all people help shape the government. The United States is a democracy that gives its citizens many rights. The Bill of Rights in the Constitution lists some rights, such as the right to speak freely, the right to practice any religion, and the right to a fair trial in court. One of the most important rights is the right to vote. When citizens vote, they help choose their government leaders. At age 18, citizens can register to vote.

Our government protects these rights. The government also protects the rights of all people to be treated fairly in housing and jobs, so that no one can discriminate against them because of religion or race. People who come to the United States from other countries can become citizens through the process of naturalization.

Citizens' Responsibilities

Our government gives citizens freedom and many rights. But citizens have responsibilities to the United States, too. Citizens must obey the law. This helps to keep our communities safe. Citizens must pay taxes. Taxes help the government pay for police, roads, and many other important services. Citizens are responsible for voting. Citizens must take turns being on a jury. Men over 18 years old have the responsibility of registering for the military. Young people have responsibilities, too. They must go to school. Education helps young people make good choices and decisions. This helps them become good citizens.

Our government works hard to make the United States a good place to live. But people need to help our democracy stay strong. Some ways to help are by learning about what is happening in the community, voting, and volunteering. Volunteers help communities in many ways. A strong democracy like the United States depends on its citizens to participate.

Before You Read

Find and underline each vocabulary word.

naturalization *noun*, the process of learning the laws of the country and the rights and duties of citizens

register *verb*, to sign up

responsibility *noun*, a duty that people are expected to fulfill

volunteer *noun*, a person who helps other people without pay

After You Read

REVIEW **At what age can citizens register to vote?** Circle the sentence that tells the answer.

REVIEW **In what ways can learning about issues prepare young people to be good citizens?** Circle the sentences that tell why education is important for young people.

Use with *United States History*, pp. 698–701

Challenge Activities

Geography Games

Make a set of flashcards that you can use for a variety of games. On one side write the word for a landform or other geographical feature, such as *lake* or *ocean*. On the reverse side of the card draw a picture to show the geographical feature, or glue a picture from a magazine. Invite a classmate to play flashcard games. Take turns showing each other the picture and saying the word. Or find the geographical features on a large map of the United States. You can also put together several sets of flashcards to play a game of Go Fish.

Trace a Product

Choose a product and find out as much as you can about how and where it was made. If you choose a food product, start by reading the ingredients. If you choose an item of clothing, read the label to find out the name of the manufacturer and where it was made. Use the library or the Internet to find out more about the company that makes the product. Write letters to the companies and ask for information. Make a flow chart that shows all the stages of production. Show your chart to the class and answer questions.

Local Regions

Think about how you could divide your home town, or neighborhood, or school. For example, you might divide a town into areas of big apartment buildings and areas of small houses. You could divide your neighborhood into areas where there are places where people live and areas where people work or shop. Make a map showing the complete region and the smaller regions that you created. Explain your map to your classmates.

Resources for Reaching All Learners
79
Use with *United States History*

Challenge Activities

Make a Poster

American Indians lived on all of the land that is now the United States. Choose a region and think about how the American Indians who lived there would think and feel about the land. Use field guides to find animals, trees, birds, and plants that live in the area. Make a poster showing the plants and animals that are found in the region. Label them. Write a sentence telling how each resource was used by American Indians. Present the poster to your classmates.

Tools for Living

You have read about how the introduction of horses in North America changed the lives of Plains Indians. When the Europeans arrived, they traded metal tools and blankets for furs and other goods. Look for more information about trade goods. Find out how American Indians made tools and goods before the Europeans came. How do you think the new tools and goods changed the lives of the Native Americans?

Write a description of how a tool or kind of clothing was made before trade with the Europeans. Include information on the material used and how Native Americans acquired it. Present your findings to your classmates.

Many Nations

You have read about Indian nations in many parts of the country. Choose one nation and find out more about them. Learn more about the people of that Indian nation now. Contrast and compare the past and the present. Write a two-part essay. In the first part describe their lives, culture, and government before the Europeans came. In the second part, describe their lives in the modern United States.

Challenge Activities

Make the Exchange

You have read about the Columbian Exchange. Act it out! Look for more information in the library or Internet about plants and animals that were brought from one continent to another. Make drawings of these plants and animals. Then set up an exchange with a partner. One represents the Americans, the other the Europeans. Take turns holding up a drawing and explaining what it can be used for, how it is grown, and so on.

From Cadiz to Tenochtitlan

The great Aztec city of Tenochtitlan amazed Cortés and his conquistadors. Use the library and Internet to learn more about Tenochtitlan and the Spanish port of Cadiz, which Spanish explorers used in the early 1500s. Compare the way of life in the two cities. For example, what kinds of houses did people live in? What food did they eat? Make two posters, one which shows the way of life of people in Cadiz and one which shows the way of life of people in Tenochtitlan. Use the posters as a starting point for telling your classmates about life in the two cities.

Make a Speech

You have read about Bartolome de las Casas. He spoke out against the mistreatment of the American Indians by the Spanish conquistadors. Use the library and the Internet to find out more about de las Casas and his ideas. What did he think was wrong with the way the Spanish treated American Indians? Organize your ideas and prepare a short speech. Pretend you are de las Casas and you are speaking to the Spanish officials. Choose at least three points to make. For each point, say what you think and why. Present your speech to your classmates. Be ready to answer questions.

Resources for Reaching All Learners
81
Use with *United States History*

Challenge Activities

A Day on the Mayflower

Use your library or the Internet to learn more details about the Pilgrims' long trip to Plymouth. Think about how the children on the *Mayflower* might have spent their time. Make a timetable that shows what an ordinary day might have been like. Draw pictures to show each activity. Share your timetable with your classmates.

Visit Fabulous New Netherland–You'll Want to Stay!!

The Dutch West India Company encouraged people to go to New Netherland. Design a travel brochure that the company could use to convince people that New Netherland is a wonderful place to visit or settle. Use pictures from magazines or the Internet to illustrate your brochure. Include information about how to travel there and where people could stay. Share your brochures with the class.

Explorers Gallery

Henry Hudson, John Cabot, La Salle and many others were famous explorers. Use your library or the Internet to learn more about an explorer that interests you. Divide a sheet of poster paper into four sections. Use one section to draw your explorer, and label it with his name and nationality. Use another section to list your explorer's goals. In the third section, list important voyages. In the fourth section, include important discoveries. Illustrate your poster and use it as a starting point to talk about your explorer with the class. Then hang the posters in the Explorers Gallery.

Challenge Activities

Make a Map

You learned about the English colonies in North America. Learn more about the physical geography of the east coast. Then trace a map of the area. Use symbols and different colors to show features, such as mountains and rivers. Mark the fall line, the tidewater, and backcountry regions. Show the map to your classmates. Present the information from a colonist's point of view.

Make a Point

You read about dissenters, such as Roger Williams and Anne Hutchinson. Look for more information about these two leaders. Read more about the Puritans and their beliefs. What did they think people should or should not do?

Work with a partner to prepare a conversation between a Puritan and a dissenter. Practice the conversation. Then perform it for the class. When you finish, take questions from the class.

Explore the Triangle Trade

Trade was important to the growth of the New England colonies. Find out what goods were exported from and imported to the colonies. How long did a voyage from Boston to London take? How long was the Middle Passage?

Use this information to create a ship's log. Include the date of the ship's departure and arrival. Explain what goods the ship is carrying. Tell about the crew and give details of life aboard the ship. Read your ship's log aloud and answer your classmates' questions.

Use with *United States History*

Challenge Activities

Examine an Experiment

You learned about the famous Philadelphia citizen, Ben Franklin. You read how he was interested in experiments. In one of these experiments, Franklin flew a kite in a lightning storm. Use books or the Internet to learn more about this experiment. Why did Franklin perform this experiment? What was he hoping to prove? What did he learn?

Make a comic strip. Draw pictures to show what Franklin's experiment was all about. Include sentences that tell what is happening and why. Share the comic strip with your classmates.

Sing a Spiritual

Slaves created spirituals to help them survive long workdays. Choose a partner. Use books or the Internet to learn more about these songs. Some websites allow you to listen to spirituals. What did a spiritual sound like? Often these songs had code words in them. Why? What did these words mean? Find out the different ways spirituals were performed.

Choose the spiritual that you like the most. Write its words on a large piece of paper. Display the paper as you perform the spiritual with your partner. Invite other classmates to join you if necessary.

Get a Job!

Many colonial children became apprentices. Boys learned skills like shoemaking and printing. Girls learned to spin thread and weave cloth. Use books or the Internet to find other jobs these children trained for. Choose a skill that you think you would have liked to learn. Make a poster that shows the different activities you would have performed in a day. Include captions that tell what is happening in each picture. Share the poster with your classmates. Tell them why you chose this job.

Challenge Activities

Personality Spotlight

You have read about some interesting people in this chapter. Choose one person you would like to know more about. Look for books or magazine articles about the person. Once you have learned more about the person, think about how he or she might have felt about the Boston Tea Party or other events affecting him or her in the early 1770s. Write a short speech on the subject in the voice of the person you choose. Practice your speech and present it to your classmates.

Make a Poster or Diorama

You have read about the events in and around Boston in the early 1770s. Think about some of the things the textbook did not tell you. Look for books or articles about Boston. What was life like for the people who lived there? What kinds of food did they eat? What were their houses like? What did they do for work? What did they do for fun? Make a poster or diorama showing a street scene in Boston in the 1770s. Include people as well as buildings. Show your poster or diorama to the class and explain what you learned.

State Your Case

You have learned about the reasons American Patriots were angry with Britain. Some were ready for war. Others signed the Olive Branch Petition and asked King George III to help find a peaceful solution. Choose a partner. Imagine that the two of you are having a conversation in Boston in 1775. Write a dialogue in which both of you state your opinions about what the colonists should do. Use details to support your case. Talk about the soldiers quartered in Boston, about the Boston Massacre, and the Boston Tea Party. Practice your dialogue and perform it for the class. Pay attention to your body language and your voice. After the dialogue, stay in character and take questions from the class.

Challenge Activities

Personality Spotlight

You have learned about many famous and interesting people in this chapter. Choose one person you would like to know more about. Look for books and magazine articles about this person. Once you have learned more about the person, write a short speech that this person might give, telling about his or her life during the American Revolution.

Make a Diorama

You have read about the Battle of Saratoga, an important American victory in 1777. Think about some facts or ideas your textbook does not tell you about this battle. For example, what was the weather like on the battlefield? Would the soldiers have been marching through mud? Would they have climbed many hills, or was the land mostly flat?

Then make a diorama or a poster that shows what the surroundings of the battle might have looked like. (Remember that the battle took place in the summer.) Include natural features, like trees or hills. Show your diorama or poster to the class and explain what you learned. Talk about how the climate and surroundings might have made the soldiers feel.

The First States

Delegates from thirteen colonies signed the Declaration of Independence. What were the names of the thirteen original colonies? Choose a colony and look for information about it during the time of the American Revolution. Draw a map of the colony you chose. Include the major natural features, like lakes, rivers, and mountains. Draw pictures on your map to show the crops or other products that came from the colony during this time. Show your map to the class and tell your classmates about the colony.

Use with *United States History,* pp. 262–289

Challenge Activities

Personality Spotlight

You have learned about some famous and interesting people in this chapter. Choose one person you would like to find out more about. Use books, or the Internet to learn more about this person. Then write a short speech that this person might give, telling about his opinions on the Constitution and the new government it created.

Make an Argument

You have read about the Constitutional Convention and the various arguments for and against a strong federal government. Use books or the Internet to find more information about these issues. Work with a partner to prepare a debate on the issues. Each partner should include reasons for their beliefs. Practice the debate and then present it to the class. Ask your classmates to vote on the issue.

Remembering George Washington

George Washington was greatly loved as a general and as President. Almost every town in the United States has a street or park named after him. Look at a map of your area to see if there is a place named after him there. Then read more about George Washington. Make a poster that could be used as a plaque to tell people why he was a great man. Include details about his accomplishments and the many things he did for the country.

George Washington

Challenge Activities

Talk About It

You learned why settlers crossed the Appalachians and why the Native Americans didn't want them there. Use books and the Internet to learn more about the settlers and the Cherokee, Choctaw, and Shawnee Indians. Find photographs and written descriptions of the land in Kentucky and Tennessee.

Write an exchange between a settler and an Indian. Have each explain why he or she wants to live in that place. Have them say how they feel about sharing the land. Have them each predict about how the area will change over time.

Coin Curiosity

In 1999, the U.S. Mint released a golden dollar with Sacagawea's picture on it. Use the library or the Internet to find out what the images on the coin mean. What do the 17 stars on the back of the coin represent? What does *E Pluribus Unum* mean?

Design your own coin with Meriwether Lewis, William Clark, or Zebulon Pike. Decide what your coin will look like. When did the expedition take place? Why was it important? Who did they meet? Draw your coin. Explain each image to your classmates.

Make a Triptych

Learn more about the Indians who were forced to move because of the Indian Removal Act. Look for images of the Indian Territory, which is now Oklahoma. Think about how the Indians felt about the land they were leaving and the new place they were moved to.

Use three pieces of paper to make a triptych. The page on the left shows the original home of the Indians. The middle picture shows the journey. The picture on the right shows their new land in Oklahoma. Show the triptych to your classmates. Use it to describe the changes the Indians endured because of the Indian Removal Act.

Challenge Activities

Make a Comic Strip

Make a comic strip about the Industrial Revolution. First, write a list of important events that happened during this time. Put them in order. Count them to know how many boxes will be in your comic strip. Then draw each event with text inside or below the comic strip box. Share your comic strip with your class.

Wagons Ho

Find out more about covered wagons and what it was like to travel a long distance in one. Then make a chart that compares and contrasts travel to the West by covered wagon with travel to the West today. Think about things all travelers do to plan and prepare for a trip. Think about possible emergencies and needed supplies. Explain your chart to your class.

Wild West

Use your classroom library or the Internet to learn more about what it was like to be a miner during the California Gold Rush. Then imagine that you are a forty-niner. Most evenings you like to write in your journal about what happened that day. Think about some of the facts you have learned about the gold rush, boomtowns, and the people who looked for gold. Include details that you learned—perhaps about the kinds of people who become miners, what happens when you find gold, and what's good and what's bad about your life as a miner. Write some entries in your journal.

Resources for Reaching All Learners
89
Use with *United States History*

Challenge Activities

Stage a Debate

You have learned about the different ideas of people who lived in the South and in the North. Work with a partner to prepare a debate. One partner should speak for the North. Include opinions on slavery, abolition, popular sovereignty in the territories, and tariffs. The other partner should speak for the South. Include opinions on slavery, the threat of slave rebellions, popular sovereignty in the territories, and high costs of manufactured goods. Use books or the Internet to read more about these issues. Work with your partner to make up four or five questions to answer. Practice your speeches. Then share the debate with your classmates. Invite the class to vote.

Meet Abe Lincoln

You have read about Abraham Lincoln's early life and political career. Use books or the Internet to find out more about him. Write an imaginary autobiography that describes Lincoln's childhood, work, and home life. Include his opinions about slavery, the Constitution, states' rights, the Union, and war. Look for pictures of Lincoln and descriptions of how he looked and sounded. Read your autobiography to your classmates in character. Stay in character to answer your classmates' questions.

Make a Map

You have read about slave states, free states, and territories. Find maps that show which states and territories were part of the United States in 1861. Use tissue paper to trace one. Mark which states and territories were free and which were slave. Then draw a line to show the boundaries of the Union and the Confederacy. Label the states, territories, and major cities. Include physical details of the land, such as mountains, bodies of water, and other important features. Show the map to your classmates and talk about the United States in 1861.

Challenge Activities

Letters from the Front

You have learned about the Civil War. Use your library or the Internet to find out about the experiences of soldiers during the war. Choose a character to represent. Write a short description explaining who you are. Are you a soldier in one of the armies? An officer? A nurse? Give information about the person you have chosen. Tell how old are you, how long have you been in the war, and who are you writing to.

Then choose a specific event during the war and imagine that you were there. Write a letter describing the event to your friends or family at home. Tell them what you saw, heard, smelled, and how you felt about the event. Read your letter aloud to your classmates. Stay in character to answer their questions.

Unpack

During the Civil War, soldiers lived in tents and walked from place to place. They carried any equipment or supplies they needed in their packs. Do some research about the uniforms, equipment, and belongings of soldiers. Did soldiers carry mess kits? Water bottles? Writing paper? Draw pictures of each item and pack them into a paper bag. Unpack your "pack" for your classmates and explain each item and how it was used.

Exploring the Home Front

Soldiers who fought in the Civil War came from all over the country. Nearly every town has a war memorial for the men who died. Find out if your town has a Civil War memorial. If possible, visit the memorial and write the names of soldiers who died. Do you live in a state that was part of the Union or Confederacy? Is your hometown far from the battlefields or was there fighting near where you live? Look for information on the Internet or at a local historical society. Make a diorama or poster showing what it was like where you live during the Civil War. Use it as a starting point. Tell your classmates about life in your community during the Civil War.

Use with *United States History*

Support for Language Development

1. Write the letter of the picture and word that goes with the definition below.

barbed wire   demand   railhead   supply

____ The amount of something that people want to sell at a certain price

____ Wire with sharp points on it

____ The amount of something that people want to buy at a certain price

____ A town where railroad tracks begin or end

2. Supply and demand affect how much things are worth. Read "Demand and Supply for Cattle" in the lesson. Write how the supply and demand affected the price of cattle.

Cause: There were many longhorn cattle in Texas. Not many people wanted to buy them.

Effect: _____

Cause: There were many people in the North and East that wanted to buy beef and leather. There were not many longhorn cattle.

Effect: _____

3. Read "The End of the Drives" in the lesson. Complete the sentence.

Many states passed laws to keep out Texas cattle because the cattle

had _____ .

Challenge Activities

First Sight of Land

You learned that many immigrants arrived in the United States between 1880 and 1924. Most of these immigrants came from eastern or southern Europe. Look at a map and choose a country from that region. Look for information about that country in books or on the Internet.

Imagine that you are an immigrant crossing land and sea to get to America. Think about how you might have felt when you first saw Ellis Island or Angel Island. Write journal entries you may have written. Include your plans. Where do you want to live? What kind of work will you look for? Share these journal entries with the class.

Time for Reform

You read about the progressives and muckrakers of the early 1900s. Choose one issue they fought for. Research it. For example, study the fight to end child labor. Learn about the dirty and dangerous work in the factories or, find out more about the fight for suffrage.

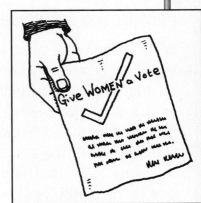

Use the information you find to write a leaflet about the issue. Share your pamplet with the class. Try to convince your classmates to think as you do.

Make a Diorama

As cities got bigger, they also got crowded, noisier, and dirtier. Find photos and descriptions of what Chicago looked like during the early 1900s. Make a diorama of a street scene. Include people and their modes of transportation. Show buildings and their physical details. What kinds of animals lived there? Present your diorama to your classmates. Use it to describe life in the big city.

Challenge Activities

Play the Stock Market

The early 1920s was a time of prosperity for many Americans. People used their money to invest in the stock market. Pretend that you are interested in buying some stock. Which company would you be interested in? Use the Internet to research that company. How old is the company? What does it produce? Has it been successful? What other companies are like it?

Many daily newspapers list the activity of the stock market. Find a newspaper. Ask an adult to help you find your company. How much does one share cost? Did the stock go up? Did it fall? By how much? Share these findings with your classmates.

People and Event Cards

Write on one side of an index card the names of important people or events that you learned about in this chapter. Draw a picture that illustrates the person or event on the other side of the card. Use your cards to play a game with a friend. Show your friend the illustration. Ask him to guess the event. If your friend answers correctly, he keeps the card. The player with the most cards at the end of the game wins.

Interview an Icon

You learned about many important men and women in this chapter. Choose a partner. Then choose one person that both of you would like to research. Write a list of questions that you have about this person.

Use your library or the Internet to research that person. Who is the person? Why is he/she important? What did he/she do? Use this information to write interview questions. Role-play the interview for your class.

Resources for Reaching All Learners
94
Use with *United States History*

Challenge Activities

Diorama of a 1950s Community

You have read about the baby boom of the 1950s. Find out what some of the new 1950s communities looked like. Search books or the Internet for pictures of communities, such as Levittown, New York and Wheaton, Maryland.

Make a diorama showing one of those communities. Include houses, roads, and schools. Share your diorama with the class and explain what you learned. Compare your community and the 1950s community.

The *Eagle* Has Landed

You learned that Neil Armstrong and Buzz Aldrin were the first humans to land on the moon. Their lunar module was called *Eagle*. When they landed on the moon, Neil Armstrong and Buzz Aldrin told people on Earth, "The *Eagle* has landed." The name of their mission was Apollo 11. Use an encyclopedia or the Internet to learn more about Apollo 11.

Write a newspaper article telling the world about this important event. Choose a headline that will attract attention. Include as much information as you can about the mission. Share your newspaper article with the class.

Vietnam Debate

You learned about the Vietnam War and the role the United States played in it. You know that some Americans supported the U.S. role in Vietnam and others did not. Use books and the Internet to find out more about the Vietnam War.

Then form two groups; one supporting the U.S. role in the Vietnam War and the other against it. Stage a debate for the class. Use facts to support your arguments. Choose a classmate to help moderate the debate.

Resources for Reaching All Learners
95
Use with *United States History*

Challenge Activities

Explore the Lives of Children in Afghanistan and Iraq

Learn more about Afganistan and Iraq, two of the countries the United States has sent soldiers to in the last few years. Work with other students. Choose one country and prepare a set of questions you would like to have answered. For example: What was it like to live there as a child before the war? What do people there eat? What kind of work do they do? What are their houses like? What are the schools like? How did the war affect children who live there? Use books, magazines, and the Internet to find information.

Write a letter to a child in the country you chose. Mention things that you have learned about life in his or her country. Then ask questions about things you would like to learn more about. Read your letter to the class. Ask if classmates can answer any of your questions.

Fight for Equal Rights

In the 1970s, women, farm workers, American Indians, and other groups of people worked hard to gain more rights. Select a group of people that interests you. Use books and the Internet to find out the types of rights the group fought for or is fighting for. Make a banner demanding equal rights. Draw pictures to illustrate it. Share your banner with the class and explain which group you represent and what you are fighting for.

Inventions

You learned about the growing computer industry and the boom of many high-tech businesses during the 1990s. You have seen how inventions change the way people live. Work with other students to brainstorm an invention that you would like to create. Talk about what it would look like and how it would work. Then draw a picture or make a model of your invention. When complete, share your invention with the class and tell classmates how it will improve their lives.

Challenge Activities

New Restaurant News Flash!

You can find Mexican art, food, and music in many places in the Southwestern United States. This is because that part of the United States used to belong to Mexico. Pretend you are going to open a restaurant in the Southwest. You want to please all your customers, so you will include some Mexican foods on your menu. You might use some Mexican art to decorate the restaurant, too. And how about Mexican music on your opening day? Make up a TV commercial that will make people want to come to your new restaurant and act it out for your classmates.

Holidays, Holidays, Holidays

You and your family probably have your own traditions for celebrating birthdays, the New Year, and other holidays. People who come to the United States from other countries celebrate many of the same holidays that Americans celebrate. But just as your family has its own traditions, immigrants often bring their own holiday customs to the United States.

An American New Year's Eve	A German New Year's Eve
Eat clam chowder with crackers	Eat split pea soup with wieners
Fireworks and noisemakers	Fireworks and bells
Toasts and kisses at midnight	Toasts and hugs at midnight

Choose your favorite holiday and find out how someone from another ethnic background celebrates that same holiday. Make a chart that compares your customs and illustrate it. Share your chart with the class.

Volunteer Army

Think about how volunteers help your community. Do people in your community give blood? Clean up parks or lakes? Walk to raise money for cures? Work together to help families with emergencies? Use your library or the Internet to find out about things volunteers do in other schools, towns, and cities. List your results and share it with your class.

Support for Language Development

1. Write in the letters that go with the pictures below.

geography

landform

plateau

climate

equator

____ the imaginary line around the middle of the Earth

____ the study of the world and the people and things that live there

____ the type of weather a place has over a long period of time

____ a high, steep-sided area rising above the surrounding land

____ a feature on the surface of the land

2. Read the section called "Landforms." Then write the names of bodies of water (rivers, lakes), mountains (ranges), and other features (plains, canyons) in the correct columns below.

Bodies of Water	Mountains	Plains/Canyons/Other

Support for Language Development

1. Write in the letters for the pictures that go with the definitions below.

capital resource

human resource

scarcity

opportunity cost

conservation

____ the skills and knowledge of the people doing the work

____ the protection and wise use of natural resources

____ not having as much of something as people want

____ a tool, machine, or building people use to produce goods and services

____ the thing you give up when you decide to do or have something else

2. Read the section of the lesson called "Other Important Resources." Then decide if the following words are capital, human, or natural resources. Write the words in the correct column.

peanuts	oven	
tractor	soil	
factory workers	water	
sunshine	farmers	

Capital	Human	Natural

Name _____ Date _____

Support for Language Development

1. Write the letter of the picture and word that goes with the definition below.

specialization

consumer

trade

economy

_____ a person who buys goods and services

_____ buying and selling of goods

_____ the way people focus on making certain goods they can produce best with resources that are nearby and plentiful

_____ a system people use to produce goods and services

2. Write the word or words that complete the sentences correctly.

A. One way to divide the United States into _____ is to group together states that are close to each other.

B. Regions can be places where people speak the same

_____ or share the same _____.

C. The United States can be divided into regions by

_____ density.

D. Most regions have plenty of some _____, such as coal, and less of others.

Use with *United States History*, pp. 22–25

Support for Language Development

1. Write the word that goes with the definition below.

environment

erosion

pollution

ecosystem

_____ Anything that makes the soil, air, or water dirty and unhealthy

_____ The surroundings in which people, plants, and animals live

_____ A community of plants and animals along with the surrounding soil, air, and water

_____ The process by which water and wind wear away the land

2. Read the section called "Changing the Land." Write the correct word or words to complete each sentence below.

Changing the _____

_____ _____, such as wind and moving _____, constantly shape and reshape the land.

_____ _____, such as digging mines and building _____, also change the land.

Support for Language Development

1. Write the letter of the picture and word that goes with the definition below.

pueblo

agriculture

civilization

glacier

_____ a group of people living together with organized systems of government, religion, and culture

_____ farming, or growing plants

_____ the Spanish word for town

_____ a huge, thick sheet of slowly moving ice

2. Read the sentences below. Which happened first? Write "1" in front of the first event. Write "2" in front of the second event. Write "3" in front of the third event. Write "4" in front of the fourth event.

_____ **A.** Ice Age ended.

_____ **B.** Ancient people crossed the land bridge between Asia and Alaska.

_____ **C.** Aztecs built Tenochtitlán.

_____ **D.** Agriculture began in Central Mexico.

Resources for Reaching All Learners
102
Use with *United States History,* pp. 38–43

Name _____ Date _____

Support for Language Development

1. Write the vocabulary word on the line next to its meaning.

| surplus | potlatch | clan |

_____ large feast that lasts
for several days

_____ group of related
families

_____ extra

2. Write the word or words that complete the sentence correctly.

A. The Northwest is close to the _____ Ocean.

B. Two key resources of the Tlingit were _____ and

_____ .

C. On special occasions Northwest Indians held a

_____ .

D. American Indians dried _____ salmon, so they had

food all year long.

Support for Language Development

1. Write the vocabulary word on the line next to its meaning.

staple	ceremony	irrigation

_____

a special event at which people gather to express important beliefs

_____

supplying water to crops using streams, ditches, or pipes

_____

main crop that is used for food

2. Write the word or words that complete the sentence correctly.

A. The _____ is mostly dry desert.

B. The _____ believe they are the caretakers of the land.

C. Hopis were among the first to fire _____ to make it strong.

D. Visitors can sometimes watch Hopi _____.

Resources for Reaching All Learners
104
Use with *United States History*, pp. 54–57

Support for Language Development

1. Write the vocabulary word on the line next to its meaning.

lodge	nomad	travois

_____ a house made of bark, earth, and grass

_____ similar to a sled, used by nomads to carry their possessions

_____ a person who moves around and does not live in one place

2. Read the sentences below. Which happened first? Write "1" in front of the first event. Write "2" in front of the second event. Write "3" in front of the third event.

_____ **A.** Comanche Indians spread across the Great Plains.

_____ **B.** Plains Indians began to ride and raise horses.

_____ **C.** Spanish introduced horses into North America.

Support for Language Development

1. Write the letter of the picture and word that goes with the definition below.

wampum

barter

longhouse

____ exchange of goods without using money

____ a large house made of wooden poles and bark

____ carefully shaped and cut seashells strung like beads

2. Write the word that completes the sentence correctly.

A. The Eastern Woodlands were rich in natural _____.

B. In the warm south, people built houses with no

_____.

C. In the cold north, people lived in _____.

3. Read the section called "Farming and Building" in your text. In the box labeled "Compare," tell how the northern and southern regions were alike. In the box labeled "Contrast," tell how the regions were different.

Compare	**Contrast**
_____, _____, and _____ were the staple crops for most woodland Indians	In _____ southern climates, people built houses without walls. Farther north, people needed protection from the _____.

Support for Language Development

1. Write the vocabulary word on the line next to its meaning.

merchant	kingdom	caravan

_____

A group of people and animals who travel together

_____

A place ruled by a king or queen

_____

Someone who buys and sells goods to earn money

2. Read "Trade with China." Write the word or words that complete the sentence correctly.

A. Before 1500 most people in Europe, Africa, and Asia did not know

that the _____ existed.

B. _____ _____

spent 16 years working for the ruler of China.

C. _____ _____

brought a giraffe from Africa back to China.

Support for Language Development

1. Write the letters of the pictures and words that go with the definitions below.

profit

astrolabe

slavery

navigation

technology

____ the use of scientific knowledge and tools to do things better and more rapidly

____ the science of planning and controlling the direction of a ship

____ a navigation tool that measures the height of the sun or a star against the horizon

____ money left after all expenses have been paid

____ a cruel system in which people are bought and sold and made to work without pay

2. Read the section of the lesson called "The Renaissance." Then write the word or words that complete the sentence correctly.

A. Europeans learned about the compass and gunpower from the

_____.

B. The _____ _____ meant ideas could spread faster.

C. New _____ tools meant new sea routes could be explored.

Use with *United States History*, pp. 90–93

Support for Language Development

1. Write the word on the line next to the definition.

settlement	circumnavigate	epidemic

_____ — a small community of people living in a new place

_____ — an outbreak of a disease that spreads quickly and affects many people

_____ — to sail completely around something

2. Read the chart in your textbook showing the Columbian Exchange. Then write the words in the box under the correct heading.

corn	bananas
pigs	beans
horses	diseases
potatoes	chocolate

From Americas	From Europe
_____	_____
_____	_____
_____	_____
_____	_____

Support for Language Development

1. Write the word on the line next to the definition.

expedition	empire	conquistador

_____ a journey to achieve a goal

_____ many nations or territories ruled by a single group or leader

_____ Spanish word for conqueror, a soldier

2. Read the section of the lesson called "Cortés Conquers the Aztecs." Then write the word or words that complete the sentence correctly.

Causes		Effects

Causes	Effects
Cortés met people who were enemies of the Aztecs.	Cortés convinced them to join him to _____ the Aztecs.
Cortés had armor, guns and horses. The Aztecs did not.	_____ defeated the _____ and claimed the land for Spain.

Use with *United States History*, **pp. 104–107**

Support for Language Development

1. Write the letter of the picture and word that goes with the definition below.

mission

colony

hacienda

_____ a territory ruled by another country

_____ a religious community where priests taught Christianity

_____ a large farm or ranch, often with its own church and village

2. Read "New Settlements." Match the Spanish explorer or priest to the description.

Pedro Menéndez de Avilés	started a settlement at Santa Fe, New Mexico, in 1598.
Junípero Serra	founded missions on the coast of California in 1769.
Don Juan de Oñate	started St. Augustine in Florida in 1565.

Support for Language Development

1. Write the vocabulary word on the line next to its meaning.

armada	claim	invasion

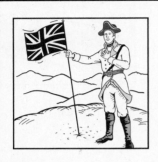	_____	to declare something as your own
	_____	a large fleet of ships
	_____	an attack by an armed force to conquer another country

2. Draw a line to match the explorer to the details that describe him.

John Cabot	Around 1534, I continued France's search for a water route to Asia. I sailed far up the St. Lawrence River.
Samuel de Champlain	In the late 1400s, the King of England paid for my voyage to find Asia. I found Canada instead.
Jacques Cartier	In 1608, I started a fur-trading post at Quebec. It became the first permanent French settlement in North America.

Use with *United States History,* pp. 122–125

Support for Language Development

1. Write the letter of the picture and the word that go with the definition below.

indentured servant

invest

cash crop

stock

charter

____ a document giving permission to a person or group to do something

____ to put money into something to earn more money

____ a crop that people grow and sell to earn money

____ someone who agreed to work for a number of years in exchange for the cost of the voyage to North America

____ a piece of ownership of a company

2. Read the section of the lesson called "The Jamestown Colony" and fill in the missing words.

Cause

| The water wasn't good for drinking. Insects carried diseases. |

Effect

| The settlers died from _____ and _____ . |

Support for Language Development

1. Write the vocabulary word on the line next to its meaning.

compact	pilgrim	cape

	_____	a person who makes a long journey for religious reasons
	_____	an agreement
 Cape Cod	_____	a strip of land that stretches into a body of water

2. Fill in the missing words in the box below.

Pilgrims and Puritans

Compare	Contrast
Separated from the Church of England; Wanted a colony based on _____ beliefs	Pilgrims arrive in November, _____ _____ to plant crops. Puritans arrive in June, in time to plant crops.

Support for Language Development

1. Write the vocabulary word on the line next to its meaning.

missionary	diversity	tolerance

_____

the variety of people in a group

_____

respect for beliefs that are different from one's own

_____

a person who teaches his or her religion to others who have different beliefs

2. Fill in the missing words in the boxes below.

Governor Stuyvesant made _____ _____ that angered the New Netherland colonists.	The colonists were so unhappy that they refused to fight the _____ _____ that came to attack and take over the Dutch land.	New Netherland became _____ _____, an English colony.

Name _____ Date _____

Support for Language Development

1. Write the letter of the picture and word that goes the definition below.

growing season

tidewater

fall line

backcountry

____ The water in rivers and streams that rises and falls every day with the ocean's tides

____ The time of year when it is warm enough to grow crops

____ The land "in back of" the area where most colonists settled

____ When rivers from higher land flow to lower lands, and often form waterfalls

2. Read about the thirteen colonies in your textbook. Then draw lines to match the colonies on the left to the sentences on the right.

In the Southern colonies	it was hard to find good farmland.
In New England	the tidewater region provided rich farmland.
In the Middle colonies	glaciers dropped fertile soil in the area.

Support for Language Development

1. Write the letter of the picture and word that goes with the definition below.

a town meeting   **b** banish   **c** dissenter   **d** self-government

_____ A gathering where colonists held elections and voted on the laws for their towns

_____ When the people who live in a place make laws for themselves

_____ A person who does not agree with the beliefs of his or her leaders

_____ To force someone to leave

2. Read about the following dissenters in your textbook. Then draw a line to connect the phrase on the left with the name on the right.

I was the leader of the Wampanoag nation.	Roger Williams
I believed government and religion should be separate.	Anne Hutchinson
I held meetings where men and women could discuss religion.	Thomas Hooker
I wanted to let all men, even those who did not belong to the church, to vote.	Metacomet

Name _____ Date _____

Support for Language Development

1. Write the letter of the picture and word that goes with the definition below.

slave trade

export

industry

Middle Passage

import

____ All the businesses that make one product or provide one service

____ A product sent to another country and sold

____ A product brought into one country from another country

____ The trip from Africa to the West Indies

____ The business of buying and selling human beings

2. Read the section of the lesson called "Using the Sea." Write the correct words to complete the sentences below.

Because farming was difficult in New England, some colonists looked for other ways to earn a _____.

Boston became a center for the _____ industry.

Many people made their living by catching and selling _____.

By the 1700s, _____ was an important industry.

Support for Language Development

1. Write the vocabulary word on the line next to its meaning.

representative	proprietor	treaty

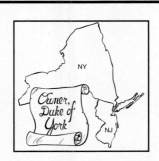

_____

A person who owned and controlled all the land in a colony

_____

Someone who is chosen to speak and act for others

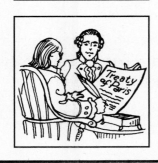

_____

An official agreement between nations or groups

2. Read the paragraphs about Benjamin Franklin in the section called "Philadelphia" in your book. Then complete the sentences.

A. He published a _____ and *Poor Richard's Almanack*.

B. He _____ a wood stove and a clock.

C. He helped start the first library, fire company, and

_____ in Philadelphia.

Support for Language Development

1. Write the letter of the picture and word that goes with the definition below.

free enterprise

artisan

laborer

apprentice

____ Someone who is skilled at making something by hand

____ Someone who studies with a master to learn a skill or business

____ A system in which people may start any business that they believe will succeed

____ A person who does hard physical work

2. Read the section in your textbook called "A Mix of People." Then write the correct word or words to complete the sentences below.

   A. The people of the Middle Colonies came from many

   _____.

   B. Colonial proprietors believed in _____ _____.

   C. Religious tolerance and _____ land attracted

   many people.

Support for Language Development

1. Write the letter of the word that goes with the definition below.

a plantation   **b** legislature   **c** refuge   **d** debtor

_____ A safe place

_____ A group of people with the power to make and change laws

_____ A large farm on which crops are raised by workers who live on the farm

_____ A person who owes money

2. Read the section in your textbook called "New Colonies in the South."
Then write the correct words to complete the sentences below.

A. 1632: Calvert hopes to make Maryland a _____ for

Catholics.

B. 1633: King Charles I forms Carolina to keep _____ and

_____ out of the area.

C. 1729: King George II divides _____ into North Carolina

and South Carolina.

D. 1732: King George II gives land to Oglethorpe. He wants Georgia

to be a place for poor people and _____.

3. Read the section in your textbook called "Governing the Colony."
Then number the sentences in the order they happened.

_____ **A.** The legislature makes the Anglican Church the official
church.

_____ **B.** The House of Burgesses becomes the first elected
legislature in the colonies.

_____ **C.** Colonists want a voice in the laws of Virginia.

Support for Language Development

1. Write the vocabulary word on the line next to its meaning.

overseer	spiritual	indigo

_____

A plant that can be made into a dark blue dye

_____

A person who watches and directs the work of other people

_____

An African American religious folk song

2. Read the section in your textbook called "Southern Agriculture." Fill in the missing crops in the chart below.

Southern Colonies and Their Crops

Virginia and Maryland:

_____

North Carolina:

_____, tobacco

South Carolina and

Georgia: _____,

_____

Support for Language Development

1. Write the letter of the picture that goes with the definition below.

proclamation

ally

congress

rebellion

_____ An official public statement

_____ A fight against a government

_____ A group of representatives who meet to discuss a subject

_____ A person or group that joins with another to work toward a goal

2. Fill in the blanks in the boxes on the left.

Causes	Effects
The British wanted to settle in the Ohio River Valley and to trade with the _____ _____ who lived there.	Britain declared war on France.
Britain and France ended the war and signed the _____ _____ _____.	France gave Britain control of Canada and most of the land east of the Mississippi River.
_____ soldiers stayed in the Ohio River Valley.	Pontiac led American Indians in a war against the British.

Resources for Reaching All Learners

123

Use with *United States History*, pp. 228–231

Support for Language Development

1. Write the vocabulary words in the correct space.

| tax | boycott | protest | liberty | repeal | smuggling |

a _____

b _____

c _____

d _____

e _____

f _____

2. Read the sentences. Write the letters and numbers for the problems and solutions.

A. British government passed the Townshend Acts.

B. The government passed the Stamp Act.

1. The Daughters of Liberty boycott all British goods.

2. Merchants agreed to boycott British goods.

Problem

A

B

Solution

1

2

Support for Language Development

1. Write the letter of the picture that goes with the definition below.

quarter

delegate

correspondence

massacre

____ Written communication

____ Someone chosen to speak and act for others

____ To give people food and shelter

____ The killing of many people

2. Read the sentences below. Number the sentences in order from first to last.

____ **A.** Parliament passed the Coercive Acts.

____ **B.** The Boston Tea Party

____ **C.** The First Continental Congress

____ **D.** The Boston Massacre

3. Read the section of the lesson called "The Boston Tea Party." Use these words to complete the following sentences.

| Tea Act | Sons of Liberty | East India Company |

A. The _____ was allowed to sell tea in America for a very low price.

B. The _____ threw the tea into Boston Harbor.

C. In 1773, Parliament passed the _____.

Support for Language Development

1. Write the letter of the picture that goes with the definition below.

militia

commander

minutemen

Patriot

petition

_____ A colonist who opposed British rule

_____ Militia with special training

_____ Officer in charge of an army

_____ Group of ordinary people who train for battle

_____ A written request from a number of people

2. Draw a line from each name to make correct sentences.

A. Paul Revere

B. George Washington

C. General Thomas Gage

D. King George III

sent 700 soldiers to destroy the Patriots' weapons.

refused to look for a peaceful solution.

warned the minutemen that the British were coming.

was the commander of the Continental Army.

3. Fill in the blanks with the correct answer.

A. At the Battle of Bunker Hill the British fought against the

_____ .

B. The Second Continental Congress created the _____

_____ .

Support for Language Development

1. Write the letter of the picture and word that goes with the definition below.

treason

independence

rights

_____ freedom from being ruled by someone else

_____ the crime of fighting against one's own government

_____ freedoms that are protected by a government's laws

2. Read the sentences below. Which happened first? Write "1" in front of the first event. Write "2" in front of the second event. Write "3" in front of the third event.

_____ **A.** Thomas Jefferson wrote the Declaration of Independence.

_____ **B.** Thomas Paine wrote *Common Sense*.

_____ **C.** Delegates signed the declaration.

3. Draw a line from the name in the left column to the correct sentence in the right column.

King George	signed the Declaration of Independence.
Congress	was a pamphlet that pushed for independence.
Patriots	had tried to take away the colonists' rights.
Common Sense	felt independence from Britain was worth fighting for.

Support for Language Development

1. Write the vocabulary word on the line next to its meaning.

Loyalists	neutral	inflation

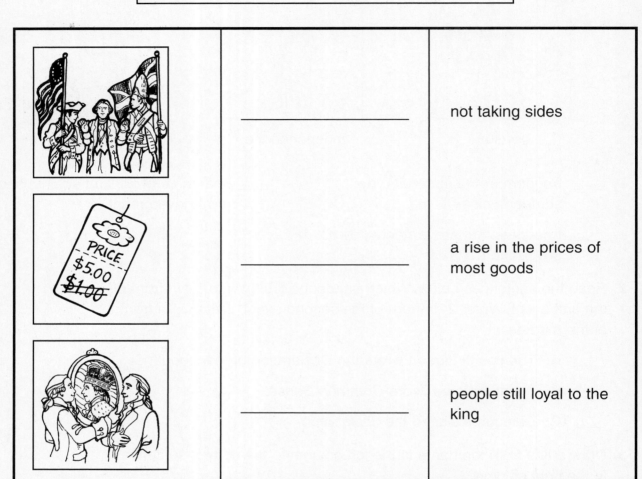

_____ not taking sides

_____ a rise in the prices of most goods

_____ people still loyal to the king

2. Read the sentences that explain why people were Patriots or Loyalists. Write the letter for each sentence in the correct column.

A. Some colonists thought Britain should rule America.

B. Many colonists wanted America to be independent.

C. Americans who worked for the British government wanted to keep their jobs.

D. Some enslaved African Americans were offered freedom if they became Patriot soldiers.

Patriots	Loyalists

Name _____ Date _____

Summary: Civil War Begins

Before You Read

Find and underline each vocabulary word.

secession *noun*, when part of a country leaves or breaks off from the rest

Confederacy *noun*, states that separated from the Union and formed a confederation

civil war *noun*, a war between two groups or regions within a nation

Abraham Lincoln

Conflict grew between the North and South. Southerners thought abolitionists would start slave rebellions. Some southerners wanted to leave the Union. Northerners were afraid slavery would spread. Americans who opposed slavery formed the Republican Party. Republicans opposed slavery in the territories.

Abraham Lincoln was a Republican. He was born in Kentucky, a slave state. He was raised on a farm in Illinois, a free state. His family was poor. He did not go to school, but he read a lot. Lincoln became a lawyer and a political leader.

Lincoln's Campaigns

In 1858, Lincoln ran for Senate in Illinois against Stephen Douglas. They debated so people could hear their ideas. He did not think slavery was wrong. Lincoln said slavery was evil, but he did not support abolition. Lincoln lost, but the debates made him famous. Many southerners thought he wanted to abolish slavery.

Lincoln ran for president in 1860. He was the only candidate against slavery. He won, but the election showed that the country was divided. No southern states voted for Lincoln. Some southerners said the federal government was too strong. They said tariffs and laws to limit slavery threatened states' rights. Some chose secession to protect their right to enslave people.

Secession Begins

In 1860, South Carolina left the union. In all, eleven southern states formed the Confederacy. Jefferson Davis was president. Lincoln wanted unity and peace but it was too late. Confederates attacked Fort Sumter on April 12, 1861. Lincolne called for men to fight the rebellion. The Civil War began.

After You Read

REVIEW Why did some southerners want their states to secede? Draw a box around three sentences that tell what southerners said about the federal government, what they thought threatened states' rights, and what right they wanted to protect.

REVIEW Why did southerners see Lincoln as an enemy? Circle what Lincoln said about slavery. Also circle what southerns thought he would do about slavery.

REVIEW What event began the Civil War? What happened on April 12, 1861? Draw a box around the answer.

Name _____ Date _____

Summary: A Nation at War

Before You Read

Find and underline each vocabulary word.

border states *noun*, slave states that stayed in the Union

casualties *noun*, soldiers who are killed or wounded in war

draft *noun*, the way a government forces people to become soldiers

emancipation *noun*, the freeing of enslaved people

North Against South

Eleven southern states left the Union and formed the Confederacy. Four border states stayed in the Union. The North wanted to keep the Union together. They planned to stop the Confederacy from trading with other nations. They would attack the South from the East and West at the same time. The North had more people, more factories, and more railroads. The South planned to fight off northern attacks until the Confederacy could survive as a nation. The South had good military leaders. They hoped France and Britain would help because these countries needed southern cotton. Most of the war was in the South, so Confederate soldiers knew the land. Both sides thought they could win quickly. In July 1861, at the Battle of Bull Run they learned the war might last a long time.

The War's Leaders

Robert E. Lee led the Confederate army. He stopped the Union army from capturing Richmond. He invaded the North. The Union army stopped him at Antietam in September 1862. There were at least 23,000 casualties in one day. Union General Ulysses S. Grant captured Confederate forts in the West and defeated the Confederates at Shiloh. Because the ports were blocked, the South was low on food, weapons, and money. The Confederacy had to draft soldiers. In the North, rich people could pay to get out of the draft. People who were too poor to pay protested. So did people who opposed the whole war.

Turning Points

In 1863, Lincoln made the Emancipation Proclamation, freeing the enslaved people. The Union captured Vicksburg and won control of the Mississippi River. Lee attacked the North, and the Union beat him at Gettysburg.

After You Read

REVIEW What was the Confederacy's plan for winning the war? Highlight the sentence that tells what the South planned to do.

REVIEW Why did people in the North oppose the draft? Underline the sentences that tell you the answer.

REVIEW Why was the victory at Vicksburg important to the Union? Circle the sentence that tells you the answer.

Support for Language Development

1. Write the vocabulary word on the line next to its meaning.

strategy	traitor	surrender

	_____	to give up
	_____	a plan of action
Benedict Arnold | _____ | someone who is not loyal |

2. Which happened first? Write "1" in front of the first event. Write "2" in front of the second event. Write "3" in front of the third event. Write "4" in front of the fourth event.

____ **A.** Greene's strategy to wear out the British forced Cornwallis to retreat.

____ **B.** The British decided to change their strategy by invading the South.

____ **C.** The United States and Britain signed the Treaty of Paris.

____ **D.** Washington's army and the French navy trapped the British at Yorktown.

Support for Language Development

1. Write the letter of the picture that goes with the definition below.

constitution   citizen   territory   ordinance

_____ A law

_____ An official member of a city, state, or nation

_____ Land ruled by a nation that has no representatives in its government

_____ A written plan for government

2. Read the section of the lesson called "Problems for the New Nation." Then write the word or words that complete each sentence correctly.

A. By 1786, it was clear that the Articles of Confederation could not

make the _____ work together.

B. Congress still owed money for the _____.

C. Congress could not raise the money because it was not allowed

to collect _____.

3. Read the section of the lesson called "The Articles of Confederation." Then circle whether each question is true or false.

A. The Articles of Confederation made Congress the national government. True / False

B. The articles created a strong national government. True / False

C. The Articles gave most of the power to the state governments. True / False

D. Congress could not declare war. True / False

Resources for Reaching All Learners
131   Use with *United States History*, pp. 296–299

Support for Language Development

1. Write the letter of the picture that goes with the definition below.

federal

ratify

republic

_____ A government in which the citizens elect leaders to represent them

_____ To officially accept

_____ A system of government in which the states share power with a central government

2. Write the word or words that complete each compromise.

Problem	Solution
The Northern states wanted an end to the slave trade. The Southern states would not accept the new government on these terms.	Northern and Southern states agreed to end the _____ _____ by 1808.
Smaller states argued that bigger states would have more delegates. This would give bigger states more power.	Each state would have the _____ number of representatives in the Senate. In the House of Representatives, the number would depend on each state's _____ .

Use with *United States History*, pp. 302–307

Support for Language Development

1. Write the letter of the word that goes with the definition below.

a unconstitutional   **b** amendment   **c** checks and balances

d veto   **e** democracy

____ A government in which the people have the power to make political decisions

____ A change made to the Constitution

____ Determined by the Supreme Court to not agree with the Constitution

____ A system in which each branch of government can limit the power of the other two branches

____ When the President rejects laws made by Congress

2. Draw a line from the name of a part of the government on the left to the name for the branch of government. Then write what job it does.

A. President   Judicial Branch _____

B. Supreme Court judge   Legislative Branch _____

C. Senator   Executive Branch _____

Support for Language Development

1. Write the letter of the picture that goes with the definition below.

inauguration   Cabinet   political party   capital

_____ The city where the government meets

_____ A group chosen by the President to help run the executive branch and give advice

_____ The official ceremony to make someone president

_____ A group of people who share similar ideas about government

2. Read the sentences below. Write numbers on the lines below to show what happened first, second, and third.

_____ **A.** Work began on the building of the new capital.

_____ **B.** George Washington was elected President.

_____ **C.** Washington retired as President.

Resources for Reaching All Learners
134
Use with *United States History*, pp. 320–323

Name _____ Date _____

Support for Language Development

1. Write the letter of the picture that goes with the definition below.

pioneer

frontier

flatboat

canal

_____ Large, rectangular boat partly covered by a roof

_____ The edge of a country or a settled region

_____ A waterway built for boat travel and shipping

_____ One of the first people to enter or settle a region

2. Read the section of the lesson called "Daniel Boone." Then read the sentences below. Write a number in front of each event to show what happened first, second, third, and fourth.

_____ Daniel Boone helped clear a new road through the Cumberland Gap.

_____ On the other side of Cumberland Gap, they found beautiful and rich land.

_____ Boone guided families across the Appalachians into Kentucky.

_____ Daniel Boone and several other men traveled to the other side of the Cumberland Gap.

3. Read the section of the lesson called "Making a Home." Then read the sentences below. Circle the main idea. Underline the details.

A. Settlers traveled to an unknown land and lived far from family and friends.

B. Pioneers cut down trees to create a clearing in the woods.

C. Frontier life was hard.

D. Settlers grew corn and other grains and raised farm animals.

Name _____ Date _____

Support for Language Development

1. Write the letter of the picture that goes with the definition below.

corps

source

interpreter

manufacturers

_____ People who use machines to make goods

_____ A team of people who work together

_____ Someone who helps people who speak different languages understand each other

_____ The place where a river begins

2. Draw a line from the name on the left column to the correct sentence on the right column.

Sacagawea	sold Louisiana to the United States.
Thomas Jefferson	led the Corps of Discovery.
Zebulon Pike	wanted to help farmers.
Meriwether Lewis and William Clark	was an interpreter for the Corps of Discovery.
Napoleon Bonaparte	led a group to find the source of the Mississippi River.

Use with *United States History*, pp. 354–357

Support for Language Development

1. Write the letter of the word that goes with the definition below.

a prosperity   **b** nationalism   **c** foreign policy

_____ A government's actions toward other nations

_____ Economic success and security

_____ Devotion to one's country

2. Read the sentences below. Write numbers on the lines below to show which event happened first, second, third, and fourth.

_____ **A.** The British navy fired at Fort McHenry.

_____ **B.** The U.S. declared war on Britain.

_____ **C.** British forces attacked Americans in New Orleans.

_____ **D.** The U.S. and Britain signed the Treaty of Ghent.

Resources for Reaching All Learners
137
Use with *United States History,* pp. 360–365

Name _____ Date _____

Support for Language Development

1. Write the vocabulary word on the line next to its definition.

ruling	campaign	suffrage

_____

A series of actions taken toward a goal

_____

An official decision

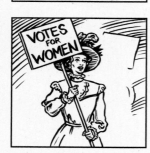

_____

The right to vote

2. Read the sentences below. Match a fact on the left with the correct event on the right.

A. Jackson helped settlers and farmers.

B. Indians continued to resist settlers moving onto their land.

C. Jackson ordered the government to take the money out of the national bank.

Jackson forced Indians to move west of the Mississippi River.

The government invested in state banks.

Settlers and farmers voted for Jackson.

Resources for Reaching All Learners

138

Use with *United States History*, pp. 368–371

Support for Language Development

1. Write the letter of the picture that goes with the definition below.

textile

interchangeable parts

mass production

productivity

entrepreneur

____ a person who takes risks to start a new business

____ making many products at once

____ cloth or fabric

____ the amount of goods and services made by a worker in a certain amount of time

____ parts made by a machine to be exactly the same size and shape

2. Read the sentences below. In the box on the right, write the letter of the sentence that explains the effect of each invention.

A. Factories and farmers could ship their goods to almost any city in the country by train.

B. Cotton was soon America's largest export.

C. The new ways of making goods increased the productivity of the United States.

Causes   **Effects**

cotton gin

interchangeable parts

steam locomotives

Resources for Reaching All Learners

139

Use with *United States History*, pp. 378–383

Support for Language Development

1. Write the letter of the picture that goes with the definition below.

famine

injustice

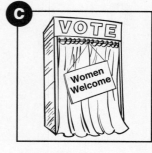

reform

____ the abuse of a person's rights

____ a widespread shortage of food

____ an action that makes something better

2. Fill in the blanks with the correct answer.

A. The Irish potato crop failed in 1846. It caused a _____,

and many people left Ireland to go to the United States.

B. Thousands of Germans left Europe because of war and crop

_____.

C. Many women who worked for _____ realized they

also faced _____ as women.

D. The _____ movement wanted people to control or cut

back the drinking of alcohol.

3. Draw a line to match the reform movement with its goal.

Antislavery Movement	Wanted to give women the same rights as men
Temperance Movement	Wanted to stop the practice of slavery
Women's Rights Movement	Wanted people to control or cut back the drinking of alcohol

140   Use with *United States History,* pp. 388–391

Support for Language Development

1. Write the letter of the word that goes with the definition below.

a annexation   **b** manifest destiny   **c** front   **d** cession

_____ something that is given up

_____ the belief that the United States should spread across North America, from the Atlantic Ocean to the Pacific Ocean

_____ joining two countries or pieces of land together

_____ where the fighting takes place in a war

2. Read the sentences below. Number them from 1 to 5 in the order that they happened.

_____ James Polk became President, and Congress voted to annex the Republic of Texas.

_____ Santa Anna led a large army to San Antonio to stop the rebellion.

_____ To gain his freedom, Santa Anna agreed to give Texas its independence.

_____ Tejanos and Texans rebelled against Mexico and fought for their independence.

_____ Sam Houston led an attack on Santa Anna's army and captured Santa Anna.

Support for Language Development

1. Write the letter of the picture that goes with the definition below.

a

wagon train

b

forty-niner

c

GOLD!

gold rush

d

HOTEL

boomtown

_____ many people hurrying to the same area to look for gold over a short time

_____ a line of covered wagons that moved together

_____ gold miner who went to California in 1849 during the gold rush

_____ a town whose population grows very quickly

2. Draw a line to connect the first part of the sentence in the left column with the best answer in the right column.

In 1843, a group of about 1,000 traveled on the Oregon Trail to find	a place where they could practice their religion.
In 1847, the Mormons traveled on the Mormon Trail to find	to dig for gold.
In 1849, forty-niners rushed to California	good, inexpensive land.

3. Fill in the blanks with the correct words from "After the Gold Rush."

   A. Miners and farmers killed large numbers of California

   _____ and took over their land.

   B. American newcomers forced many _____ property owners

   off their land.

   C. _____ such as San Francisco grew.

   D. By 1850, California had enough people to become a

   _____.

Support for Language Development

1. Write the letter of the word that goes with the definition below.

a tariff   **b** states' rights   **c** sectionalism

____ Loyalty to one part of the country

____ A tax on imported goods

____ The idea that states, not the federal government, should make decisions about matters that affect them

2. Read the section of the lesson called "Resistance to Slavery." Then write the word or words that best complete each sentence.

A. After Nat Turner's rebellion, _____ states passed laws

to _____ both enslaved and free blacks.

B. Slavery became a source of deep _____ between the

North and South.

C. Many Southerners thought that slavery was too

_____ to their _____ to give up.

Resources for Reaching All Learners
143   Use with *United States History*, pp. 416–419

Support for Language Development

1. Write the letter of the word that goes with the definition below.

a discrimination　　　　**b** Underground Railroad　　　**c** abolitionist

_____ Someone who joined the movement to end slavery

_____ A series of escape routes and hiding places used to bring people out of slavery

_____ The unfair treatment of particular groups

2. Write the name of the person being described in the boxes on the right.

I told white people what it was like to be enslaved.	**I am** →	
I spoke for abolition and women's rights.	**I am** →	
I was a conductor on the Underground Railroad.	**I am** →	

144　　　**Use with *United States History*, pp. 424–427**

Name _____ Date _____

Summary: Twenty-First Century Begins

Before You Read

Find and underline each vocabulary word.

millenium *noun,* a period of 10 centuries, or 1,000 years

popular vote *noun,* the vote of individual citizens

Electoral College *noun,* representatives, called electors, from each state

terrorism *noun,* the use of violence against ordinary people to achieve a political goal

The 2000 Election

On December 31, 1999, people all over the world celebrated the beginning of a new millenium. The new millenium really began on January 1, 2001. In a presidential election, the vote of individual citizens is called the popular vote. The candidate who wins the popular vote in a state wins all of that state's Electoral College votes. To win the election you have to win the electoral vote.

The 2000 presidential election was an example of a close popular and electoral vote. The race was very close in Florida, where George W. Bush won the first count. Al Gore said the votes were not counted properly. Finally, the Supreme Court said that the Florida votes would not be recounted. Bush became President. In 2004, Bush ran again, and won both the electoral and popular votes.

Attack on the Nation

On September 11, 2001, nearly three thousand people were killed by acts of terrorism in the United States. Terrorists hijacked four airplanes. They crashed two airplanes into the World Trade Center in New York, and one into the Pentagon in Washington, D.C. A fourth plane crashed in Pennsylvania.

The terrorists were from a group called al-Qaeda. They were against the United States' involvement in the Middle East. After the attacks, Bush accused the country of Afghanistan of hiding the leader of al-Qaeda, Osama bin Laden, and his followers. In October, 2001, a coalition of nations led by the United States went to war in Afghanistan. They defeated the government, but they did not find bin Laden.

In 2003, Bush said Saddam Hussein, the leader in Iraq, was a danger to his neighbors and to the United States. In March, 2003, the United States went to war in Iraq. After defeating Hussein's army and arresting Hussein, the military stayed in Iraq while a new Iraqi government formed.

After You Read

REVIEW **What is the difference between the popular vote and the electoral vote?** Circle the words that tell what a popular vote is. Highlight the words that tell what the votes in the Electoral College are. Underline the words that explain how a presidential election is won.

REVIEW **How did the United States respond to the terrorist attacks of September 11, 2001?** Circle the sentences that tell you the answer.

Name _____ Date _____

Summary: Life in the 1990s

Before You Read

Find and underline each vocabulary word.

Internet *noun,* links computers around the world with each other

high-tech *adjective,* or high-technology, uses the most recent knowledge and equipment

interdependent *adjective,* to depend, or rely, on each other.

free-trade agreement *noun,* treaties among countries that trade with one another

Clinton's Presidency

In 1992, Bill Clinton was elected President. He believed government money should be used to help people. There was not enough money because of the budget deficit from the Reagan years. The economy grew and more taxes were collected. Clinton put more money into social programs. By 1998, the United States had a budget surplus. The government had more money than it spent.

Clinton helped start peace processes in Northern Ireland and the Middle East. In the former country of Yugoslavia, different groups fought to form separate nations. The United States and other countries sent troops to stop the fighting there in 1999.

Clinton's second term was hurt by a scandal. He was impeached by the House of Representatives. The Senate found him not guilty.

A Changing Economy

During the 1990s, the United States had the longest period of economic growth in its history. Many people had more income to save, spend, or invest. Changes in computers and the development of high-tech businesses helped the economy grow. Computer programs were invented that people could use at home, at school, and at work. The Internet made it possible for people to get information, shop, and communicate quickly and easily.

New technology made the U.S. economy more productive. Jobs changed with the economy. More people did service jobs. Some companies moved factories overseas where they could make products at a lower cost. People with more education did better in the 1990s than people with less education.

A Connected World

Improved communication and transportation made trade between countries easier and less expensive. Nations are now more interdependent. Mexico, Canada, and the United States signed free-trade agreements in the 1990s.

After You Read

REVIEW **In which places in the world did President Clinton help settle conflicts?** Circle the names of three places where President Clinton helped settle conflicts.

REVIEW **What effect did computers have on the economy in the 1990s?** Circle the sentence that answers the question.

REVIEW **In what ways did better communication change life for people during the 1990s?** Highlight the sentence that tells you the answer.

Answers *continued*

Name _____ Date _____

Summary: United States Today

A Nation of Immigrants

Millions of immigrants come to the United States. Some come for a better life, and some come for religious or political freedom. Until 1965, most immigrants came from Europe or Mexico. (In 1965, Congress changed the immigration laws.) Now immigrants come from many nations. Spanish-speaking immigrants come from Central and South America and the Caribbean. Refugees from wars in El Salvador and Nicaragua came during the 1980s.

People also come from Africa and the West Indies. Today almost one-third of America's immigrants are Asians from India, China, the Philippines, and other countries. Immigrants often live in communities where other people from their country live. They influence the culture and government of the places where they live.

Many People, One Nation

Many immigrants to the United States find the freedom they need to start successful careers. The United States has a diverse population, with many different ethnic groups. People bring music, food, language, art, and customs from their countries. Each person brings knowledge, skills, and talents. These things improve the United States. Ethnic diversity is one of the greatest strengths of the United States.

All people in the United States share a heritage of democracy. All United States citizens share the Constitution and the Bill of Rights. The Constitution and the Bill of Rights explain the rights of U.S. citizens. Our democratic heritage unites us into one nation. You can see the Latin motto "E Pluribus Unum" on American money. These Latin words mean "out of many, one." These words remind us that the United States became one nation by joining together 13 colonies. Today 50 states and many ethnic groups are joined together into one nation.

Before You Read

Find and underline each vocabulary word.

refugee *noun*, a person who escapes war or other danger and seeks safety in another country

heritage *noun*, something that is passed down from one generation to the next

motto *noun*, a short statement that explains an ideal or goal

After You Read

REVIEW **Why did immigration to the United States change after 1965?** Circle the sentence that tells the answer.

REVIEW **What do all United States citizens share?** Draw a box around the sentence that tells the answer.

Name _____ Date _____

Summary: Neighbors in North America

Canada

Canada is the United States' neighbor to the north. It has three territories and ten provinces. Its history is similar to American history. American Indians lived first in both countries. Europeans colonized both countries. (In Canada, the colonists were mostly French.) After a French-British war in 1754, Canada became a British colony. Many people in Canada speak both French and English. Both languages are now official languages there. In 1867, Canada gained its independence from Britain. Canada is a democracy. Like the United States, Canada is multicultural.

In 1992, Canada signed the North American Free Trade Agreement (NAFTA) with the United States and Mexico. NAFTA increased trade among the three nations. Canada is the United States' biggest trade partner. The two countries also work together to solve environmental problems that affect both countries.

Mexico

Mexico is the United States' neighbor to the south. It has 31 states and one federal district. The Maya and Aztecs lived in Mexico first, and they built large, beautiful cities. Spain began to colonize Mexico in the 1520s. In 1821, Mexico fought Spain for its independence and won. Mexico has a representative government that gives a lot of power to the President. Most Mexicans have a mixture of Spanish and Mexican Indian heritage. Spanish is the official language, but many people speak Indian languages. Mexican art, building styles, and food are common in the Southwest United States, which was once part of Mexico.

Many Mexicans work in maquiladoras, and many Mexicans come to the United States to work. This helps the U.S. economy. In 1992, Mexico signed NAFTA with the United States and Canada. Mexico's most important trading partner is the United States. After Canada, Mexico is the United States' second most important trading partner.

Before You Read

Find and underline each vocabulary word.

province *noun*, a political region of a country that is similar to a state

multicultural *adjective*, having many cultural traditions

maquiladora *noun*, a factory in Mexico near the U.S. border

After You Read

REVIEW **Why is French one of the two official languages in Canada?** Circle the sentence that tells the answer.

REVIEW **How and when did Mexico gain its independence?** Draw a box around the sentence that tells how and when Mexico gained its independence.

REVIEW **What are some of Mexico's connections with the United States?** Circle the sentences that tell about connections with Mexican culture, work, and trade.

Support for Language Development

1. Write the letter of the picture and word that goes with the definition below.

border states

casualties

draft

emancipation

_____ the freeing of enslaved people

_____ soldiers who are killed or wounded in war

_____ the way an army forces people to be soldiers

_____ slave states that stayed in the Union

2. Read the sentences below. Which happened first? Write "1" in front of the first event. Write "2" in front of the second event. Write "3" in front of the third event. Write "4" in front of the fourth event.

_____ **A.** Emancipation Proclamation

_____ **B.** Battle of Antietam

_____ **C.** Battle near Gettysburg, Pennsylvania

_____ **D.** Formation of the Confederacy

3. Read the section in the lesson called "North Against South." In the box labeled "Compare," write how the Union and the Confederacy were alike. In the box labeled "Contrast," write how they were different.

Compare	Contrast
Both the North and the South thought they could _____ quickly.	The _____ had more people and more factories for making weapons and supplies than the _____.

Support for Language Development

1. Write the vocabulary word on the line next to its meaning.

home front	civilian	camp

_____ a group of temporary shelters, such as tents

_____ all the people who are not in the military when a country is at war

_____ a person who is not in the military

2. Read the section in the lesson called "On the Home Front." In the box labeled "Effect," complete the sentence about people on the home front.

Cause

Families were left behind on the home front.

Effect

_____ ran farms and businesses. They sewed uniforms, knitted socks, made _____, and _____ money.

Support for Language Development

1. Write the letter of the word that goes with the definition below.

a telegraph　　　　**b** total war　　　　**c** desert

____ The strategy of destroying an enemy's resources

____ To leave the army without permission

____ A machine that sends electric signals over wires

2. Read the section of the lesson called "Grant and Lee." In the box labeled "Cause," tell which army was getting stronger. In the box labeled "Effect," fill in the word that tells what happened.

Causes　　　　　　　　　　　　**Effect**

The _____ suffered terrible losses, but Grant kept attacking.

Lee _____ to Grant at Appomattox.

Support for Language Development

1. Write the letter of the picture and word that goes with the definition below.

assassination   Freedmen's Bureau   impeach

_____ an agency set up to provide food, clothing, medical care, and legal advice to poor blacks and whites

_____ the murder of an important leader

_____ to charge a government official with a crime

2. Read the section of the lesson called "The Constitution Changes." Draw a line to connect the number of each amendment with what the amendment did.

Thirteenth Amendment		Gave full citizenship to African Americans
Fourteenth Amendment		Gave African American men the right to vote
Fifteenth Amendment		Ended slavery in the United States

Name _____ Date _____

Support for Language Development

1. Write the vocabulary word on the line next to its meaning.

sharecropping	Jim Crow	segregation

_____ laws that segregated African Americans from other Americans

_____ forced separation of races of people

_____ system where farmers used land and gave landowners a share of the crop

2. Read the section of the lesson called "Responses to Reconstruction." Then write the word or words that complete the sentences correctly.

A. _____ angered some people in the South.

B. Some people wanted to stop _____

_____ from taking part in government.

C. The _____ _____

_____ threatened, beat, and even killed African

Americans to keep them from voting.

Support for Language Development

1. Write the letter of the word that goes with the definition below.

a prejudice   **b** transcontinental

____ From one edge of a continent to the other

____ A negative opinion of a group of people, not based on fact

2. Read the section of the lesson called "The Telegraph Helps Communication." For each sentence, circle whether it is true or false.

Using horses, stagecoaches, or steamboats were   True   False
quick ways to send messages across the country.

The telegraph carried messages from the East   True   False
Coast to the West Coast in just a few minutes.

3. Read the sentences. Write the letters in the boxes to show what happened first, second, third, and fourth.

A. The transcontinental railway was completed.

C. Former soldiers, African Americans, and immigrants laid the tracks.

B. Congress provided land and money to build the transcontinental railroad.

D. Western farmers made money by shipping cattle and wheat to the East.

☐ first   ☐ second   ☐ third   ☐ fourth

Support for Language Development

1. Write the letter of the picture and word that goes with the definition below.

drought

Exodusters

homestead

_____ A long period with little or no rain

_____ A settler's home and land

_____ African Americans who moved to the Great Plains

2. Read the sentences below. The sentences with letters are problems. The sentences with numbers are solutions. Match each problem with a solution. Write the letters and numbers in the boxes below.

A. There were not many people on the Great Plains to do farm work.

B. The land was dry. There were frequent droughts.

C. There wasn't a lot of wood on the Great Plains.

1. Homesteaders used sod to build homes.

2. Homesteaders dug wells and used windmills to pump water.

3. Homesteaders invented new farm machines.

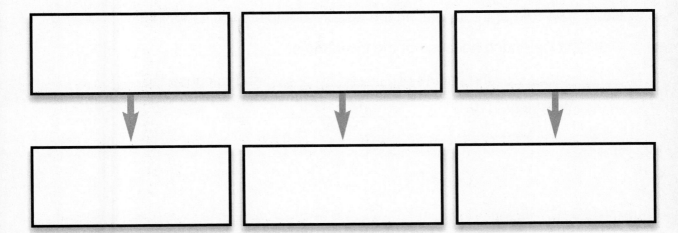

Support for Language Development

1. Write the letter of the word that goes with the definition below.

a barbed wire   **b** demand   **c** railhead   **d** supply

____ The amount of something that people want to sell at a certain price

____ Wire with sharp points on it

____ The amount of something that people want to buy at a certain price

____ A town where railroad tracks begin or end

2. Supply and demand affect how much things are worth. Read "Demand and Supply for Cattle" in the lesson. Write how the supply and demand affected the price of cattle.

Cause: There were many longhorn cattle in Texas. Not many people wanted to buy them.

Effect: _____

Cause: There were many people in the North and East that wanted to buy beef and leather. There were not many longhorn cattle.

Effect: _____

3. Read "The End of the Drives" in the lesson. Complete the sentence.

Cattle drives ended because of the invention of _____

_____, the growth of _____, and because too

many cattle grazed on _____ _____.

Support for Language Development

1. Write the letter of the word that goes with the definition
below.

a assimilate　　**b** extinct　　**c** habitat　　**d** reservation

____ When a certain type of plant or
animal no longer exists

____ Land the government reserved for
Indians

____ The area where an animal or
plant normally lives or grows

____ To take in a group and change its
culture and traditions

2. Read "War on the Plains" in the lesson. Fill in the missing words
below.

Plains Indians fought _____ who tried to force them

onto _____ .

3. Read the "Government Policy" section. Then complete the sentences.

┌───┐
│ The government tried to force American Indians to change.   │
└───┘

┌──────────────────┐ ┌──────────────────┐ ┌──────────────────┐
│ The government   │ │ They were not   │ │ They were not   │
│ made Indian   │ │ allowed to speak │ │ allowed to wear   │
│   │ │   │ │   │
│ _____   │ │ _____   │ │ _____   │
│   │ │   │ │   │
│ _____   │ │ _____ .   │ │ _____ .   │
│   │ │   │ │   │
│ illegal.   │ │   │ │   │
└──────────────────┘ └──────────────────┘ └──────────────────┘

Support for Language Development

1. Write in the letter of the picture and word that goes with each definition.

competition

corporation

labor union

strike

____ A business in which many people own shares, or parts, of the business

____ Occurs when more than one business sells the same goods or service to customers

____ An organization of workers that tries to improve pay and working conditions for its members

____ When workers refuse to work in order to force business owners to make changes

2. Read the section of the lesson called "A Time of Invention." Draw a line from the invention on the left to its job on the right.

A. telephones   kept machines running longer

B. oil cups   saved office workers time

C. typewriters   were cleaner, brighter, and safer than gas lamps

D. electric light bulbs   let people talk to people in other places

Use with *United States History*, pp. 534–539

Support for Language Development

1. Write the letter of the word that goes with the definition below.

a persecution　　　　**b** ethnic group　　　　**c** tenement

_____ Unfair treatment or punishment

_____ A poorly built apartment building

_____ A group of people who share a culture or language

2. Read the section in the lesson called "Arriving in America." Write the word or words that complete each sentence correctly.

A. Some immigrants came to the United States to escape _____.

B. Other immigrants were looking for _____.

C. Most immigrants found _____ _____ in America.

3. Read the section of the lesson called "Laws Against Immigration." Then read the main idea below. Complete the details with two other jobs that immigrants had in the United States.

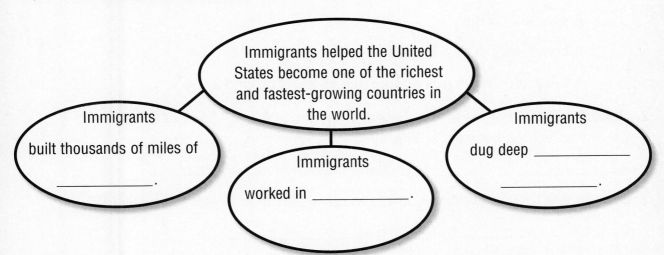

Immigrants helped the United States become one of the richest and fastest-growing countries in the world.

Immigrants built thousands of miles of _____.

Immigrants worked in _____.

Immigrants dug deep _____ _____.

Support for Language Development

1. Write in the letters of the picture and word that goes with each definition.

stockyard

rapid transit

settlement house

skyscraper

_____ Fenced area where large numbers of animals are kept until they are used for food or moved

_____ A very tall building

_____ A community center for people in the city

_____ A system of trains that people use to travel around a city

2. Read the section of the lesson called "Changes in Cities." Then fill in the blanks with the correct answers.

A. _____ _____ were used to attract shoppers.

B. _____ needed electricity to carry people in skyscrapers.

C. _____ _____ and _____ _____ invented ways to send electricity through wires.

D. Theaters used _____ _____ to light their stages.

E. _____ cities were exciting places.

Name _____ Date _____

Support for Language Development

1. Write the letter of the picture and word that goes with the definition below.

barbed wire   demand   railhead   supply

d The amount of something that people want to sell at a certain price

a Wire with sharp points on it

b The amount of something that people want to buy at a certain price

c A town where railroad tracks begin or end

2. Supply and demand affect how much things are worth. Read "Demand and Supply for Cattle" in the lesson. Write how the supply and demand affected the price of cattle.

Cause: There were many longhorn cattle in Texas. Not many people wanted to buy them.

Effect: ___The price of cattle was low.___

Cause: There were many people in the North and East that wanted to buy beef and leather. There were not many longhorn cattle.

Effect: ___The cattle were worth more money in those regions.___

3. Read "The End of the Drives" in the lesson. Complete the sentence.

Many states passed laws to keep out Texas cattle because the cattle had ___ticks, bugs, or insects___.

Name _____ Date _____

Support for Language Development

1. Write the letter of the picture and word that goes with the definition below.

drought   Exodusters   homestead

a A long period with little or no rain

b African Americans who moved to the Great Plains

c A settler's home and land

2. Read the sentences below. The sentences with letters are problems. The sentences with numbers are solutions. Match each problem with a solution. Write the letters and numbers in the boxes below.

A. There were not many people on the Great Plains to do farm work.

B. The land was dry. There were frequent droughts.

C. There wasn't a lot of wood on the Great Plains.

1. Homesteaders used sod to build homes.

2. Homesteaders dug wells and used windmills to pump water.

3. Homesteaders invented new farm machines.

A	B	C
3	2	1

Support for Language Development

1. Write the letter of the word that goes with the definition below.

a imperialism   **b** isthmus

_____ When nations gain colonies to build empires

_____ A narrow strip of land with water on two sides

2. Read the section of the lesson called "Building the Panama Canal."
   Then complete the sentences below.

The United States built the Panama Canal at the _____ of Panama.	_____ no longer had to travel around South America.	Ships sailing from the east or west coasts of the United States saved thousands of miles. So, trade _____.

Resources for Reaching All Learners
160   Use with *United States History*, pp. 572–575

Support for Language Development

1. Write the letter of the word that goes with the definition below.

a alliance   **b** trench warfare   **c** armistice   **d** isolationism

____ An agreement to stop fighting

____ A type of fighting in which soldiers crouch down in trenches and fire their weapons from there

____ When a country stays out of other countries' affairs

____ An agreement between nations to work together and to defend each other

2. Read the section of the lesson called "America Enters the War." Then read the sentences below. Write a T if the sentence is true and an F if the sentence is false.

____ The United States entered the war because Austria-Hungary attacked Serbia.

____ The United States joined the war after Germany began attacking American ships.

____ The United States joined the Central Powers to make the world safe for democracy.

3. Read the sentences below. Number the events in the order they happened.

____ **A.** The United States joined the Allies.

____ **B.** Austria-Hungary declared war on Serbia.

____ **C.** Nations made alliances.

____ **D.** The Allies and the Central Powers declared war on one another.

____ **E.** The Allies won the war.

Resources for Reaching All Learners

161

Use with *United States History*, pp. 578–583

Support for Language Development

1. Write the vocabulary word on the line next to its meaning.

assembly line	credit	division of labor

_____

Getting an item today, but paying for it later with small payments

_____

A line of workers or machines that puts a product together piece by piece

_____

When workers perform different parts of a large task

2. Read the section of the lesson called "Consumer Goods and Credit." Then write the correct word to complete the sentence.

Causes

The economy boomed during the 1920s. Americans believed it would keep growing.

Effects

Many people used _____ to buy refrigerators and washing machines.

Others _____ their money in things such as land and paintings.

Support for Language Development

1. Write the letter of the word that goes with the definition below.

a stock market   **b** depression   **c** unemployment

_____ The number of people without a job

_____ A period when many people can't find work and many others have no money to keep businesses going

_____ A place where people can buy and sell shares of a company's stock

2. Write the correct words to complete the sentences.

Cause

After the _____ _____ crashed, the economy became weaker.

Effect

Stores could not sell their goods and factories did not need as many workers. Many businesses closed, and people lost their jobs.

This time of hardship was named the Great _____.

Support for Language Development

1. Write the letter of the word and picture next to the correct definition.

dictator

war bonds

internment camp

_____ A place where prisoners are held during wartime

_____ A ruler who has total power over a country and its people

_____ A loan from the American people to the federal government

2. Read the sentences below. Number the events in the order they happened.

_____ Japanese Americans were sent to live in internment camps.

_____ Japan joined the Axis Powers.

_____ The Nazis took power.

_____ The United States dropped atomic bombs on Japan.

Name _____ Date _____

Support for Language Development

1. Write the vocabulary word on the line next to its meaning.

| communism | capitalism | arms race |

_____

a contest between nations to build bigger and more powerful weapons

_____

a system in which the government controls production and owns the nation's natural and capital resources

_____

a system in which ordinary people and businesses control the production of goods and services

2. The United States and the Soviet Union had several conflicts during the Cold War. Reread "Cold War Conflicts" and write the names of two other conflicts in the boxes.

After World War II, the United States and the Soviet Union fought a war of ideas called the Cold War.

Berlin Airlift

Support for Language Development

1. Write the letter of the word that goes with the definition below.

a veteran   **b** baby boom   **c** budget

_____ Increase of babies born after World War II

_____ A plan for saving and spending income

_____ A person who has served in the military

2. Read the sentences below. Then write a letter for each problem (the cause) in the boxes on the left. Write a number for the sentence that tells the effect (what happened because of the cause) in the boxes on the right.

Causes   **Effects**

A. Businesses grew and workers had more income.

B. People bought cars in record numbers.

  1. People drove to national parks, movies, and restaurants.

  2. Families could make more choices about what to buy.

Resources for Reaching All Learners
166   Use with *United States History*, pp. 620–623

Support for Language Development

1. Write the vocabulary word on the line next to its meaning.

| civil rights | desegregation | nonviolent protest |

_____ a way of bringing change without using violence

_____ the rights and freedoms that countries guarantee their citizens

_____ ending the separation of people by racial or ethnic group

2. Reread the section of the lesson called "Civil Rights Victories." In the boxes, write the names of two more Acts that were passed to recognize equal rights.

1	
1	
3	
4	

Support for Language Development

1. Write the vocabulary word on the line next to its meaning.

space race	demonstration	cease-fire

	_____	a gathering of people who want to tell the public and the government their opinion
	_____	a struggle between the United States and the Soviet Union to be the first country to send people into space
	_____	an agreement to stop all fighting

2. Read the sentences below. Which happened first? Write "1" in front of the first event. Write "2" in front of the second event. Write "3" in front of the third event. Write "4" in front of the fourth event.

____ The North Vietnamese defeated South Vietnam.

____ People for and against the war held demonstrations in cities around the country.

____ The United States sent soldiers to fight in the Vietnam War.

____ In 1973, North Vietnam, South Vietnam, and the United States agreed to a cease-fire.

Support for Language Development

1. Write the letter of the word that goes with the definition below.

a accord   **b** resign   **c** migrant worker

_____ To give up your job

_____ A person who moves from place to place to find work, mostly on farms

_____ An agreement

2. Read the section called "The Carter Years" in your textbook. In the box labeled "Solution," tell what President Carter did to help solve the conflict in the Middle East.

Problem   **Solution**

| Israel and Egypt had been enemies for 30 years. | In 1978, President Carter helped the leaders sign a _____ _____ . |

Support for Language Development

1. Write the vocabulary word on the line next to its meaning.

| coalition | deficit | deregulation |

_____

the process of removing rules about what businesses can and cannot do

_____

a group of allies that work together to achieve a goal

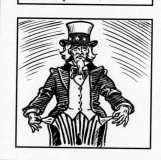

_____

shortage caused by a government spending more money than it collects in taxes

2. Read the section of the lesson called "Reagan Becomes President." Read the main idea below. Fill in the blanks with words that tell some details.

President Reagan cut taxes and government spending on social programs, while building a stronger military.

He removed _____ rules about what businesses could or could not do.

He believed a _____ _____ would help people more than government programs could.

Use with *United States History*, pp. 656–659

Support for Language Development

1. Write the letter of the picture and word that goes with each definition below.

high-tech

free-trade agreement

Internet

_____ links computers around the world with each other

_____ treaties among countries that trade with one another

_____ uses the most recent knowledge and equipment

2. Read the sentences below. Which one happened first? Write "1" in front of the first event. Write "2" in front of the second event. Write "3" in front of the third event.

_____ **A.** By 1998, the United States had a budget surplus.

_____ **B.** Clinton was impeached by the House of Representatives.

_____ **C.** There was a budget deficit from the Reagan years.

3. Write the word or words that complete the sentence correctly.

A. During the Clinton presidency the economy _____.

B. In the 1990s, more people in the United States found work

in _____ _____ than in manufacturing

or farming.

C. Trade between nations increased as new technology improved

_____ and _____.

D. In the 1990s free-trade agreements were signed by the United

States, _____, and _____.

Support for Language Development

1. Write the letter of the word that goes with the definition below.

a popular vote   **b** millennium   **c** terrorism   **d** Electoral College

____ Representatives, called electors, from each state

____ The vote of individual citizens

____ The use of violence against ordinary people to achieve a
political goal

____ A period of 10 centuries, or 1,000 years

2. Read the section of the lesson called "The 2000 Election." In the box labeled
"Cause" tell who decided that the votes would not be counted again.

Causes

The _____ _____
decided that the votes in Florida would
not be counted again.

Effects

Bush won the first count, so he won
Florida's electoral votes and became
President.

3. Read the sentences below. Which happened first? Write "1" in front of
the first event. Write "2" in front of the second event. Write "3" in front
of the third event. Write "4" in front of the fourth event.

____ **A.** Bush becomes President of the United States.

____ **B.** United States goes to war in Iraq.

____ **C.** Terrorist attacks on New York and Washington, D.C.

____ **D.** United States goes to war in Afghanistan.

Support for Language Development

1. Write the letter of the word that goes with the definition below.

a multicultural   **b** province   **c** maquiladora

____ A political region of a country that is similar to a state

____ Having many cultural traditions

____ A factory in Mexico near the U.S. Border

2. Choose the best words to complete the sentence.

Canada	Mexico
With many immigrants, Canada is a _____ society.	Most _____ are mestizos, people of both Spanish and Mexican Indian ancestry.

Support for Language Development

1. Write the letter of the word that goes with the definition below.

a heritage   **b** refugee   **c** motto

_____ A person who escapes war or other danger and seeks safety in another country

_____ Something that is passed down from one generation to the next

_____ A short statement that expresses an ideal or a goal

2. Fill in the blank with the correct word.

> Everyone in the United States lives under the Constitution and the Bill of Rights.

> The Constitution and the Bill of Rights are the democratic
>
> _____ of all people in the United States.

Support for Language Development

1. Write the letter of the picture that goes with the definition below.

naturalization

register

responsibility

volunteer

____ the process of learning the laws of the country and the rights and duties of citizens

____ a person who helps other people without being paid

____ to sign up

____ a duty that people are expected to fulfill

2. Fill in the blanks with the correct word.

A. Immigrants can become citizens after they go through a legal process called _____.

B. At age 18, citizens can _____ to vote.

C. Organizations in every community depend on the time and talent of _____

D. Citizens have a _____ to serve on juries in law courts.

3. Read the sections in the lesson called "Voting and Other Rights" and "Citizens' Responsibilities." Then read the phrases below. Write the letter that is in front of the phrase in the column under "Rights" or "Responsibilities."

A. obeying the law

B. speaking freely

C. paying taxes

D. practicing religion

Rights	Responsibilities

Answers

Name _____ Date _____

Summary: Our Nation's Resources

Natural Resources

Many things we eat, wear, or use come from nature. Gasoline comes from oil found underground. Cars are made of iron ore from mines. Water to drink, air to breathe, and soil and sun for farming also come from nature. Without nature, humans could not survive.

Some resources are renewable. Trees are cut down for wood to make paper, furniture, or other things. New trees can be planted to replace the trees cut, so they are a renewable resource.

Oil and coal are mineral resources from the earth. They give us energy to heat our homes, cook our food, and run our cars. They cannot be replaced. They are nonrenewable.

Wind and water are flow resources. They can only be used at a certain time or place. For example, people can only use wind when it is blowing.

Other Important Resources

It takes many steps to turn natural resources into things we use. Capital resources are tools, such as tractors, computers, or other machines. Human resources are the skills and knowledge of the people doing the work. Without people, nothing would get done.

If many people want a product but there aren't enough for all of them, it is called scarcity. Sometimes people have to decide what they want most. If you can buy either a jacket or sneakers, but not both, you must choose one. The one you give up is the opportunity cost.

People need to be careful using resources so that there will be enough for the future. Everyone can practice conservation to use our natural resources wisely. Companies can use containers made from materials that can be recycled, such as metal or cardboard. People can recycle paper, cans, and bottles and not waste water, gas, and electricity.

Before You Read

Find and underline each vocabulary word.

capital resource *noun*, a tool, machine, or building people use to produce goods and services

human resource *noun*, a person and the skills and knowledge he or she brings to the job

scarcity *noun*, not having as much of something as people want

opportunity cost *noun*, the thing you give up when you decide to do or have something else

conservation *noun*, the protection and wise use of natural resources

After You Read

REVIEW What is the difference between renewable and nonrenewable resources? Highlight a sentence that describes each kind of resource.

REVIEW What is the difference between capital resources and human resources? Draw a box around the sentence that tells what capital resources are. Circle the sentence that tells what human resources are.

REVIEW Why do people practice conservation? Circle the sentences that tell the answer.

2

Use with *United States History*, pp. 14–19

Name _____ Date _____

Summary: Land and Climate

A Varied Land

To understand the United States, we must learn geography. Geographers ask where a place is and what it is like. They want to know how the land affects people, and how people affect the land. Geography helps us understand our past, present, and future.

There are many different landforms in the United States. The Sierra Nevada Mountains and the Coast Ranges are near the Pacific coast. The Basin and Range area is to the east of these mountains. This region has many high mountains and plateaus. A plateau is a high, steep-sided area rising above the land. Rivers running over plateaus have worn away rock to make canyons like those at Bryce Canyon National Park.

Further east are the Rocky Mountains. East of the Rockies are wide, flat plains that slope toward a valley in the center of this huge valley. East of the Mississippi, the Central Plains rise again to the Appalachian Mountains. These mountains go from Maine to Alabama. East of the Appalachians is the Atlantic Coastal Plain, which meets the Atlantic Ocean.

Climate

The United States has many climates. Climate is the type of weather a place has over a long period of time. It includes temperature and how much rain, snow, or sleet falls. The southern part of the country is usually warmer than the northern part. The closer a place is to the equator, the warmer it is.

Landforms affect climate. Lower places are usually warmer than places high in the mountains. Plants and trees also affect climate. Their leaves release water and make shade. A place with many plants or trees has a cooler temperature.

Before You Read

Find and underline each vocabulary word.

geography *noun*, the study of the world and the people and things that live there

landform *noun*, a feature on the surface of the land

plateau *noun*, a high, steep-sided area rising above the surrounding land

climate *noun*, the type of weather a place has over a long period of time

equator *noun*, the imaginary line around the middle of the Earth

After You Read

REVIEW What questions do geographers ask? Underline two sentences that tell the answer.

REVIEW What is climate? Circle the sentence that tells the answer.

1

Use with *United States History*, pp. 6–9

Answers

Name _____ Date _____

Summary: People and the Land

Before You Read

Find and underline each vocabulary word.

environment *noun,* the surroundings in which people, plants, and animals live

erosion *noun,* the process by which water and wind wear away the land

pollution *noun,* anything that makes the soil, air, or water dirty and unhealthy

ecosystem *noun,* a community of plants and animals along with the surrounding soil, air, and water

How Land Affects People

Geography affects how cities grow. San Diego, California, is one of the largest cities in the United States. It has a big (harbor)on the Pacific Ocean.(Shipping)and(trade)helped San Diego grow. It has the location and resources that allow many people to live there.

Denver, Colorado, began to grow when gold and silver were found nearby. Businesses opened when more people came to work in the mines. The city grew as its economy grew.

People live where they can find jobs. Others live in places because they like the environment. Geography affects what people do for fun. In mountainous places, people ski in the winter and hike in the summer. In warm places, people waterski.

Changing the Land

Natural forces, such as wind and water, change the land slowly over time. The Colorado River has carved the Grand Canyon through erosion. Water and wind can also form new land. Soil that is washed away or blown away can collect in another place. Much of Louisiana was formed by soil the Mississippi River carried there.

Humans also change the land. Some human activities make things easier for people. They can also hurt the environment or change how it is used. Highways make travel easier, but then the land can no longer be farmed. Mines provide jobs and mineral resources, but the chemicals used can cause pollution. This can make the environment unsafe for fish, wildlife, and people.

All parts of an ecosystem are connected. People can change an ecosystem without knowing it. Zebra mussels attached themselves to ships. The ships carried the mussels to the Great Lakes from a different ecosystem. Now, they have spread throughout the Great Lakes. The mussels clog pipes and eat food that local fish depend on. Today, people are more aware of the way their activities change the environment.

After You Read

REVIEW In what ways did San Diego's location cause it to grow? Which two industries helped San Diego grow? Which geographical feature made this possible? Circle the words that tell the answers.

REVIEW What is one example of how natural forces can change the land? Draw a box around the sentences that tell how the Grand Canyon and Louisiana were formed.

Name _____ Date _____

Summary: Regions of the United States

Before You Read

Find and underline each vocabulary word.

region *noun,* an area that has one or more features in common

economy *noun,* the system people use to produce goods and services

specialization *noun,* the result of people making the goods they are best able to produce with the resources they have

consumer *noun,* someone who buys goods and services

trade *noun,* the buying and selling of goods

What Is a Region?

The United States can be divided into regions.(States that are close to one another can be included in a region.)The United States can be divided into four regions: Northeast, South, Midwest, and West.(States in a region often share landforms.)The Midwestern states have wide plains and few mountains. The West has many mountains.

The United States can also be divided into political regions, such as states.(Regions can also be divided by)climate. Another way to divide the country is by common activities, such as the work people do, or a common custom or language.(For example, the Dairy Belt is a region that raises cows that produce a lot of milk. It includes parts of the Midwest and Northeast.

People's ideas about regions can change. The Great Plains region used to be called a desert, but today it has many farms.

Regions and Resources

(Regions can also be grouped by the resources they have.)For example, the Appalachian Mountain region has a lot of coal. Resources are important for a region's economy. The resources in a region help people decide what crops to grow and what goods to produce.

When a region makes a lot of one product, it is called specialization. In the South, the climate and soil are good for growing cotton. This can be made into clothing. In North Dakota, the climate is better for growing wheat.

Trade between regions lets consumers all over the country buy goods they want or need. Countries also specialize in producing goods. They trade for goods made in other countries. For example, the United States buys oil from Mexico and sells cars to Mexico. Trade connects businesses around the world.

After You Read

REVIEW What are the different ways the United States can be divided into regions? Circle the sentences that tell different ways of dividing the country into regions.

REVIEW Why do people in regions trade with each other? Highlight the sentence that tells why there is trade between regions.

Answers continued

Summary: Ancient Americans

Before You Read

Find and underline each vocabulary word.

glacier *noun*, a huge, thick sheet of slowly moving ice

migration *noun*, movement from one region to another

agriculture *noun*, farming, or growing plants

civilization *noun*, a group of people living together with organized systems of government, religion, and culture

pueblo *noun*, the Spanish word for town

After You Read

REVIEW **According to scientists, how did people first come to North America?** Circle the sentences that tell how scientists think people came to North America.

REVIEW **Where did the mound building civilizations live?** Underline the sentence that tells you the answer.

REVIEW **What were kivas?** Highlight the sentence that tells how kivas were used.

People Arrive in the Americas

During the Ice Age much of the world's water was frozen in glaciers. The ocean floor between Alaska and Asia was a grassy land bridge. Many scientists think people followed migrating animal herds across it. Migration stopped about 10,000 years ago when the glaciers melted and the seas rose. People who had crossed from Asia, called Paleo-Indians, spread out over North and South America. They are the ancestors of modern American Indians.

Civilizations Develop

Early Paleo-Indians hunted big animals. About 11,000 years ago the big animals began to die out. People learned new ways to get food. They hunted smaller animals, fished, and gathered wild plants.

About 9,000 years ago some Paleo-Indians began to use agriculture. Scientists think people in present-day Mexico grew the first crops of corn, beans, and squash. People's lives changed as they stopped migrating to grow crops. More people survived because of the supply of food.

Paleo-Indians farmed and built villages and cities. The Adena, Hopewell, and Mississippians were Mound Builders. They built giant earth mounds and large villages in North America. Their civilization lasted for about 2,500 years.

The Ancient Pueblo civilization lived in the Southwest region for about 800 years. The Ancient Pueblo built big buildings made of stone with many rooms. The Ancient Pueblo also built underground rooms, called kivas, used for religious ceremonies. Around 1300, the Ancient Pueblo left their villages. No one knows why they left.

The Aztec civilization controlled Central Mexico around 1300 and was strong for 200 years. American Indian groups developed civilizations in almost every region of North America.

Summary: Peoples of the Northwest

Before You Read

Find and underline each vocabulary word.

surplus *adjective*, extra

potlatch *noun*, large feast that lasts for days

clan *noun*, group of related families

After You Read

REVIEW **What two important resources helped the Northwest Indians live?** Underline the words that tell where the Indian people in the Northwest got the things they needed. Highlight two important resources.

REVIEW **How were clans important to the Tlingit?** Draw a box around the words that say what a clan is. Underline the sentence that tells how clans influenced how people lived.

The Pacific Northwest

The Pacific Northwest region stretches from Alaska to northern California. It lies between the Pacific Ocean on the west and the mountains to the east. There are many islands and bays. Thick forests cover much of the land. American Indians who lived in the area around 1500 got everything they needed from the land and water. On land they gathered berries and fern roots. They hunted deer, geese, elks, and bears. One key resource was salmon. They caught so much salmon that the surplus was dried to eat during the year. They also ate seals, whales, and shellfish. The forests were another important resource. People made houses from wood and decorated them with carvings. They used cedar logs to make totem poles and placed them in front of their houses. The tall poles told the history of families who lived there. Canoes were also carved from cedar and used to carry goods. On important occasions, families held potlatches. Families demonstrated their wealth by giving gifts to the rest of the community.

The Tlingit

The Tlingit (KLINK-it) were one of the largest American Indian groups in the Pacific Northwest. They lived near the coast or on rivers. They shredded bark to make clothes. In cold weather they wore animal skins.

The Tlingit society is divided into clans. A clan is a group of related families. Strict rules told people how to act toward other clans. Several families from the same clan lived together in big houses. Each family had its own area. Families gathered by a central fire to talk and cook. During the winter, people stayed inside. They had time then to weave, carve, paint, and sew. They held ceremonies and potlatches.

About 17,000 Tlingit live in southeastern Alaska now. Their clans and traditions are strong. They still have potlatches for important occasions.

Answers

Summary: Peoples of the Plains

The Great Plains

The Great Plains stretch from the Mississippi River to the Rocky Mountains, and from Texas into Canada. They used to be grassland. In the east, where there was more rain, the grass grew eight feet high. In the west, where the land was drier, the grasses were shorter.

American Indians have lived on the Plains for thousands of years. Their most important resource was the great herds of buffalo that used to roam the Plains. The Pawnee and Omaha farmed the Eastern Plains. They lived in villages near rivers and built earth lodges. In the spring and fall they worked their farms. In the winter and summer they hunted buffalo. American Indians used all parts of the buffalo. They ate the meat and used the skins for teepee covers, blankets, clothing, drums, and shields. Buffalo bones were carved to make tools. Buffalo hair was used for rope.

Plains Indians decorated their belongings with paint and porcupine quills. The dry Western Plains were not good farmland. The Western Plains Indians were nomads. They followed the herds of buffalo, carrying their belongings from place to place on travois. The Lakota once farmed the Eastern Plains, but they fought with the Ojibwa. The Lakota migrated west and became nomads.

The Comanche

Spanish explorers brought horses to North America in the 1500s. Horses made it easier to hunt, travel, and fight. The Comanche moved to the Great Plains in the 1600s. By the 1700s they had spread across what is now Texas and Oklahoma. They were nomads and fierce warriors. They controlled a large area of the Plains.

The Comanche nation was divided into smaller groups that lived and hunted together. Each group chose war and peace chiefs. The chiefs met to discuss issues that affected all Comanche. About 8,500 Comanche live in the United States now. They have their own government and continue to value their traditions.

Before You Read

Find and underline each vocabulary word.

lodge *noun,* a house made of bark, earth, and grass

nomad *noun,* a person who moves around and does not live in one place

travois *noun,* similar to a sled, used by nomads to carry their possessions

After You Read

REVIEW In what ways were the lives of the Eastern and Western Plains Indians different? Circle the names of the Indian nations that lived in the Eastern Plains. Highlight the sentences that describe how they lived. Then draw a box around the name of Indians who lived on the Western Plains. Highlight the words that describe how they lived.

REVIEW Why were horses important to Western Plains Indians? Circle the sentence that tells how horses helped the Plains Indians.

Summary: Peoples of the Southwest

The Southwest

The Southwest region includes New Mexico and Arizona, and parts of Utah, Nevada, Colorado, Texas, southern California, and northern Mexico. The Southwest is mostly low, flat desert or desert on high plateaus. There are some mountains and deep canyons. There is almost no rain and the land is very dry. Streams are fed by snow melting in the mountains. There are few trees.

Native Americans in the Southwest built houses of sticks, stones, and clay called adobe. They built their homes on top of steep mesas to keep them safe from attacks. They planted their corn deep in the ground so the roots could get moisture from the earth. They developed irrigation to water their crops in order to get good harvests. They also planted crops on land that was flooded in the spring.

The Hopi

The Hopi have lived in the Southwest for hundreds of years. They are Pueblo Indians. Early Hopi used irrigation to grow corn, beans, and squash. Corn was the staple food. Hopi grew red, blue, yellow, white, and purple corn. They grew enough to store so it would last all year. They also made clay pottery. They were among the first people to fire pottery. Firing pottery with coal makes the clay hard and strong.

Through their religion the Hopi acted as caretakers of the land. They believed that when the land is healthy, the harvest would be good. Throughout the year the Hopi prayed and held ceremonies as part of taking care of the land. For instance, at a ceremony called the Bean Dance, the Hopi danced and prayed for a good harvest.

Modern Hopi follow many traditions of their culture. They continue to take part in ceremonies. Visitors are sometimes allowed to watch. Many Hopi are skilled at traditional pottery, weaving, and jewelry making. Others hold jobs, are teachers, or run their own businesses.

Before You Read

Find and underline each vocabulary word.

irrigation *noun,* supplying water to crops using streams, ditches, or pipes

staple *noun,* main crop that is used for food

ceremony *noun,* special event at which people gather to express important beliefs

After You Read

REVIEW Why was irrigation necessary for the Southwest Indians? Highlight the sentence that describes the climate of the region.

REVIEW What is the Bean Dance? Underline the sentence that tells you the answer.

Answers continued

Name _____ Date _____

Summary: World Travel and Trade

Trade with China

Before 1500, there was almost no contact between the Eastern and Western hemispheres. Most people in Europe, Asia, and Africa did not know the Americas existed. Often, merchants were the first to travel to distant places looking for new goods to trade.

In 1271, Marco Polo traveled from Italy to China. He wrote a book about his adventures. He told about a trade route that connected Europe and China. It was called the Silk Road. He described inventions, such as paper, printing, and gunpowder. Merchants became rich by bringing silks, spices, and other goods to Europe.

In 1405, the Chinese began exploring and trading with people in distant places. Admiral Zheng He sailed with hundreds of ships throughout Southeast Asia to the east coast of Africa. In 1434, the new ruler of China stopped all Chinese exploration.

African Trading Kingdoms

People in Africa also traded. Some West African kingdoms became powerful through trade. In the 700s, Ghana was rich in gold but did not have enough salt. Salt was used to keep food from spoiling. Merchants from Arabia crossed the Sahara in big caravans to trade salt for gold.

Arab merchants taught people in Ghana about their religion, Islam. Many people in Ghana became followers of Islam. In 1234, the kingdom of Mali conquered Ghana. Mali's cities became new trade centers. One of its most important cities was Timbuktu. In 1324, Mali's ruler, Mansa Musa, traveled to Mecca. Mecca was the most holy city in Arabia. He set up trading agreements.

When he returned to Mali, he brought scholars and artists from Arabia with him. They made Timbuktu an important center for learning and art. In 1468, a new kingdom called Songhai took over most of Mali. The kingdom grew weaker after Mansa Musa's rule, but trade continued for over a hundred years.

Before You Read

Find and underline each vocabulary word.

merchant *noun*, someone who buys and sells goods to earn money

kingdom *noun*, a place ruled by a king or queen

caravan *noun*, a group of people and animals who travel together

After You Read

REVIEW **What was the importance of the Silk Road?** The Silk Road connected Europe to which country? Underline the sentence that tells you the answer.

REVIEW **What effect did trade with North Africa have on Ghana's culture?** What did Arab merchants teach the people of Ghana? What did the people of Ghana convert to? Highlight the sentences that tell the answer.

Name _____ Date _____

Summary: Peoples of the East

The Eastern Woodlands

The Eastern Woodlands stretched from the Atlantic coast to the Mississippi River and from the Gulf of Mexico to the Great Lakes. It had plenty of rain and was rich in natural resources. There were many sources of food. Forests covered the region. Many American Indian nations lived in the mountains, valleys, and plains. They hunted deer, bears, and rabbits. They made syrup from the sap of maple trees.

Near the Great Lakes American Indians gathered wild rice. Most were also farmers. Their staple crops, called the "three sisters," were corn, beans, and squash. Woodland Indians made houses appropriate to the climate. In the warm south, houses could have no walls, just roofs for shade and protection from rain. They wore light clothing woven from grasses. In the cold north, Woodland Indians built longhouses. Many families lived together in a longhouse. They wore warm deerskin clothing.

The Haudenosaunee

Five Haudenosaunee nations stopped warring and formed a confederation between 1100 and 1600. The confederation, known as the Haudenosaunee League, included Mohawks, Oneidas, Onondagas, Cayugas, and Senecas. Later, the Tuscarora joined. The Haudenosaunee, also called the Iroquois, lived in clans. Clan mothers, who were the oldest women in the clan, chose chiefs. The League was governed by chiefs from each nation. To make a decision, all of the chiefs had to agree. They discussed issues until they reached agreement.

The Haudenosaunee traded with other American Indians. They used wampum to symbolize agreements and show important events. When the Europeans came into the region they bartered furs for blankets and knives. More than 50,000 Haudenosaunee live in North America now. Some live in their homelands in Canada and New York State. Some live in cities. Many follow traditional customs and ceremonies. Some Mohawks are steelworkers. They helped build landmarks such as the Empire State Building and the Golden Gate Bridge.

Before You Read

Find and underline each vocabulary word.

longhouse *noun*, a large house made with wooden poles and bark

confederation *noun*, a type of government in which separate groups of people join together, but local leaders make most decisions for their group

wampum *noun*, carefully shaped and cut seashells strung like beads

barter *noun*, exchange of goods without using money

After You Read

REVIEW **What were the three sisters?** Circle the sentence that tells about the three sisters.

REVIEW **Why did the Haudenosaunee use wampum?** Circle the sentence that tells how the Haudenosaunee used wampum.

Answers

Name _____ Date _____

Summary: Europeans Arrive in the Americas

Before You Read
Find and underline each vocabulary word.

settlement *noun*, a small community of people living in a new place
epidemic *noun*, an outbreak of a disease that spreads quickly and affects many people
circumnavigate *verb*, to sail completely around something

After You Read
REVIEW Why did Ferdinand and Isabella finally agree to give Columbus money for his voyage in 1492?** Highlight the sentences that tell two reasons Ferdinand and Isabella wanted to pay for Columbus's explorations.

REVIEW How did the Columbian Exchange change the diet of Europeans?** Underline the words that tell which food became important in Europe.

REVIEW Who named the Pacific Ocean and why?** Circle the name of the explorer. Highlight the sentence that tells the answer.

Christopher Columbus

Christopher Columbus believed he could reach Asia by sailing west across the Atlantic Ocean. He asked King Ferdinand and Queen Isabella of Spain to pay for the trip. They were at war with North African Muslims. These North Africans had ruled southern Spain for 700 years. The Spanish rulers needed the money to pay for the war. They hoped Columbus would find riches. They also wanted to tell people about Roman Catholicism. Columbus landed on an island in the present-day Bahamas. He thought it was close to India. He called the peaceful Taino people who lived there Indians.

The Columbian Exchange

The Spanish rulers wanted Columbus to start a settlement and look for gold. His ships carried horses, cows, pigs, wheat, barley, and sugar cane. These animals and plants were new to the Americas. The Spanish also carried new diseases. People died in epidemics. Most of the Taino died. The settlement destroyed many plants and animals. Columbus took home new foods, including potatoes, corn, beans, peanuts, and cacao. This movement of plants and animals between Europe, Asia, Africa, and the Americas is called the Columbian Exchange. Potatoes became an important food in Europe.

Exploration Continues

Other European rulers soon sent their own explorers to the Americas to claim lands and find riches. Pedro Alvares Cabral claimed eastern South America for Portugal in 1500. In 1513, de Balboa saw the Pacific Ocean from Panama. Ferdinand Magellan tried to circumnavigate the Earth. He named the ocean Pacific, which means peaceful, because it looked so calm. Magellan was killed, but his crew was the first to sail around the world.

Name _____ Date _____

Summary: New Ideas in Europe

Before You Read
Find and underline each vocabulary word.

technology *noun*, the use of scientific knowledge and tools to do things better and more rapidly.
navigation *noun*, the science of planning and controlling the direction of a ship
astrolabe *noun*, a navigation tool that measures the height of the sun or a star against the horizon
profit *noun*, money left after all expenses have been paid
slavery *noun*, a cruel system in which people are bought and sold and made to work without pay

After You Read
REVIEW What did new technology do to make exploration easier?** Underline the sentence that tells why a compass was useful. Highlight the sentence that tells why Europeans liked guns.

REVIEW Why was sailing around the Cape of Good Hope important?** Underline the sentence that tells why Europeans wanted to find a sea route to Asia.

The Renaissance

Many changes took place in Europe in the 1300s and 1400s. This period was called the Renaissance, which means rebirth. People explored the ideas of ancient Greeks, Romans, and other peoples.

Learning led to new technology. The printing press was developed in 1454. Before then people copied books by hand. A printing press could print a page of type quickly. More books were made, and new ideas spread widely and rapidly.

New ideas also changed navigation. North Africans taught Europeans to use the astrolabe. It told them how far north or south they were. The Chinese taught Europeans to use a compass. It allowed sailors to steer without seeing stars or sun.

Gunpowder was another Chinese invention. Europeans used it in guns and cannons. They felt they could protect themselves if they were attacked when exploring new places.

A Sea Route to Asia

Europeans were eager to trade with Asia. Merchants could make big profits selling Asian goods, such as spices and silk. People in Europe loved spices like pepper.

Europeans knew a sea route would be faster than the Silk Road. In Portugal, Prince Henry started a navigation school to encourage explorers. Mapmakers, shipbuilders, and sea captains worked together to share their knowledge. They designed and built faster ships that were good for exploring. Portuguese traders exploring the coast of West Africa captured Africans and forced them into slavery. Enslaved people were sold in Europe.

In 1487, Bartolomeu Dias was blown off course by a storm. His ship reached the eastern side of Africa. The Portuguese named the tip of Africa the Cape of Good Hope. They knew then that they could sail around Africa to get to Asia. In 1497, Vasco da Gama first took that route to India. Portuguese ships soon used the route to trade spices.

Answers *continued*

Name _____ Date _____

Summary: New Spain

New Spain Grows

By the 1570s, Spain ruled Mexico as a <u>colony</u>. Spanish settlers farmed and built mines to find gold and silver. Soon more Spanish soldiers, government officials, and priests came. Over the next 200 years, the soldiers and priests traveled north and started <u>missions</u>. Priests wanted to <u>convert</u> American Indians to Roman Catholicism. Other European nations sent explorers and settlers to the Americas. The Spanish wanted to stop these nations from claiming land. They built forts called presidios to protect Spanish claims and guard against attacks. In 1565, Pedro Menéndez de Avilés started St. Augustine in Florida. It was the first town built in the present-day United States by Europeans. In 1598, Don Juan de Oñate started a settlement at Santa Fe, New Mexico. In 1769, a priest named Junípero Serra founded missions on the California coast.

Life in New Spain

The Spanish did not find much gold in North America. They started farms called <u>haciendas</u> to make money. They forced American Indians to work on farms and in mines. Many Indians died from overwork and bad treatment. A priest, Bartolomé de las Casas, spoke out against this bad treatment. Most settlers ignored him. Later, the Spanish imported enslaved Africans to replace the many American Indians who died. Most of the enslaved Africans worked on sugar cane plantations in the Caribbean colonies. By 1650, about 130,000 enslaved Africans and their descendants had been brought to New Spain. Some American Indians moved to missions, converted to the Spanish religion, and learned to speak Spanish. Others refused. In 1680, Pueblo Indian leader Popé led a <u>revolt</u> against the Spanish in New Mexico. They killed hundreds of Spanish and kept the Spanish out of the area until 1692. Then Spanish soldiers reconquered the area.

Before You Read

Find and underline each vocabulary word.

colony *noun*, a territory ruled by another country

mission *noun*, a religious community where priests teach Christianity

convert *verb*, to change a religion or a belief

hacienda *noun*, a large farm or ranch, often with its own church and village

revolt *noun*, a violent uprising against a ruler

After You Read

REVIEW **Why did the Spanish build presidios in New Spain?** Highlight the sentence that describes the Spanish forts.

REVIEW **What did some American Indians do when they moved to Spanish missions?** Highlight the sentence that gives the answer.

Name _____ Date _____

Summary: Conquest of the Americas

Cortés Conquers the Aztecs

European rulers wanted explorers to find riches to bring back to Europe. Hernán Cortés led an <u>expedition</u> to Mexico in 1519. His ships carried 600 conquistadors with horses and weapons. They wanted fame and riches. Cortés had heard about the Aztecs. The Aztecs ruled an <u>empire</u> that covered much of present-day Mexico. Its capital city, Tenochtitlán, was beautiful and huge. It was twice as big as any European city. The Aztec ruler, Moctezuma, welcomed Cortés, but Moctezuma soon sent the Spaniards away. The conquistadors were greedy for gold. Cortés got help from neighboring Indian nations that had been conquered by the Aztecs. His soldiers had horses, guns, and armor, and the Aztecs did not. Smallpox made the Aztecs weak. Cortés defeated them. In 1535, Spain controlled the Aztec empire and named it New Spain. After Cortés, conquistadors explored Central and South America to find gold and treasure. Pizarro conquered the Inca empire in South America in the 1530s.

Exploring North America

Conquistadors went north looking for gold. Juan Ponce de León claimed present-day Florida for Spain in 1513. He was looking for a "fountain of youth." A legend said it would make an old person young again. Spain sent <u>(de Soto)</u> to search for gold in the area beyond Florida in 1539. He traveled as far as the Mississippi River. He found no gold. The conquistadors fought against and enslaved the American Indians they met. In 1540 <u>(Francisco Vásquez de Coronado)</u> and his men traveled <u>3,500 miles looking for gold.</u> Spanish explorers were the first Europeans to see most of North America. They learned about the geography and peoples of the region.

Before You Read

Find and underline each vocabulary word.

expedition *noun*, a journey to achieve a goal

conquistador *noun*, Spanish word for conqueror

empire *noun*, many nations or territories ruled by a single group or leader

After You Read

REVIEW **Why did people inside the Aztec empire help Cortés defeat the Aztecs?** Highlight the sentence that tells why some Indian nations helped Cortés fight Moctezuma.

REVIEW **What did the Spanish hope to find in the lands north of Mexico?** Underline the words that tell why conquistadors made expeditions to the north. Circle the names of the leaders of the expeditions.

Answers

Name _____ Date _____

Summary: Roanoke and Jamestown

The Lost Colony

The English wanted a colony in North America. They wanted to find gold and silver there. In 1585, about 100 English men arrived in Roanoke Island, near North Carolina. In 1587, more settlers came to Roanoke. Their leader, John White, returned to England to buy supplies. When he returned to Roanoke, the colonists were gone. No one ever found them.

The Jamestown Colony

In 1606, English merchants started the Virginia Company. They wanted to build a settlement in North America. The king gave the company a charter for their colony. The merchants asked people to invest in the company. If the colonists found treasure, the people who bought stock would make money.

In 1607, more than 100 men and boys sailed to present-day Virginia. They named their colony Jamestown. The settlers looked for gold. They did not know how to farm. Jamestown was damp and hot. The insects carried diseases. The water wasn't good for drinking, and the settlers ran out of food. Many died from hunger and disease.

John Smith, a new leader, ordered the men to stop looking for gold and plant crops. Life was hard in Jamestown. In 1609, most of the colonists died in the winter. It was known as the "starving time."

In 1612, a settler named John Rolfe found that tobacco grew well in Jamestown. Soon tobacco became a cash crop. Settlers sold tobacco to England. They bought food and supplies from England. In 1619, the first women and Africans arrived. The first Africans probably came as indentured servants.

Powhatan Indians also lived in the area. The Powhatans saw that the English wanted their land. They fought. The two sides made peace when John Rolfe married Pocohantas, daughter of the Powhatan leader. The peace was short. The English tried to take more Powhatan land. They fought again. In 1646, the English killed many of the Powhatan and took control of most of their land.

Before You Read

Find and underline each vocabulary word.

charter *noun*, a document giving permission to a person or group to do something

invest *verb*, to put money into something to try to earn more money

stock *noun*, a piece of ownership of a company

cash crop *noun*, a crop that people grow and sell to earn money

indentured servant *noun*, someone who agreed to work for a number of years in exchange for the cost of the voyage to North America

After You Read

REVIEW Why did the Jamestown colonists run out of food? Underline the sentence that tells the answer.

REVIEW Why did colonists in Jamestown fight the Powhatans? Highlight the words that say what the English wanted.

Name _____ Date _____

Summary: A Northwest Passage

Searching for a Passage to Asia

In the 1500s and 1600s, explorers looked for a Northwest Passage through North America to Asia. They wanted a fast way to bring back riches from Asia. In 1497, the English king sent John Cabot to look for the passage. Cabot sailed to Canada, but he only found a rich fishing area. The French king also sent sailors to look for the passage. They did not find it, but they explored new lands.

Jacques Cartier explored the St. Lawrence River in Canada. Giovanni da Verrazano explored the east coast of North America. Samuel de Champlain traveled up the St. Lawrence River. He started a fur-trading post called Quebec. Quebec was the first permanent French settlement in North America.

In 1606, a Dutch trading company sent Henry Hudson to find the passage. Hudson sailed up what is now the Hudson River in New York. The Dutch claimed the land and started a colony in the Hudson River Valley. In 1610, Hudson explored for the English. He found what is now Hudson Bay in Canada. England claimed the land around Hudson Bay. None of the explorers found a Northwest Passage, but they did find lands with forests, rivers, and wildlife.

Spain and England

King Philip of Spain was angry with England. An English sea captain, Francis Drake, attacked many Spanish ships and took the gold and silver. He gave it to the Queen of England. The king was also angry because England was a threat to Spain's power in the Americas. Spain and England also had had religious differences. England broke away from the Catholic Church and became Protestant. King Philip wanted England to be Catholic again.

In 1588, the king ordered an armada of 130 warships to attack England. Francis Drake was ready for the invasion. The English ships sank many of the Spanish ships and defeated the Spanish Armada. Then they used their new power to claim more land in the Americas.

Before You Read

Find and underline each vocabulary word.

claim *verb*, to declare something as your own

armada *noun*, a large fleet of ships

invasion *noun*, an attack by an armed force to conquer another country

After You Read

REVIEW What did John Cabot find during his exploration of Canada? Circle the words that say what Cabot was looking for. Underline the sentence that tells what he found.

REVIEW Why did the king of Spain attack England? Highlight three reasons why the king of Spain wanted to attack England.

Answers *continued*

Name _____ Date _____

Summary: New England Settlements

The Plymouth Colony

People called Separatists were unhappy with the Church of England. They decided to *separate* and start their own church. This was against English law. One Separatist group called Pilgrims went to the Netherlands for religious freedom. They practiced their religion freely in the Netherlands, but they wanted an entire community based on their religious beliefs. The Virginia Company of London agreed to let the Pilgrims build a community in the colony of Virginia.

In 1620, about 100 Pilgrims sailed across the Atlantic on the *Mayflower*. Bad weather blew the ship to Cape Cod, in Massachusetts. The Pilgrims built their settlement near there and named it Plymouth. The Virginia Company did not control Massachusetts, so the Pilgrims wrote a plan for their own government. They called it the Mayflower Compact. In it, the Pilgrims agreed to make laws for the good of the colony and to obey them.

Life was hard. The Pilgrims arrived in November. It was too late in the year to plant crops. They did not have enough food, and many colonists died in the winter. In the spring, a Wampanoag man named Squanto showed the Pilgrims how to plant crops, and how to hunt and fish. In the fall, the Pilgrims and Wampanoags celebrated to give thanks for the Pilgrims' first harvest. This feast is remembered during Thanksgiving.

Massachusetts Bay Colony

The Puritans were another religious group that did not agree with the Church of England. The Puritans wanted to build a community based on their religious beliefs. In 1630, the Puritans landed in Salem, Massachusetts. They decided to settle in present-day Boston. They named their colony the Massachusetts Bay Colony, after the Massachuset Indians. The Puritans were better prepared than the Pilgrims. They arrived in June and planted crops. By the 1640s, 20,000 Puritans settled in the area. The area was called New England because so many people from England lived there.

Before You Read

Find and underline each vocabulary word.

pilgrim *noun*, a person who makes a long journey for religious reasons

compact *noun*, an agreement

cape *noun*, a strip of land that stretches into a body of water

After You Read

REVIEW **Why did the Pilgrims leave the Netherlands for North America?** Underline the sentence that tells the answer.

REVIEW **How did Squanto help the Plymouth Colony succeed?** Highlight the sentence that tells what Squanto taught the Pilgrims.

Name _____ Date _____

Summary: Dutch and French Colonies

New Netherland

In the 1500s and 1600s, European explorers claimed land in North America. Henry Hudson claimed land for the Dutch. They named it New Netherland. The first settlements were fur-trading posts along rivers in present-day New York. In 1626, the colony's governor, Peter Minuit, bought Manhattan Island from the Manhates Indians. He started a settlement and named it New Amsterdam. He also set up a colony for Sweden on the present-day Delaware River.

The Dutch West India Company controlled both settlements. The company encouraged people of different religions and nationalities to go to New Netherland. The diversity of the population grew, and the settlers practiced tolerance. In 1647, Peter Stuyvesant became governor. He was unpopular because he was not tolerant and he made harsh laws. In 1664, English ships sailed to New Amsterdam. The settlers were so unhappy with Stuyvesant that they refused to fight the English. The English renamed the colony New York.

New France

In the 1600s, France claimed land in present-day Canada and named it New France. Few settlers lived there. The cold climate was bad for farming. Most settlers were young men. They lived near Quebec, a fur-trading post. Fur was an important business. New France had many animals with thick fur. American Indians trapped them and traded the fur to the French for goods like tools, pots, and cloth. The French sold the furs to Europeans to make into hats and coats.

The French were partners with the Huron and Algonquin Indians, who were at war with the Haudenosaunee, a group of five Indian nations. The fur traders helped the Huron fight their enemies. Missionaries also went to New France to teach the Catholic religion. In 1673, a missionary named Marquette and an explorer named Jolliet traveled by canoe down the Mississippi River. In 1682, an explorer named La Salle claimed the Mississippi and the land around it for France. He called it Louisiana after King Louis XIV.

Before You Read

Find and underline each vocabulary word.

diversity *noun*, the variety of people in a group

tolerance *noun*, respect for beliefs that are different from one's own

missionary *noun*, a person who teaches his or her religion to others who have different beliefs

After You Read

REVIEW **Why was Stuyvesant an unpopular governor?** Underline the sentence that tells about Peter Stuyvesant.

REVIEW **How did the traders of New France get fur to sell to Europeans?** Circle the sentence that tells who trapped the animals to get their fur. Underline the words that tell what the French gave the Indians in exchange for furs.

Answers

Summary: Geography of the Colonies

The Thirteen Colonies

The English colonies in North America were located between the Atlantic Ocean and the Appalachian Mountains. France had colonies to the north. Spain had colonies to the south. The thirteen colonies can be separated into three parts, or regions, by geography and climate: New England, the Middle Colonies, and the Southern Colonies.

The land in New England was shaped by glaciers. During the Ice Age, thick sheets of ice cut through the mountains. Glaciers pushed rocks and rich soil south. A thin layer of rocky dirt was left. Crops did not grow well in the rocky, sandy soil. Forests and hills made it hard to farm. In New England the summers were warm, but winters were long and cold. The growing season was only about five months long.

Colonists in New England used other natural resources to make a living. They cut down trees to make buildings and boats. They caught fish and whales for food and other products.

Glaciers pushed the soil from New England into the Middle Colonies. The soil was rich and deep. It was good for farming. The growing season was longer than in New England. There was more sun and lots of rain. Colonists used riverboats on long, wide rivers such as the Hudson and Delaware. They sent crops to sell in nearby towns. Colonists also hunted deer and beaver for food and fur.

The Southern Colonies had the best climate and land for farming. The climate was warm almost all year long. The soil was rich. The growing season lasted for seven or eight months. The many waterways along the southern coast formed the tidewater region. Ocean tides made rivers rise and fall as much as 150 miles inland. The fall line was along the Appalachian Mountain range. There, rivers flowed from higher lands to lower lands. The backcountry was the land in back of the area where most colonists settled. It was steep and covered with forests. Farms were small. Colonists hunted and fished for food.

Find and underline each vocabulary word.

growing season *noun*, the time of year when it is warm enough for plants to grow

tidewater *noun*, the water in rivers and streams that rises and falls every day with the ocean's tides

fall line *noun*, the area in which rivers flowing from higher land to lower lands often form waterfalls

backcountry *noun*, the land "in back of," the area along the coast where most colonists settled

REVIEW Why was farming difficult for New England colonists? Draw a box around the sentence that tells why crops did not grow well. Circle the sentence that tells why it was hard to farm. Underline the sentence that tells about the climate.

REVIEW Why was farming in the Middle and Southern colonies better than in New England? Draw a box around the sentences that describe the soils in these colonies. Underline the sentences that tell about the climates.

Summary: New England

Massachusetts

In the 1600s, English Puritans settled in New England. People in their communities obeyed the rules of the Bible. Puritan religion shaped the government of the Massachusetts Bay Colony. All settlers had to go to church.

A town meeting was held once a year. Only men with property could vote on laws for their town. Puritan towns had more self-government than most colonies.

Some colonists thought Puritans should not tell them what to believe or how to act. Roger Williams was a dissenter. He did not believe the government should make laws about religion. Williams wanted religious freedom. The Puritans banished him from Massachusetts Bay.

In 1636, Williams started a new colony that became Rhode Island. Rhode Island's government was separate from the church. Anne Hutchinson also disagreed with Puritan ministers. She held meetings that allowed men and women to discuss religion. Puritans did not think women should teach men about religion. Hutchinson was banished and went to Rhode Island.

Thomas Hooker also disagreed with the Puritans. He wanted to start a place where men who did not belong to the church could vote. He started the colony of Connecticut. Other colonists settled the area that became New Hampshire and Maine.

Conflicts over Land

The Puritans lived on American Indian land. Colonists bought the land from the Indians and expected them to leave. Indians believed land could be shared, but not owned. Colonists and the Pequot Indians fought over the land. Colonists killed most of the Pequot Indians and took their land. More colonists arrived. The Wampanoag Indian leader Metacomet, called King Philip, felt his people had to defend their land. In 1675, another war began. A year later the colonists won King Philip's War. They enslaved some Wampanoags and forced the rest to leave. Few American Indians remained in eastern New England after the war.

Find and underline each vocabulary word.

town meeting *noun*, a gathering where colonists held elections and voted on the laws for their towns

self-government *noun*, a system of government that lets people make laws for themselves

dissenter *noun*, a person who does not agree with the beliefs of his or her leaders

banish *verb*, to force someone to leave

REVIEW In what ways were Roger Williams and Anne Hutchinson alike? Circle the words that tell what Roger Williams did not believe. Circle the words that tell what Anne Hutchinson did.

REVIEW What caused the Pequot War? Draw a box around the sentence that tells why the colonists and Pequot Indians fought.

Answers *continued*

Name _____ Date _____

Summary: The Middle Colonies

New York and New Jersey

In 1664, England captured the colony of New Netherland. King Charles II gave the colony to his brother, James the Duke of York. James kept some of the land and named it New York. He gave the rest of the land to two friends. They divided the land into East Jersey and West Jersey. In 1702, the two colonies joined to form New Jersey.

The proprietors of New York and New Jersey picked governors to rule the colonies. The proprietors allowed the colonists to be part of the government in two ways. First, the governors chose a council that helped make decisions. Second, colonists elected representatives to an assembly. The assembly did not have much power, but it was a step toward self-government.

Pennsylvania and Delaware

William Penn belonged to a religious group called the Quakers. In England, people who did not belong to the Church of England were punished. Penn wanted a colony where all Christians could live in peace.

In 1681, King Charles gave Penn land in the Middle Colonies. This land was named Pennsylvania. The Duke of York gave Penn more land, which later became Delaware.

In Pennsylvania, colonists worshiped freely. They also had a more powerful elected assembly that could approve or reject laws. Penn bought land and made treaties with the Lenni Lenape Indians. His fairness helped everyone live together peacefully.

Penn planned the colony's first city, Philadelphia. This city became a big trade center because it had a good harbor. Ships brought goods from other colonies and from Europe.

Benjamin Franklin was Philadelphia's most famous citizen. He published a newspaper. He also helped to start Philadelphia's first fire company, hospital, and library. Franklin became famous for his inventions.

Resources for Reaching All Learners
Copyright © Houghton Mifflin Company. All rights reserved.

22   Use with *United States History*, pp. 186–191

Before You Read

Find and underline each vocabulary word.

proprietor *noun*, a person who owned and controlled all the land in a colony

representative *noun*, someone who is chosen to speak and act for others

treaty *noun*, an official agreement between nations or groups

After You Read

REVIEW How did colonists in New York and New Jersey take part in government? Highlight two sentences that tell how the proprietors allowed the colonists to take part in the government.

REVIEW How did the government of Pennsylvania differ from those of New York and New Jersey? Circle the sentence that describes the government of Pennsylvania.

Name _____ Date _____

Summary: Life in New England

Using the Sea

Most colonists in New England grew just enough crops to feed their families. The rocky coast had good harbors. The thick forests provided wood to build ships. Boston became the center for the shipbuilding industry. The fishing industry grew rapidly in the 1600s. Cod and whales were key resources. By the 1700s, whaling was an important industry.

Merchants shipped exports of fish and lumber to Europe, the West Indies, and Africa. They traded for imports of tea, spices, and manufactured goods. These shipping routes were called the triangular trade. The slave trade was part of the triangular trade. Merchants forced captured people from Africa to travel the Middle Passage from Africa to the West Indies. They were packed in crowded ships. Many died on the way. During the 1600s and 1700s, hundreds of thousands of Africans were forced to work as slaves in the colonies.

Home and Community Life

Most New England families lived in small houses with one main room. They cooked on the fireplace and slept on mattresses on the floor. Colonial homes were like busy workshops. Almost everything people wore, ate, or used was made by hand at home. Men and boys worked the farm, cared for animals, and fixed buildings. Women and girls cooked and preserved food. They made soap, candles, and the family's clothing. They also helped at planting and harvest time.

Some Puritans taught their children to read the Bible at home. Many New England towns had schools. In the early 1700s, colonists no longer had strong religious beliefs. In the 1730s, new ministers convinced people to return to religion. This movement was called the Great Awakening. It caused people to join new churches and to see religion in new ways.

Resources for Reaching All Learners
Copyright © Houghton Mifflin Company. All rights reserved.

21   Use with *United States History*, pp. 174–179

Before You Read

Find and underline each vocabulary word.

industry *noun*, all the businesses that make one kind of product or provide one kind of service

export *noun*, a product sent to another country and sold

import *noun*, a product brought into one country from another country

Middle Passage *noun*, the voyage from Africa to the West Indies

slave trade *noun*, the business of buying and selling human beings

After You Read

REVIEW What was triangular trade? Highlight three sentences that tell what the merchants traded in the triangular trade.

REVIEW How did boys and girls help their families? Draw a box around the sentence that tells what work the boys did. Underline the sentences that tell what work the girls did.

REVIEW Why did many New England colonists return to religion in the 1730s? Circle the name given to the renewed interest in religion.

Answers

Name _____ Date _____

Summary: Life in the Middle Colonies

Before You Read
Find and underline each vocabulary word.

free market economy *noun*, an economy in which the people, not the government, decide what will be produced

free enterprise *noun*, a system in which people may start any business that they believe will succeed

artisan *noun*, someone who is skilled at making something by hand

laborer *noun*, a person who does hard physical work

apprentice *noun*, someone who studies with a master to learn a skill or business

A Mix of People

In the 1600s, the Middle Colonies accepted people of different religions and cultures. The colonists were German, Dutch, Scots-Irish, Scandinavian, English, and enslaved Africans. Some were Catholic or Jewish. Proprietors allowed them to practice different religions. Proprietors allowed this religious tolerance for two reasons. First, leaders like William Penn believed that people of all religions should live together in peace. Second, some proprietors did not care about the colonists' religious beliefs. They just wanted colonists to buy or rent land.

Making a Living

Many families in the Middle Colonies were farmers. Men, women, and children all worked long hours in the fields and in the home. Boys helped plant and harvest crops. Girls did housework, cooking, and sewing.

The climate and soil of the Middle Colonies were very good for farming. Many farmers grew more than they needed for their families. They sold extra grain and livestock in the cities. Farmers used the long, wide rivers to ship their goods to Philadelphia and New York. Merchants there sold the farmers' goods to other cities and nations.

As in the other English colonies, the Middle Colonies had a free market economy. Proprietors did not tell the colonists what to do. Colonists could make what they thought would earn them the most money. This is called free enterprise.

Philadelphia and New York became busy ports and trade centers. Many artisans and laborers found work in these cities. Some of the laborers were enslaved Africans.

Many colonial children became apprentices to learn useful skills. Boys learned things like shoemaking and printing. Girls learned to spin thread and weave cloth.

After You Read
REVIEW **Why did proprietors allow religious tolerance?** Highlight two reasons that proprietors allowed religious tolerance.

REVIEW **Why did colonial children become apprentices?** Highlight the sentence that tells the answer.

Name _____ Date _____

Summary: The Southern Colonies

Before You Read
Find and underline each vocabulary word.

plantation *noun*, a large farm on which crops are raised by workers who live on the farm

legislature *noun*, a group of people with the power to make and change laws

refuge *noun*, a safe place

debtor *noun*, a person who owes money

Virginia

In 1607, Virginia became the first permanent English colony. Early settlers started plantations. Plantation owners grew rich by growing and selling tobacco and rice. Many workers were enslaved Africans. Early settlers built their plantations on the best farmland near the ocean. Later, settlers moved inland.

In 1619, Virginia became the first colony to have an elected legislature. This assembly was called the House of Burgesses. Colonists elected the burgesses. Only white men who owned land could vote or be elected. Most of them belonged to the Anglican Church. In 1632, the legislature made this church the official church of Virginia. People who were not Anglican had to leave the colony.

New Colonies in the South

England settled four more colonies in the South: Maryland, North Carolina, South Carolina, and Georgia. Maryland began in 1632 when King Charles I gave land to a Catholic named Cecilius Calvert. Calvert wanted Maryland to be a refuge for Catholics. In 1649, Maryland passed the Toleration Act. This law promised that all Christians could worship freely.

In 1663, King Charles II formed a colony south of Virginia. France and Spain claimed this area. The king hoped that an English settlement would keep the French and Spanish away. The settlement was called Carolina. Later it was divided into North Carolina and South Carolina. South Carolina had good farmland and harbors. North Carolina did not.

In 1732, King George II gave land to James Oglethorpe. Oglethorpe formed Georgia as a place for English debtors. Oglethorpe made strict rules for the colonists. Later, these rules changed. In time, Georgia became a rich plantation colony.

After You Read
REVIEW **Who were burgesses?** Underline the sentence that says who could be elected as burgesses.

REVIEW **What were differences between North Carolina and South Carolina?** Circle two things that South Carolina had that North Carolina did not have.

Answers *continued*

Name _____ Date _____

Summary: Life in the South

Southern Agriculture

The Southern Colonies had an agricultural economy. The climate was good for growing crops. Planters used enslaved Africans to do the hard work needed to grow tobacco and rice.

In Virginia and Maryland, tobacco was the most important crop. In North Carolina, colonists used sticky pine sap to make pitch. Pitch was used to seal the boards of a ship to keep out water. In South Carolina and Georgia, the main crops were rice and indigo.

The Southern Colonies had fewer towns and cities than other colonies. Charles Town was the capital of South Carolina. It was the biggest southern city and a busy trade center.

Plantations and Small Farms

Plantations were huge, with many buildings and workers. Planters' children had private teachers. They learned reading, writing, and dancing. Later, parents taught their children how to manage a large plantation.

However, most colonists lived on small farms in the backcountry, away from schools and towns. Farmers' children only learned to read and write if their parents taught them.

Southern Slavery

Slaves lived in all the colonies by 1750. Most lived in the Southern Colonies. Enslaved Africans were treated as if they were property, not people. Plantation owners used cruel laws and punishments to make slaves work hard. Some overseers whipped and even killed workers. Many slaves died young because of this bad treatment. Some ran away. Others created a new culture that blended African traditions to help them survive. They formed close communities. Many adopted Christianity. They combined African music with their religious beliefs to make powerful spirituals.

Resources for Reaching All Learners
Copyright © Houghton Mifflin Company. All rights reserved.

25   Use with *United States History*, pp. 210–215

Before You Read
Find and underline each vocabulary word.

indigo *noun,* a plant that can be made into a dark blue dye

overseer *noun,* a person who watches and directs the work of other people

spiritual *noun,* an African American religious folk song

After You Read

REVIEW Why was Charles Town an important city? Highlight the sentences that describe Charles Town.

REVIEW How did the children of planters and the children of backcountry farmers learn how to read and write? Who taught planters' children? Who taught farmers' children? Find two sentences that tell the answers and underline them.

REVIEW What did slaves do to survive the hardships of slavery? Draw a box around the sentences that tell the answer.

Name _____ Date _____

Summary: The French and Indian War

War Between France and Britain

In the 1750s, Britain and France had colonies in North America. The British wanted to settle in the Ohio River Valley and to trade with the Native Americans who lived there. The French built forts to protect their trade with the Indians. In 1754, George Washington led an army against the French. He was defeated.

Britain declared war on France. The war for control of the valley was called the French and Indian War. Most American Indians in the region were allies of the French. The American Indians liked the French because they traded but did not settle on the land.

In 1754, a congress of the British colonies met in Albany, New York. Benjamin Franklin thought the colonies should work together to defeat France. Each colony would still have its own government. They would also create one government together to decide important issues. His idea was called the Albany Plan of Union. The colonists rejected it. They did not want to join together under one government.

Victory for Britain

In 1757, Britain sent more soldiers to North America. This helped defeat the French in Canada. In 1763, Britain and France ended the war and signed the Treaty of Paris. France gave Britain control of Canada and most of the land east of the Mississippi River.

British soldiers stayed in the Ohio River Valley. The Indians wanted the soldiers to leave. An Ottawa chief named Pontiac led the Indians in a war against the British. This was called Pontiac's Rebellion. The British defeated the Indians in less than a year.

To avoid more conflict with American Indians, Britain made the Proclamation of 1763. It recognized the Indians' right to the land. It did not allow colonists west of the Appalachian Mountains. The colonists were angry. They wanted to settle on the land. They did not want the British soldiers to live among them.

Resources for Reaching All Learners
Copyright © Houghton Mifflin Company. All rights reserved.

26   Use with *United States History*, pp. 228–231

Before You Read
Find and underline each vocabulary word.

ally *noun,* a person or group that joins with another to work toward a goal

congress *noun,* a group of representatives who meet to discuss a subject

rebellion *noun,* a fight against a government

proclamation *noun,* an official public statement

After You Read

REVIEW What was the Albany Plan? Underline the sentence that describes what Franklin thought the British colonies should do in order to defeat France.

REVIEW Why were colonists upset with Britain after the French and Indian War? Highlight two reasons the colonists were angry.

Answers

Name _____ Date _____

Summary: Early Conflicts with Britain

Britain Needs Money

Britain spent a lot of money to defeat the French. The British government said that the colonies should pay for the War. The government raised money by taxing goods brought into the colonies. The Sugar Act of 1764 taxed goods like sugar, coffee, and cloth. When a colonist bought cloth, part of the money went to the government as a tax. Some merchants avoided the tax by <u>smuggling</u> goods into the country.

In 1765, Britain passed the Stamp Act. This act taxed anything printed on paper. Many colonists said the new taxes were unfair. Colonists had no say in making tax laws because they did not have representatives in Parliament. Men like Samuel Adams in Boston formed groups to protest the Stamp Act. Adams was the leader of a group called the Sons of Liberty. Sometimes this group and others used violence to resist new taxes.

Conflict over Taxes

In 1765, the nine colonies met to discuss the taxes at the Stamp Act Congress. They decided that only colonial governments should tax the colonies. Merchants in ports like New York and Philadelphia held a boycott of British goods. The protests and boycott worked. Britain repealed the Stamp Act.

In 1767, Britain needed money to pay for the services of (colonial governors) and (soldiers.) Parliament created the Townshend Act. This Act made colonists pay taxes on tea, glass, paper, and other items. Colonists boycotted British goods again. They threatened to use violence against tax officials. British troops were sent to protect the officials. A group of women called the Daughters of Liberty made their own cloth instead of buying British cloth.

By 1770, the protests worked. The British repealed most of the taxes, but left the tax on tea. They wanted to show that they still had the power to tax the colonies. Anger grew toward the British government.

Before You Read
Find and underline each vocabulary word.

tax *noun*, money people pay their government in return for services

smuggling *noun*, to import goods illegally

liberty *noun*, freedom from being controlled by another government

protest *noun*, an event at which people complain about an issue

boycott *noun*, a refusal to buy, sell, or use goods

repeal *verb*, to cancel a law

After You Read
REVIEW **What was the goal of Samuel Adams and other Sons of Liberty?** Underline the sentence that explains why Samuel Adams formed the Sons of Liberty.

REVIEW **Why did the British Parliament pass the Townshend Acts?** Circle two services the government needed to pay for.

Name _____ Date _____

Summary: Conflicts Grow

Trouble in Boston

Britain sent soldiers to Boston when colonists resisted taxes. Colonists did not want soldiers in their city. On March 5, 1770, a crowd yelled and threw snowballs at some of the soldiers. The soldiers started to shoot. Five colonists were killed. Colonists called the fight a <u>massacre.</u>

News traveled slowly. (Samuel Adams started the Committees of Correspondence to share news and ideas) with people in other colonies. Members wrote letters that told what the British were doing. Members suggested action colonists could take.

The Boston Tea Party

In 1773, the Tea Act allowed the East India Company of Britain to sell tea for a very low price. But if colonists bought the cheap tea, they also paid a tax to Britain. Many colonists did not want to pay taxes to Britain at all. They also didn't want one company to control the tea trade. Merchants refused to sell the tea or unload it from the ships. On December 16, 1773, some Sons of Liberty illegally boarded the ships. They threw the tea into the harbor. This protest was called the Boston Tea Party.

The British government was angry. It passed laws called the Coercive Acts. These laws stopped all trade between Boston and Britain, did not allow town meetings, and gave Britain control of the colony. Britain sent soldiers back to Boston. Colonists were forced to quarter them. Colonists called the laws the "Intolerable Acts" and said they were too harsh.

On September 5, 1774, delegates from most colonies met in the First Continental Congress. Delegates discussed the Intolerable Acts. [They asked King George III to stop taxing the colonies without their agreement.] They stopped trade with Britain. Colonists gathered weapons in case they needed to fight. King George sent more soldiers. He said the colonists had started a rebellion.

Before You Read
Find and underline each vocabulary word.

massacre *noun*, the killing of many people

correspondence *noun*, written communication

quarter *verb*, to give people food and shelter

delegate *noun*, someone chosen to speak and act for others

After You Read
REVIEW **What was the importance of the Committees of Correspondence?** Circle the sentence that tells why Samuel Adams started the Committees of Correspondence.

REVIEW **Why did the First Continental Congress meet?** Draw a box around the sentence that tells what the delegates wanted King George III to do.

Answers continued

Name _____ Date _____

Summary: War Begins

Moving Toward War

Colonists who opposed British rule called themselves Patriots. They were angry about the Intolerable Acts. Throughout the colonies, militias prepared for war against Britain.

General Thomas Gage was the British official in Massachusetts. He learned that Patriots were storing (cannons) and (gunpowder) in Concord. He sent soldiers to destroy the supplies. Patriots Paul Revere and William Dawes learned of the plan. They rode through the night to warn the minutemen that the British were coming.

The First Battles

On April 19, 1775, British soldiers and minutemen in Lexington began shooting. Colonists were killed and wounded. Hundreds of minutemen gathered in Concord. They forced the British soldiers back to Boston. Along the way, colonists killed or wounded more than 250 British soldiers.

Colonists heard of the battles. Militias trapped British soldiers in Boston. Patriots planned to build a fort on Bunker Hill. They built it on Breed's Hill instead. British soldiers marched up the hill. They fought until the Patriots ran out of gunpowder. The British captured the fort. This was called the Battle of Bunker Hill. Even though they lost the battle, the Patriots showed they could plan and fight well.

A Colonial Army

The Second Continental Congress met in 1775. It created an army to go to war against Britain. George Washington was commander of the Continental Army. Many delegates did not want a war. They sent the Olive Branch Petition to King George III. It asked him to help end the conflict peacefully. But the king sent more soldiers. The Continental Army captured Fort Ticonderoga. The army used cannons it found there to force the British to leave Boston.

Before You Read

Find and underline each vocabulary word.

Patriot *noun,* a colonist who opposed British rule

militia *noun,* a group of ordinary people who train for battle

minutemen *noun,* militia with special training

commander *noun,* an officer in charge of an army

petition *noun,* a written request from a number of people

After You Read

REVIEW Why did General Gage send British soldiers to Concord? Circle the words that tell what the colonists were storing near Boston.

REVIEW Why was the Battle of Bunker Hill important for the colonists? Underline the sentence that tells what the Patriots showed they could do.

REVIEW What was the Olive Branch Petition? Underline what the petition asked King George to do.

Name _____ Date _____

Summary: Declaring Independence

The Steps to Independence

After the battles of 1775, the American colonies and Britain were at war. Some colonists were Patriots. They wanted independence. Others still thought of King George as their king. One famous Patriot, Thomas Paine, wrote a pamphlet called *Common Sense.* He wrote that the king treated the colonists unfairly. He said the only way to stop this was to become independent. He also wrote that the colonists had nothing to gain and much to lose by staying tied to the king. Thousands of people read the pamphlet, and support for independence grew.

Declaration of Independence

Congress asked Thomas Jefferson and others to write a declaration of independence. Jefferson wrote about the rights of all people in the Declaration of Independence. Jefferson wrote that people have the right to live, the right to be free, and the right to seek happiness. He wrote that if a government does not protect these rights, people have the right to form a new government. He wrote that King George had tried to take away rights and force taxes on the colonies. The Declaration said the colonies should separate from Britain and that only free colonies could protect the colonists' rights.

Importance of the Declaration

On July 4, 1776, the Congress accepted the Declaration. The delegates knew it was dangerous to sign it. Britain would say it was treason. But delegates signed. The Declaration is still important because it says the American people believe in equal rights for all. Today we know that the words "all men are created equal" include everyone: women, men, children, and every race and group. But in 1776, people's ideas were different. Only white men who owned property had the right to vote. Laws that recognized equal rights of other groups were passed later.

Before You Read

Find and underline each vocabulary word.

independence *noun,* freedom from being ruled by someone else

declaration *noun,* a statement that declares or announces an idea

rights *noun,* freedoms that are protected by a government's laws

treason *noun,* the crime of fighting against one's own government

After You Read

REVIEW What were Thomas Paine's arguments for independence? Underline the sentences that tell you Paine's ideas.

REVIEW According to the Declaration, why did the colonies have the right to their own government? Underline the sentences that say why the colonies had a right to their own government.

REVIEW Why is the Declaration so important to Americans? Underline the sentence that says why the Declaration is still important.

Answers

Name _____ Date _____

Summary: The War in the North

Before You Read
Find and underline each vocabulary word.

retreat *verb*, to move away from the enemy

mercenary *noun*, a soldier who is paid to fight for a foreign country

victory *noun*, the defeat of an enemy

After You Read
REVIEW **Why did Washington decide to attack Trenton?** Circle the sentence that tells why George Washington wanted to win in Trenton.

REVIEW **What happened at Valley Forge to make the Continental Army better soldiers?** Underline two sentences that tell who joined the soldiers at Valley Forge and how he helped them become better soldiers.

Washington's First Battles

The Continental Army was not as large or strong as the British army when the War for Independence started. British soldiers had better weapons and training. But the Americans had a great leader, George Washington. They were on their own land, which made it easier to plan attacks and defend themselves.

The Americans forced the British to leave Boston in the spring of 1776. In August, the British won the Battle of Long Island in New York. The Americans retreated and marched into Pennsylvania. George Washington planned an attack on the British in Trenton, New Jersey. (He wanted to win a battle so his soldiers would not give up.) On the night of December 25, the Americans rowed across the Delaware River. They attacked at dawn. The soldiers in Trenton were German mercenaries. They were still sleepy from celebrating Christmas, and the soldiers surprised them. The Americans won the battle and took almost 1,000 prisoners. The Patriots were very happy about this victory.

A Turning Point

The British marched into New York from Canada. They met the Americans at Saratoga. It was a hard battle, but the Americans won. After the Battle of Saratoga, France decided to help the Americans. They sent money, soldiers, and a navy. Later, Spain, the Netherlands, and Russia also helped the Americans.

The British captured Philadelphia and stayed there for the winter of 1777. The Americans stayed in tents at Valley Forge, about 20 miles away. Soldiers slept on the cold ground, and many men had no shoes. There was not enough food. Many soldiers died. Washington worked hard to get more food and uniforms. In the spring, Friedrich von Steuben, a German soldier, joined the army at Valley Forge. He trained the Americans to march and use their weapons better. They became better soldiers because of their training.

Name _____ Date _____

Summary: Life During the War

Before You Read
Find and underline each vocabulary word.

Loyalists *noun*, people still loyal to the king

neutral *noun*, not taking sides

inflation *noun*, a rise in the prices of most goods

After You Read
REVIEW **Why did enslaved African Americans fight on both sides in the war?** Circle the two sentences that tell the answer.

REVIEW **Why was inflation a problem for Americans?** Highlight the sentence that tells how inflation made it hard for people.

Taking Sides

On July 4, 1776, Congress declared independence. Not everyone thought this was a good idea. Many people thought Britain should rule America. When the Revolutionary War began, about half of the colonists were Patriots who supported independence. About one-fifth were Loyalists. The rest of the colonists were neutral.

Most Americans who worked for the British government were Loyalists because they wanted to keep their jobs. Many wealthy Americans were Loyalists because they thought war would hurt their businesses.

Some enslaved African Americans became Loyalists. (The British offered them freedom if they helped the British in the war.) A few fought in the army, and others built forts, drove carts, or worked as spies. Most American Indians stayed neutral. A few Indian nations fought for the Patriots, but more American Indians helped the British. They wanted the British to win and stop American settlers from taking their land.

Many enslaved African Americans were Patriots. (Some were offered freedom if they became soldiers.) Free African Americans also became soldiers. Some women Patriots worked as spies or messengers. Others helped at the soldiers' camps.

The Challenges of War

The War for Independence created many problems. People who lived near battlefields had to leave their homes. Both armies destroyed houses and robbed farms. Food, clothing, and supplies cost more. Inflation made it hard for people to buy things they needed. Some store and farm owners would not sell their goods. They wanted to wait for the prices to go higher so they could then sell their goods for more money. There were not enough supplies for soldiers and other people. Congress passed a law to stop store owners and farmers from waiting to sell their goods.

Answers *continued*

Name _____ Date _____

Summary: Winning the War

The War in the South and West

After more than three years of war, the British had not defeated the Patriots. They decided on a new strategy. They thought the South had more Loyalists than the North. They hoped these Loyalists could help them. The British invaded the South. At first, the new strategy worked. By the summer of 1780, the British had won Georgia and South Carolina. Many Loyalists helped them, including Benedict Arnold, a famous Patriot hero who secretly changed sides and became a British general. Today he is known as a <u>traitor</u>.

The British won many battles in the South, but the Patriots fought back. One officer used surprise attacks. His soldiers sneaked up on the British, attacked, and quickly retreated. Another Patriot, Nathanael Greene, forced the British to chase his small army. This tired the British and used up their supplies. Patriots in the West fought back too. They captured British forts in the Ohio River Valley. Spain also joined the war and captured British forts.

The War Ends

The Patriots fought the last big battle against the British in Yorktown, Virginia. Washington marched his army from New York to Virginia, where the British leader Cornwallis and his men were. French ships helped the Patriots. Washington's army and the French navy trapped the British army. Cornwallis hoped that British soldiers and ships in New York would help him. But the British could not defeat the French navy. Cornwallis's men fought for a week, but Cornwallis knew they could not win. On October 19, 1781, the British army at Yorktown surrendered. The war continued for two more years, but there was not much fighting. In September 1783, the United States and Britain signed the Treaty of Paris. The treaty said America was independent. Now Americans needed a government for their new country.

Find and underline each vocabulary word.

strategy *noun*, a plan of action

traitor *noun*, someone who is not loyal

surrender *verb*, to give up

Check your understanding.

REVIEW **What was Greene's strategy to defeat the British?** Circle the two sentences that explained Greene's strategy.

REVIEW **What did the Treaty of Paris say?** Draw a box around the sentence that tells what the treaty said.

Name _____ Date _____

Summary: A New Nation

The Articles of Confederation

The 13 colonies had fought for self-government. Each new state had a <u>constitution</u> to protect its <u>citizens</u>. Americans did not want to give up their power to a strong, central government.

In 1781, the Articles of Confederation made Congress the national government. Each state had one vote in Congress. The states had more power than the national government. Congress could declare war, borrow and print money, and make treaties with other nations. It could not start an army, create taxes, or control trade.

People wanted to settle on land won in the Revolutionary War. Congress passed two <u>ordinances</u> to control what happened in the Northwest <u>Territories</u>. The Land Ordinance of 1785 explained how the land would be measured, divided, and sold. The Northwest Ordinance of 1787 described how a territory could become a state. It also outlawed slavery in the territories.

Problems for the New Nation

Congress owed money to banks and to other countries for the Revolutionary War. Congress could not raise money because it could not collect taxes. The states were not working together. They printed their own money. People could not agree on how much the money was worth.

In Massachusetts, many farmers did not earn enough money to pay their debts and high state taxes. If farmers did not pay, the state took their farms. In 1786, Daniel Shays led a rebellion of armed farmers. They demanded more time to pay debts. The state militia stopped them. Shays's Rebellion showed that a weak national government could not keep order. George Washington worried the government was not strong enough to protect people's rights. In February 1787, Congress invited state delegates to meet and change the Articles of Confederation to make the nation stronger.

Find and underline each vocabulary word.

constitution *noun*, a written plan for government

citizen *noun*, an official member of a city, state, or nation

territory *noun*, land ruled by a national government but which has no representatives in that government

ordinance *noun*, a law

REVIEW **What did Congress do to organize the Northwest Territory?** Highlight the names of each ordinance. Underline what each ordinance said.

REVIEW **Why did farmers in western Massachusetts protest?** Circle the sentences that tell why the farmers had trouble paying taxes and what happened if they did not pay.

Answers

Name _____ Date _____

Summary: The Constitution

A Plan for Government

The Constitution tells us that our government is a democracy. It divides the government into three branches. The legislative branch, or Congress, makes laws. Congress also collects taxes to pay for services. The executive branch carries out the laws. The President is the head of this branch. A new President is elected every four years. The judicial branch is made up of courts. They decide what laws mean and whether they have been followed. Everyone, including the government and its officials, must follow the laws.

Limits on Government

The Constitution includes checks and balances. They keep one branch from becoming stronger than the others. The President makes treaties and chooses judges. Congress makes laws. The President can veto these treaties or judges. The courts can decide if a law follows the Constitution. A law that is found unconstitutional is no longer in effect.

The Constitution creates a federal system. The national government has power over national issues. This includes defense, printing money, the postal service, and trade. State governments have power over local issues. States control education and elections. Both systems collect taxes and set up courts. Federal laws are stronger than state laws. The highest law is the Constitution itself.

Changing the Constitution

The Constitution was written so that it can be changed as the country changes. An amendment becomes law when two-thirds of the members of the House and Senate vote for it. Three-fourths of the states also have to ratify it. The first ten amendments are the Bill of Rights. They protect rights, such as freedom of speech. The tenth amendment limits the power of the federal government. In 1790, the Constitution did not protect the rights of all Americans. People have fought for their rights and won. Today the Constitution gives equal protection to more citizens.

Before You Read

Find and underline each vocabulary word.

democracy *noun,* a government in which the people have the power to make political decisions

checks and balances *noun,* a system in which each branch of government can limit the power of the other branches

veto *verb,* to reject

unconstitutional *adjective,* does not agree with the Constitution

amendment *noun,* a change made to the Constitution

After You Read

REVIEW What are the jobs of each branch of the national government? Circle the jobs of each branch.

REVIEW Why did the authors of the Constitution create checks and balances and a federal system? Circle the sentence that explains checks and balances.

REVIEW Why does the Constitution include a way to make amendments? Circle the sentence that tells what happens as the country changes.

Name _____ Date _____

Summary: Constitutional Convention

Leaders of the Convention

The Constitutional Convention met in 1787. Delegates met to give Congress more power. Delegates included only white, male landowners. Some delegates wanted a republic. They thought a republic would protect citizens' rights. Others wanted a federal system. In a federal system, Congress could share power with the states.

Creating a New Government

James Madison suggested that the government should have three branches. One branch, the Congress, would make laws. A second branch would carry out laws. A third branch would settle legal arguments. States compromised in order to support the Constitution. Madison wanted the number of delegates from each state to be based on the state's population. Delegates from smaller states thought this would give bigger states more power. Roger Sherman suggested dividing Congress into two parts. Each state would have the same number of representatives in one house, the Senate. In the other house, the House of Representatives, the number of representatives would depend on the state's population. Southern delegates wanted to count enslaved people in their populations. Northern delegates believed they should not be counted. The states compromised. Every five enslaved persons were counted as three free people. Some states wanted to end slavery. Southern states would not accept this. The states agreed to end the slave trade by 1808.

Ratifying the Constitution

Federalists supported the Constitution. Antifederalists wanted a Bill of Rights added to the Constitution. The Bill of Rights would protect people's liberties. Federalists agreed. Nine of thirteen states needed to ratify the Constitution for it to become law. In June 1788, nine states agreed to ratify the Constitution. The country had a new government.

Before You Read

Find and underline each vocabulary word.

federal *adjective,* a system of government in which the states share power with a central government

republic *noun,* a government in which the citizens elect leaders to represent them

compromise *noun,* both sides give up something they want to settle a disagreement

ratify *verb,* to officially accept

After You Read

REVIEW What was the advantage of a federal system? Circle the words that tell how the federal system was better.

REVIEW Why did delegates argue over representation in Congress? Highlight a sentence that tells why small states worried. Circle the sentence that tells about counting enslaved people.

REVIEW Why did Antifederalists demand a Bill of Rights? Circle the sentence that tells what a Bill of Rights would do.

Answers continued

Name _____ Date _____

Summary: People on the Move

Exploring the Frontier

When Europeans came to America, they settled between the Atlantic coast and the Appalachian Mountains. These mountains were difficult to cross. The British government also did not allow colonists to cross the mountains. Land on the western side of the mountains belonged to the Indians. As land in the East filled with farms and towns, colonists wanted more land. By the late 1700s, many settlers crossed the Appalachians. Daniel Boone was a pioneer. In 1769, he explored an Indian trail that led through the Cumberland Gap over the Appalachians. Boone helped build a road through the Gap, called the Wilderness Road. He helped settlers across the mountains to the frontier. They found land that was rich and beautiful.

Life on the Frontier

Going across the mountains was hard. Settlers traveled in large wagons with food and supplies. The wagons often broke on the rocky paths. Others traveled on flatboats. They floated down the Mississippi and Ohio rivers or through canals. When pioneers got to the frontier, they saw that American Indians had already built villages and farms.

Life on the frontier was hard and lonely. Settlers left behind their families to move to a new land. Pioneers did many kinds of work on the frontier. Settlers cut down trees and used the wood to build houses. They grew grain and vegetables for their families. They also raised farm animals. Men hunted for meat. Women worked at home and watched the children.

American Indians believed that the land belonged to everyone. They did not believe it could be bought or sold. The Indians signed treaties with the government. The treaties said colonists could hunt on the land, but they could not live on it. The colonists wanted to stay. They fought with the Indians. One American Indian chief, Chief Logan, was friendly to the colonists. Then settlers killed his family in 1774. After that he fought against the colonists for many years.

Find and underline each vocabulary word.

pioneer *noun*, one of the first people to enter or settle a region

frontier *noun*, the edge of a country or a settled region

flatboat *noun*, large, rectangular boat partly covered by a roof

canal *noun*, a waterway built for boat travel and shipping

REVIEW In which river valleys did people look for farmland on the frontier? Circle the names of the rivers the settlers traveled and settled near.

REVIEW What kinds of transportation did settlers use to move west? Draw a box around the sentences that tell how settlers traveled west.

Name _____ Date _____

Summary: President Washington

The First President

The Constitution set up the system for electing the President. Each state chose representatives for the Electoral College. They voted for the President. George Washington's inauguration as the first President was in 1789. He promised to "preserve, protect, and defend the Constitution of the United States." Every President makes the same promise.

Congress created departments to help the President run the executive branch. The leader of a department was called its Secretary. The Secretary of State decided how the United States would act toward other countries. The Secretary of the Treasury made decisions about the nation's money. The Secretary of War was in charge of protecting the country. The Attorney General made sure federal laws were obeyed. These men formed the President's Cabinet. They advised the President.

Arguments in the Cabinet

Jefferson and Hamilton often disagreed. Both had supporters who started political parties. Hamilton's supporters started the Federalist Party. It wanted a strong national government that would support manufacturing and trade. Jefferson's supporters started the Democratic-Republican Party. It wanted to limit the national government, and to support farming instead of trade.

Hamilton wanted to start a national bank. Jefferson said the government did not have the power to start a bank. Washington approved the national bank. People put money in bank accounts. The bank borrows money from people's savings to make loans. The borrower pays interest for the loan.

Hamilton and Jefferson agreed to locate the new nation's capital between Virginia and Maryland.

After eight years, Washington retired as President. He warned Americans to avoid forming political parties. He also did not want the nation to take sides in foreign wars.

Find and underline each vocabulary word.

inauguration *noun*, the official ceremony to make someone President

Cabinet *noun*, a group chosen by the President to help the President run the executive branch and give advice

political party *noun*, a group of people who share similar ideas about government

interest *noun*, what people pay to borrow money

capital *noun*, the city where the government meets

REVIEW What is the purpose of the Cabinet? Circle the words that tell what the Cabinet does.

REVIEW Why did Hamilton and Jefferson disagree about creating a national bank? Circle the words that say why Jefferson opposed the bank.

Answers

Name _____ Date _____

Summary: The War of 1812

Trouble with Britain

In 1808, Britain and France were at war. The U.S. did not take either side, but Britain and the U.S. became enemies. British officers raided American ships to look for British sailors on the ships. American sailors were caught and forced to serve in the British Navy. This was called impressment. The government was angry about impressment. It was also angry that the British were helping Indians fight Western settlers. The Indian chief Tecumseh wanted Indians to unite to keep settlers away. In 1811, the Indians were defeated at their Tippecanoe settlement.

Fighting the War

In 1812, the U.S. declared war on Britain. Americans wanted to stop impressment. They also wanted Britain to stop arming the Indians.

In 1814, the British navy fired at Fort McHenry. Francis Scott Key watched the battle. He saw the American flag flying above the fort and wrote "The Star-Spangled Banner." This became the national anthem. Later that year, the U.S. and Britain signed a peace treaty. The Treaty of Ghent did not give either country any new land. Unaware of the treaty, British forces attacked Americans in New Orleans. The British were defeated.

A New Sense of Pride

After the war Americans had a time of prosperity. They developed a sense of nationalism and became interested in the American flag. In 1818, Congress passed a law that said the flag should have 13 stripes for the 13 original colonies. A star would be added for each state that joined the Union. Today there are 50 stars on the flag.

In 1816, President James Monroe worried that other European countries would invade America. He created a new foreign policy. The Monroe Doctrine warned European countries to stay out of North and South America. The United States would also stay out of Europe.

Before You Read

Find and underline each vocabulary word.

prosperity *noun*, economic success and security

nationalism *noun*, a devotion to one's country

foreign policy *noun*, a government's actions toward other nations

After You Read

REVIEW Why did **Tecumseh want American Indian nations to unite?** Circle the sentence that tells the answer.

REVIEW What inspired **Francis Scott Key to write the poem that became "The Star-Spangled Banner"?** Highlight the sentence that tells what Francis Scott Key saw.

REVIEW How did the law **passed in 1818 change the appearance of the national flag?** Circle the number of stripes on the flag. Underline the reason for that number. Underline what each star represents on the flag. Circle the number of stars the flag has today.

Name _____ Date _____

Summary: The Nation Grows

President Jefferson

John Adams was the second President of the United States. He belonged to the Federalist party. This group believed the national government should be stronger than the state governments. The Federalists wanted to make laws to help manufacturers. When Thomas Jefferson became President, the Federalists gave up power. Jefferson belonged to the Democratic-Republican party. This group believed state governments should be stronger than the federal government. They wanted to help farmers.

Farmers wanted to ship their products down the Mississippi River to Louisiana. This land belonged to France. President Jefferson sent representatives to meet with the French ruler, Napoleon Bonaparte. They asked Napoleon if Americans could keep trading on the river. Napoleon needed money to go to war against Great Britain. He sold Louisiana to the United States. The Louisiana Purchase doubled the size of the country.

Exploring the West

Jefferson sent soldiers to explore Louisiana. Meriwether Lewis and William Clark led the group. It was called the Corps of Discovery. Jefferson wanted them to study the land, plants, animals, and climates of the West. He also wanted the corps to learn about the cultures of the western American Indians and to look for a water route to the Pacific. Sacagawea, the group's interpreter, was an American Indian woman. She helped the corps speak to American Indians. The corps left in 1804 and returned in September 1806. They learned about the land and the people, but did not find a water route to the Pacific.

In 1805 Zebulon Pike led a group to find the source of the Mississippi River. They explored Missouri and went north to Minnesota. They learned about the land, but did not find the river's source. Later they explored the Arkansas and Red rivers. The Corps of Discovery and Pike's explorers led the way for traders and pioneers in the west.

Before You Read

Find and underline each vocabulary word.

manufacturer *noun*, people who use machines to make goods

corps *noun*, a team of people who work together

interpreter *noun*, someone who helps people who speak different languages understand each other

source *noun*, the place where a river begins

After You Read

REVIEW Why did **Jefferson send representatives to France?** Circle what the representatives asked Napoleon Bonaparte.

REVIEW What tasks did **Lewis and Clark complete on their expedition?** Highlight the sentence that tells what the Corps of Discovery expedition learned.

Answers *continued*

Name _____ Date _____

Summary: Age of Jackson

A New Kind of President

The first six Presidents of the United States were wealthy and well educated. In 1828, Andrew Jackson became President. He grew up poor in Carolina. Then he took the Wilderness Trail to Tennessee. He became a lawyer, politician, and business owner. He was the first President to come from a state west of the original 13 colonies.

Farmers, frontier settlers, and working men who lived on the territories were given suffrage when the territories became states. Women and African Americans could not vote. Only white men who had land or money could vote. Jackson supported the new voters. They liked his campaign. Their votes helped to elect him President.

As President, Jackson supported working people. He thought the bank only helped rich people and that the poor were not allowed to borrow money from the national bank. Jackson ordered the government to take its money out of the national bank and put it into state banks.

Indian Removal Act

As settlers came to the frontier, conflicts increased with American Indians there. Jackson believed the Indians slowed the growth of the United States. In 1830, Congress passed the Indian Removal Act. This law forced American Indians living east of the Mississippi River to leave their homes and businesses. The Indians had to move to Indian Territory in present-day Oklahoma. The Cherokee Indians objected. Cherokee Indian Chief John Ross took their case to the Supreme Court. Chief Justice John Marshall ruled that it was against the law to force the Cherokee to move. Jackson ignored the ruling. In 1838, the U.S. Army forced the Cherokee to travel 1,000 miles to Indian Territory. About one-fifth of the Cherokee died during this journey, called the Trail of Tears. The army also tried to force the Seminole Indians to leave Florida. Chief Osceola led their resistance. He was put in jail and died. Indians continued the struggle to keep their homes.

Before You Read

Find and underline each vocabulary word.

suffrage *noun*, the right to vote

campaign *noun*, a series of actions taken toward a goal

ruling *noun*, an official decision

After You Read

REVIEW What types of people did Jackson want to help? Circle words that describe the people who voted for Jackson.

REVIEW What did the Cherokee do to fight against removal? Underline the sentence that tells what Indian chief John Ross did to fight the Indian Removal Act.

Name _____ Date _____

Summary: The Industrial Revolution

The Industrial Revolution Begins

The Industrial Revolution began with textile machines. These machines turned cotton into yarn. In 1793, Eli Whitney invented the cotton gin, a machine that cleaned cotton quickly. Cotton became America's biggest export. Then the government hired Whitney to make thousands of guns. At that time guns were made by hand. Whitney thought of a way to make them quickly and cheaply. He used interchangeable parts and mass production. Soon factories began using his ideas. The nation's productivity increased.

Machines Bring Change

Entrepreneurs used machines to change how people worked. Francis Lowell built a mill that turned cotton into cloth. Soon other factories opened. New inventions, like reapers and steel plows, made farm work easier and faster. Before the Industrial Revolution, people worked on farms or in workshops. Now many people worked in factories.

Changes in Transportation

In the 1800s, dirt roads could not be used in bad weather. The government built a paved road from Maryland to Ohio. People built towns and opened businesses to sell goods. Robert Fulton invented a steamboat that could travel without wind or currents. Soon there were many steamboats. In 1825, the Erie Canal opened. This canal made it easier to ship goods between Lake Erie and the Hudson River. Many canals were built. Rivers and canals became the fastest and cheapest way to ship goods.

Steam locomotive trains were even faster than steamboats. Trips that took 32 hours by steamboat took only 10 hours by train. Soon the United States had thousands of miles of railroad track. Factories and farmers sent their goods faster to places all over the country.

Before You Read

Find and underline each vocabulary word.

textile *noun*, cloth or fabric

interchangeable parts *noun*, parts made by a machine to be exactly the same size and shape

mass production *noun*, making many products at once

productivity *noun*, the amount of goods and services made by a worker in a certain amount of time

entrepreneur *noun*, a person who takes risks to start a new business

After You Read

REVIEW What did Whitney do to manufacture guns more quickly and cheaply? Circle the sentence that tells the answer.

REVIEW In what ways did the workday change for many people during the Industrial Revolution? Underline two sentences that tell the answer.

REVIEW Why were steam locomotives better than other forms of transportation? Underline 3 sentences that give reasons why.

Answers

Name _____ Date _____

Summary: Texas and the Mexican War

The Texas Revolution

In 1821, Texas was part of Mexico. The land was cheap, so many Americans settled in Texas. Mexico tried to stop them, but they still came. Slavery was against Mexican law, but Americans brought slaves to Texas. Many American settlers and Tejanos, or Mexicans who lived in Texas, wanted to break away from Mexico. They did not like laws made by Santa Anna, Mexico's president. The Tejanos and Texans decided to fight for independence.

In 1836, Santa Anna took an army to San Antonio to take a fort called the Alamo. Fewer than 200 Texans and Tejanos met him. Most of them died in battle. After this, Texans declared independence and formed the Republic of Texas. Sam Houston led their army in a surprise attack at San Jacinto. They won, and captured Santa Anna. For his freedom, Santa Anna gave Texas its independence.

Texans elected Sam Houston president and voted to join the United States. They also made slavery legal. President Van Buren was against annexation. Mexico wanted to keep Texas, and Van Buren feared it would cause war. He also didn't want to add a new state to the Union that allowed slavery. People who wanted to annex Texas said it was the manifest destiny of the United States to spread from the Atlantic to the Pacific Ocean. In 1845, James Polk became President. Congress voted to annex Texas.

War with Mexico

The United States and Mexico disagreed on the border between Texas and Mexico. Congress declared war in 1846. Soldiers fought on three fronts. Americans captured Mexico City in 1847. In 1848, Mexico signed the Treaty of Guadalupe Hidalgo. Mexico agreed to the annexation of Texas and the Rio Grande as the border between Texas and Mexico. Mexico also gave a large area of land, the Mexican Cession, to the United States.

Before You Read
Find and underline each vocabulary word.

annexation *noun,* joining two countries or pieces of land together

manifest destiny *noun,* the belief that the United States should spread across North America

front *noun,* where the fighting takes place in a war

cession *noun,* something that is given up

After You Read

REVIEW **Why didn't President Van Buren want to annex Texas?** Underline the two sentences that tell the answer.

REVIEW **What did Mexico agree to under the Treaty of Guadalupe Hidalgo?** Circle the sentence that tells the answer.

Name _____ Date _____

Summary: Immigrants and Reformers

German and Irish Immigrants

Millions of Europeans came to the United States in the mid-1800s. Almost half were Irish and about one-third were German. Thousands of Germans left Europe because of crop failures and war. Many settled in the Midwest of the United States. Germans with money, education, and skills bought land to farm. Others worked in Chicago, St. Louis, and Milwaukee.

Many Irish people left Ireland because of the Irish Potato Famine. When a disease destroyed the potato crop in 1846, there was not enough food. Many people died. In the next 10 years, about 1.5 million Irish people came to the United States. Most of them didn't have enough money to leave the Northeast cities where they landed. They built canals and railroads or worked in factories or as servants.

Some people did not like immigrants because their customs seemed different. People also thought immigrants were taking their jobs. Many immigrants worked for little money because they needed jobs. Craftspeople who made goods by hand lost jobs because factories produced goods faster and cheaper. Many Americans left farms to look for jobs in cities.

Making a Better Society

In the 1820s, thousands of people joined Christian churches. This was the Second Great Awakening. During this time, many people tried to reform society. Antislavery and temperance were reform movements. The temperance movement wanted people to stop drinking alcohol.

Women who worked for reform, especially antislavery, saw that they were treated with injustice too. They could not vote, speak in public meetings, or have high-paying jobs. In 1848, women had a meeting in Seneca Falls to talk about their rights. This began the women's rights movement. Newspapers attacked the women's ideas, but many more women joined the movement.

Before You Read
Find and underline each vocabulary word.

famine *noun,* a widespread shortage of food

reform *noun,* an action that makes something better

temperance *noun,* controlling or cutting back the drinking of alcohol

injustice *noun,* unfair treatment that abuses a person's rights

After You Read

REVIEW **Why did Irish immigrants usually stay in Northeastern cities, while most Germans moved to the Midwest?** Circle the sentence that tells the answer.

REVIEW **Why did women reformers decide to start a movement to protect their own rights?** Draw a box around two sentences that tell the answer.

Answers *continued*

Name _____ Date _____

Summary: Moving West

Trails West

In 1843, about 1,000 people traveled west by wagon train. They wanted to find cheap land. They traveled on the Oregon Trail, which started in Missouri and went through the Rocky Mountains to what is now Oregon. The trip was hard, but by the end of the 1850s, thousands of pioneers had settled in Oregon. In 1846, Britain and the United States agreed on a border between the United States and Canada. The land south of this became the Oregon Territory.

A religious group, the Mormons, traveled west on the Mormon Trail. In 1847, the Mormons traveled to what is now Utah. They could settle and practice their religion freely there.

The California Gold Rush

Before the 1700s, American Indians lived in California. After Spain claimed California, the Spaniards forced Indians to live and work on their missions. In 1821, California became part of Mexico. The Californios, Mexicans who lived in California, forced Indians to work on their ranches.

In 1848, California became part of the United States. Gold was discovered, and more than 250,000 people, called forty-niners, rushed to California to find it. The gold rush changed California. People built boomtowns near the gold mines. Merchants sold goods to the miners. Bankers and innkeepers opened businesses. Lawyers found jobs settling arguments.

The gold rush ended about five years later. Most of the miners did not find gold, but thousands of people stayed in California. Miners and farmers killed Indians and took their land. Other Americans took the Californios' land, forcing them to leave. Cities such as San Francisco grew. By 1850, only two years after becoming a territory of the United States, California had enough people to become a state.

Before You Read
Find and underline each vocabulary word.

wagon train *noun*, a line of covered wagons that moved together

forty-niner *noun*, gold miner who went to California in 1849 during the gold rush

gold rush *noun*, many people hurrying to the same area to look for gold over a short time

boomtown *noun*, a town whose population grows very quickly

After You Read
REVIEW Why did the first large group of people set out on the Oregon Trail?
Circle the sentence that tells the answer.

REVIEW Who lived in the boomtowns around the gold mines? Draw a box around four words that name people who lived in the boomtowns and did business with the miners.

Name _____ Date _____

Summary: Worlds Apart

Slavery in the United States

All 13 colonies allowed slavery, but it was more common in the South. Some northern states made slavery illegal after the Revolution. Some delegates to the Constitutional Convention tried to abolish slavery. They failed.

The cotton gin was invented in 1793. It made growing cotton easier. Southern planters bought more land and enslaved more people to do the work. By 1860, there were nearly 4 million enslaved African Americans in the South. Cotton became the South's most important crop. Textile mills in the North and Britain needed more cotton. The price for cotton went up.

Some enslaved people fought against slavery. In 1831, Nat Turner led a rebellion. New laws were passed to control all African Americans. By 1853, they had fewer rights than ever. In the South many people thought slavery was necessary. In the North some people thought slavery was wrong.

North and South

In the South, farming was the most important business. Huge plantations had many enslaved workers. Small farmers grew food and crops. The North also had farms, but many people moved to cities. They worked in factories, making textiles, shoes, tools, and other things. By 1860, more than half of Northerners lived in cities.

Congress passed tariffs on imported goods. These tariffs helped factories in the North. There were few factories in the South. Prices for manufactured goods were high. People blamed high prices on the tariffs and on the North.

Vice President John Calhoun said the tariffs were unfair. He argued for states' rights. He said the Constitution did not let the federal government set tariffs. People in the North and South continued to argue about tariffs and slavery. This increased sectionalism throughout the country.

Before You Read
Find and underline each vocabulary word.

tariff *noun*, a tax on imported goods

states' rights *noun*, the idea that states, not the federal government, should make decisions about matters that affect them

sectionalism *noun*, loyalty to one part of the country

After You Read
REVIEW What led to the growth of slavery in the early 1800s? Circle the new invention that changed the South. Then underline the sentence that tells the effect of this invention on slavery in the South. What was the most important crop in the South? Underline the sentence that tells the answer.

REVIEW Why did southerners dislike tariffs?
Underline the sentence that tells who the tariffs helped. Circle the sentence that tells you what people blamed on the tariffs.

Answers

Name _____ Date _____

Summary: Compromise and Conflict

Would Slavery Spread?

A territory became a state when it had enough people. New states could be slave states or free states. Northerners wanted free states. They tried to make slavery illegal. Southerners wanted slave states. In 1820 Missouri wanted to enter the Union as a slave state. To keep the number of free and slave states equal, Congress let Maine join as a free state. This was the Missouri Compromise.

Congress drew an imaginary line. Only those states south of the line could be slave states. The Compromise of 1850 let territories choose to be slave states or free states by popular sovereignty. In 1854, Congress gave popular sovereignty to the Kansas and Nebraska territories. Abolitionists objected because both territories were north of the line. Settlers for and against slavery traveled to Kansas to vote. In 1861, Kansas became a free state.

The Growing Crisis

The Fugitive Slave Law was part of the Compromise of 1850. It ordered people to return runaways to slavery. Many northerners would not obey the law. Harriet Beecher Stowe wrote the book *Uncle Tom's Cabin*. It was about the cruelty of slavery. The story convinced northerners to oppose slavery. Southerners said the book was false. The conflict over slavery pushed the North and South apart.

In 1857, the Supreme Court ruled on the Dred Scott case. It said that slaves were property. Living in a free state did not make them citizens. The court also said it could not ban slavery in any of the territories. Abolitionists feared slavery would spread.

Abolitionist John Brown thought that slavery was wrong. He tried to start a rebellion against slavery by attacking an Army post in Harpers Ferry, Virginia. Brown was captured, convicted, and hung. Many northerners said he was a hero. By 1860, some southerners wanted to leave the Union to defend their way of life.

Before You Read
Find and underline each vocabulary word.

slave state *noun*, a state that permitted slavery
free state *noun*, a state that did not permit slavery
Union *noun*, another name for the United States
popular sovereignty *noun*, the right of people to make political decisions for themselves
fugitive *noun*, a person who is running away

After You Read
REVIEW **What compromises did Congress make as the nation grew?** Circle the date and name of each compromise.

REVIEW **Why did John Brown attack Harpers Ferry?** Draw a box around the sentence that tells what John Brown thought about slavery.

Use with *United States History*, pp. 432–435

Name _____ Date _____

Summary: The Struggle for Freedom

The Antislavery Movement

Some Americans felt slavery was necessary. In the South, as cotton growing spread, many people also wanted slavery to spread. Other Americans felt slavery was wrong. Some thought that enslaving people went against their religious beliefs.

The Abolitionist movement to end slavery grew in the 1830s and 1840s. There were Abolitionists in the North and the South. Abolitionists were free blacks and whites, women and men. They wrote and spoke against slavery. William Lloyd Garrison started an Abolitionist newspaper called *The Liberator*. Free blacks gave most of the money to support the newspaper.

Frederick Douglass escaped slavery. He spoke to white people about what it was like to be enslaved. Sojourner Truth also escaped slavery. She spoke for abolition and women's rights. Sarah and Angelina Grimké grew up in a Southern slaveowning family. They traveled North and spoke out against slavery.

By 1860, about 500,000 free blacks lived in the United States. They faced discrimination in both the North and South. Free blacks joined whites in creating the American Anti-Slavery Society in 1833.

The Underground Railroad

Some Abolitionists worked in secret. Free blacks gave most of the money and did most of the work to support the Underground Railroad. The Underground Railroad was a series of escape routes and hiding places called "stations." Runaways could leave the United States and go north to Canada or south to Mexico, Florida, or the Caribbean. If they were caught, they were returned to slavery and punished. People who guided runaways were called "conductors." The most famous conductor was Harriet Tubman. She escaped slavery and then returned 19 times to the South to lead others to freedom.

Before You Read
Find and underline each vocabulary word.

abolitionist *noun*, someone who joined the movement to end slavery
discrimination *noun*, the unfair treatment of particular groups
Underground Railroad *noun*, a series of escape routes and hiding places to bring people out of slavery

After You Read
REVIEW **What did free blacks in the North do to convince people that slavery was wrong?** Circle the names of people who took an active part in the abolitionist movement. Underline the actions these people took to help enslaved people. Also underline sentences that tell what all free blacks did to fight slavery.

REVIEW **What was the purpose of the Underground Railroad?** Draw a box around two sentences that explain what the Underground Railroad was and what it was used for.

Use with *United States History*, pp. 424–427

Answers *continued*

Name _____ Date _____

Summary: A Nation at War

North Against South

Eleven southern states left the Union and formed the Confederacy. Four border states stayed in the Union. The North wanted to keep the Union together. They planned to stop the Confederacy from trading with other nations. They would attack the South from the east and west at the same time. The North had more people, more factories, and more railroads. The South planned to fight off northern attacks until the Confederacy could survive as a nation. The South had good military leaders. They hoped France and Britain would help because these countries needed southern cotton. Most of the war was in the South, so Confederate soldiers knew the land. Both sides thought they could win quickly. In July 1861, at the Battle of Bull Run they learned the war might last a long time.

The War's Leaders

Robert E. Lee led the Confederate army. He stopped the Union army from capturing Richmond. He invaded the North. The Union army stopped him at Antietam in September 1862. There were 22,000 casualties in one day. Union General Ulysses S. Grant captured Confederate forts in the West and defeated the Confederates at Shiloh. Because the ports were blocked, the South was low on food, weapons, and money. The Confederacy had to draft soldiers. In the North, rich people could pay to get out of the draft. People who were too poor to pay protested. So did people who opposed the whole war.

Turning Points

In 1863, Lincoln made the Emancipation Proclamation, freeing the enslaved people. The Union captured Vicksburg and won control of the Mississippi River. Lee attacked the North, and the Union beat him at Gettysburg.

Before You Read
Find and underline each vocabulary word.

border states *noun*, slave states that stayed in the Union
casualties *noun*, soldiers who are killed or wounded in war
draft *noun*, the way a government forces people to become soldiers
emancipation *noun*, the freeing of enslaved people

After You Read
REVIEW What was the Confederacy's plan for winning the war? Highlight the sentence that tells what the South planned to do.
REVIEW Why did people in the North oppose the draft? Underline the sentences that tell you the answer.
REVIEW Why was the victory at Vicksburg important to the Union? Circle the sentence that tells you the answer.

Name _____ Date _____

Summary: Civil War Begins

Abraham Lincoln

Conflict grew between the North and South. Southerners thought abolitionists would start slave rebellions. Some southerners wanted to leave the Union. Northerners were afraid slavery would spread. Americans who opposed slavery formed the Republican Party. Republicans opposed slavery in the territories.

Abraham Lincoln was a Republican. He was born in Kentucky, a slave state. He was raised on a farm in Illinois, a free state. His family was poor. He did not go to school, but he read a lot. Lincoln became a lawyer and a political leader.

Lincoln's Campaigns

In 1858, Lincoln ran for Senate in Illinois against Stephen Douglas. They debated so people could hear their ideas. He did not think slavery was wrong. Lincoln said slavery was evil but he did not support abolition. Lincoln lost, but the debates made him famous. Many southerners thought he wanted to abolish slavery.

Lincoln ran for President in 1860. He was the only candidate against slavery. He won, but the election showed that the country was divided. No southern states voted for Lincoln. Some southerners said the federal government was too strong. They said tariffs and laws to limit slavery threatened states' rights. Some chose secession to protect their right to enslave people.

Secession Begins

In 1860, South Carolina left the union. In all, eleven southern states formed the Confederacy. Jefferson Davis was president. Lincoln wanted unity and peace but it was too late. Confederates attacked Fort Sumter on April 12, 1861. Lincoln called for men to fight the rebellion. The Civil War began.

Before You Read
Find and underline each vocabulary word.

secession *noun*, when part of a country leaves or breaks off from the rest
Confederacy *noun*, states that separated from the Union and formed a confederation
civil war *noun*, a war between two groups or regions within a nation

After You Read
REVIEW Why did some southerners want their states to leave the Union? Draw a box around three sentences that tell what southerners said about the federal government, what they thought threatened states' rights, and what right they wanted to protect.
REVIEW Why did southerners see Lincoln as an enemy? Circle what Lincoln said about slavery. Also circle what southerners thought he would do about slavery.
REVIEW What event began the Civil War? What happened on April 12, 1861? Draw a box around the answer.

Answers

Name _____ Date _____

Summary: The War Ends

Before You Read
Find and underline each vocabulary word.

telegraph *noun*, a machine that sends electric signals over wires

total war *noun*, the strategy of destroying an enemy's resources

desert *verb*, to leave the army without permission

After You Read

REVIEW Why did Sherman decide to use total war against the South? Highlight the sentence that tells you the answer.

REVIEW Why did Lee have to surrender? Underline the sentences that tell about fighting in Richmond and after the Union soldiers captured Richmond. Circle the sentences that tell about the Confederacy's supplies and soldiers.

Union Victories

After Vicksburg and Gettysburg in 1863, the North hoped they would win the war. The South kept fighting. Lincoln needed a tough army general to defeat the South. He chose Ulysses S. Grant. Grant sent General William Tecumseh Sherman to lead the Union army in Tennessee. In September 1864, Sherman captured Atlanta and sent Lincoln a message by telegraph, telling of his victory. The Union navy also captured Mobile Bay in Alabama. Lincoln needed victories to win voters' support for reelection. Sherman's army marched from Atlanta to the coast and into South Carolina. He ordered his troops to use total war so the southerners would give up. His soldiers destroyed any resources the Confederacy could use to fight. They stole food and killed livestock. They wrecked factories and railroad lines. They burned homes and barns.

Grant and Lee

While Sherman marched through Georgia and South Carolina in 1864, General Grant led a huge army toward Richmond, Virginia. They were opposed by Robert E. Lee and his army. The Union army suffered many casualties, but Grant kept attacking. Lee was forced to retreat farther south. In June 1864, the two armies faced each other near Richmond. They fought for almost a year. The Union army was getting stronger. They had plenty of supplies and soldiers. Lee's army was getting weaker. The Confederacy had no more money for supplies. They had no more soldiers to send to the front. The soldiers were hungry and tired. Some decided to desert. In April 1865, Grant captured Richmond. Grant's soldiers chased Lee's army west. Lee's army was starving and almost surrounded. On April 9, 1865 Lee surrendered to Grant at Appomattox Court House. The Union soldiers saluted their enemies as they marched past. The war was finally over.

Name _____ Date _____

Summary: The Human Face of War

Before You Read
Find and underline each vocabulary word.

camp *noun*, a group of temporary shelters, such as tents

home front *noun*, all the people who are not in the military when a country is at war

civilian *noun*, a person who is not in the military

After You Read

REVIEW What did women on both sides of the war do to help their side? Draw a box around the sentences that tell how women helped in the Civil War.

REVIEW What happened to prices in the South during the Civil War? Underline the sentence that tells how the price of food changed during the Civil War. Then highlight the effect of higher prices for civilians and soldiers.

The Soldier's Life

Men from all over the country fought in the Civil War. Many soldiers hoped for excitement but found terror on the battlefield. Life in the camp was hard. Soldiers lived in tents. The food was not good. Confederate soldiers didn't have enough food. Many soldiers were killed by new rifles. However, twice as many died from diseases. At first almost all the soldiers were white men. About 180,000 African Americans served in the Union army. Immigrants from Ireland, Germany, and Italy also fought for the Union. American Indians fought on both sides. Thousands of boys went into battle even though they were too young. Some boys were drummers who sent signals during battles. Women on both sides disguised themselves as men and joined the army. Women also worked as spies. More than 3,000 women in the North and many women in the South nursed the sick and wounded. One nurse, Clara Barton, later founded the Red Cross.

On the Home Front

Soldiers left their families to go to war. The families made up the home front. With men gone, women took on new tasks. They ran farms and businesses. They sewed uniforms, knitted socks, made bandages, and raised money. Most of the battles were in the South. Civilians in the North could not see the war happening. Mathew Brady used the new technology of photography to show them. He took pictures of soldiers in camp and on the battlefield. People in the South saw their cities, homes, and barns destroyed in the war. Inflation, or a rise in prices, made food very expensive. Soldiers and civilians in the South often did not have enough to eat. Enslaved people also suffered, but they thought the war would bring freedom. The Emancipation Proclamation in 1863 gave them hope. News of emancipation did not get to Texas until June 19, 1865. That day is celebrated as Juneteenth, the day slavery ended, in many parts of the South.

Name _____ Date _____

Summary: The Challenge of Freedom

Freedom and Hardship

Reconstruction was a time of hope for African Americans. Slavery was over. New laws protected their rights. The plantation system was over. African Americans knew how to farm, but they could not afford to buy land. Some landowners let freed African Americans farm on their land. This system was called sharecropping. Landowners loaned sharecroppers tools and seeds. Sharecroppers gave the landowners a share of the crop. Often sharecroppers did not make enough money to pay their debts.

Some southerners opposed Reconstruction. They did not like that federal troops in their states. They did not support laws that gave rights to African Americans. People formed secret organizations, like the Ku Klux Klan, to stop African Americans from taking part in government. They threatened, beat, and killed African Americans to stop them from voting.

The End of Reconstruction

By 1877 many people thought Reconstruction had not reunited the nation. President Rutherford B. Hayes told the federal troops to leave the South. Without soldiers to protect them, many African Americans could not vote. They lost their political power. Southern states passed Jim Crow laws to keep African Americans separate. Segregation was enforced in schools, hospitals, even cemeteries. The states usually spent less money on schools and hospitals for African Americans. Many African Americans believed education was important. In 1881, a former slave named Booker T. Washington opened the Tuskegee Institute where students studied and learned useful skills. The teachers and students were African Americans. Washington believed that educated African Americans would get equal treatment. Churches became important centers in African American communities.

Before You Read

Find and underline each vocabulary word.

sharecropping *noun*, system where farmers used land and gave landowners a share of the crop

Jim Crow *noun*, laws that kept African Americans separate from other Americans

segregation *noun*, forced separation of races of people

After You Read

REVIEW **Why did many freed African Americans become sharecroppers?** Underline the sentence that tells the answer.

REVIEW **What was the purpose of the Tuskegee Institute?** Circle the name of the man who started the Tuskegee Institute. Then highlight the words that tell what people did at the Institute.

Resources for Reaching All Learners
54   Use with *United States History*, pp. 482–485

Name _____ Date _____

Summary: Reconstruction

Plans for Reconstruction

After the war, the country had to be reunited. This period was called Reconstruction. Some northerners wanted to punish the South. Lincoln asked people to forget their anger. He wanted the defeated states to set up state governments and rejoin the Union quickly. Radical Republicans in Congress wanted to change the South and protect the rights of African Americans. Lincoln was shot on April 14, 1865 by John Wilkes Booth. His assassination shocked the country.

Reconstruction

Vice President Andrew Johnson became president. He put Lincoln's plan into action. Southern states had to abolish slavery. Most passed Black Codes to limit the rights of African Americans. Congress set up the Freedmen's Bureau to provide support for poor blacks and whites. In 1867, Congress put the South under military rule. Soldiers forced states to obey Congress and pass laws letting all men vote. In 1868, Congress impeached Johnson. They said he broke laws. Some southerners supported Congress. They were called scalawags. Some northerners went to the South just to make money. They were called carpetbaggers.

The Constitution Changes

During Reconstruction, Congress created three amendments to the Constitution. They gave the national government more power over the states. The Thirteenth Amendment ended slavery. Black Codes still limited the rights of African Americans. To protect those rights Congress passed the Fourteenth Amendment. It gave blacks full citizenship. Southern states had to ratify this amendment to rejoin the Union. The Fifteenth Amendment recognized the right of African American men to vote. But African Americans faced a long struggle for equality.

Before You Read

Find and underline each vocabulary word.

Reconstruction *noun*, period when the South rejoined the Union

assassination *noun*, the murder of an important leader

Freedmen's Bureau *noun*, an agency set up to provide food, clothing, medical care, and legal advice to poor blacks and whites

impeach *verb*, to charge a government official with a crime

After You Read

REVIEW **What was Lincoln's plan for Reconstruction?** Underline the sentence that tells you the answer.

REVIEW **Why were soldiers sent to the South?** Circle the sentence that tells the answer.

REVIEW **Why did Congress pass the Fourteenth Amendment?** Highlight the sentences that tell you the answer.

Resources for Reaching All Learners
53   Use with *United States History*, pp. 472–477

Answers

Name _____ Date _____

Summary: Linking East and West

The Telegraph Helps Communication

In the early 1800s the only way to get a message or news from one place to another was to travel there. Sometimes news from one part of the country didn't reach another part for several weeks. In 1844, a new kind of communication was introduced. The new telegraph machine sent electric signals through wires to a distant location. Samuel Morse invented a code for sending messages. People could send and get messages in just a few minutes. By 1861, telegraph wires stretched from coast to coast. Reporters sent news stories to their newspapers, and people sent personal messages and business information. During the Civil War, battle plans were made using the telegraph.

A Transcontinental Railroad

Many Americans began moving west by the 1840s. They were looking for gold and for farmland. There were only two good ways to travel. One way was to sail around the tip of South America. The other way was to travel to the end of the railroad line and take a rough trail on land in wagons pulled by horses, mule, or oxen. Both ways were long, difficult, and expensive. In 1862, railroad companies got money and land from Congress to build a transcontinental railroad to connect the coasts. The Union Pacific hired former Civil War soldiers, formerly enslaved African Americans, and Irish immigrants to build track from east to west. They started in Nebraska with existing railroad lines from the east coast. The Central Pacific hired many Chinese immigrants to lay tracks from California toward the east. Because of prejudice, these workers were paid less than other workers and given the most dangerous jobs.

The two tracks met at Promontory Point, Utah on May 10, 1869, to make a 1,800 mile long transcontinental railroad. It was the first of several railroads. It was easier to cross the continent by train. Western farmers made money by shipping cattle and wheat to the east.

Before You Read

Find and underline each vocabulary word.

transcontinental *adjective*, from one edge of a continent to the other

prejudice *noun*, an unfair negative opinion that can lead to unjust treatment

After You Read

REVIEW How did people travel west in the 1840s? Circle the two sentences that tell how people traveled.

REVIEW What kinds of goods were shipped on transcontinental railroads? Circle the words that describe what Western farmers sold to the east in order to make money.

Name _____ Date _____

Summary: Life on the Great Plains

Settling the Great Plains

In the early 1800s, few people lived on the Great Plains. The Great Plains are in the middle of the United States. People did not think the land was good for farming. It was very dry and flat.

In 1862 the Homestead Act was passed. The government helped people to settle on the Great Plains. The government sold adults 160 acres of land for a small amount of money. If they could farm the land for five years, they could own it. A settler's home and land was called a homestead. Many homesteaders came from the east coast, where farmland cost a lot. In the Great Plains, land was cheaper. Settlers also came from Europe, where there was not much land to buy. There was a lot of land to buy in the Great Plains. African Americans also wanted to start farms. Many African Americans were poor. They faced prejudice and violence after the Civil War. They started their own towns in Kansas. African Americans were called Exodusters, after a book in the Bible that tells the story of how people escaped slavery.

Settlers Face Hardships

Settlers had to learn how to farm on the Great Plains. The soil was held together by grass roots. It was called sod. Settlers were called sodbusters because they had to break through the sod to plant crops. There was not a lot of wood so, settlers used sod to build homes. Winters were long and cold. Summers were hot and dry. There were many droughts. There were grass fires because it was so dry. Farmers had to grow crops that did not need much water. They carried water from streams. Some farmers used windmills to pump water from underground. In the 1870s millions of grasshoppers ate the crops. There weren't many people in the area to do farm work, so farmers made new and better farm machines. New machines made it faster and easier to grow more crops.

Before You Read

Find and underline each vocabulary word.

homestead *noun*, a settler's home and land

Exodusters *noun*, African Americans who moved to the Great Plains

drought *noun*, a long period with little or no rain

sodbusters *noun*, name given to settlers who had to break through sod to build houses and plant crops

After You Read

REVIEW Why was life on the Great Plains so difficult? Underline sentences that describe the land.

REVIEW How did settlers adapt to the lack of extra workers on the Great Plains? Underline what the settlers did to make growing crops easier and faster.

Answers *continued*

Name _____ Date _____

Summary: Cattle Ranchers

Texas Cattle

In the 1860s, millions of longhorn cattle lived in Texas. They were strong animals. They ate grass and they did not need a lot of water. Cowhands made sure the cows did not run away. They herded the cattle. Cowhands burned brands into the cattles' skin. The cowhands knew which cattle they owned by looking at these marks.

Cattle ranchers could not make much money selling their cattle in Texas. There was a big supply, or lots, of cattle. There were not many people to buy them. There was a big demand. The price of cattle was low. The cattle ranchers herded their cattle onto trains. They sent the cattle to cities in the North and East. There were many people in the cities who wanted to buy beef and leather. The demand was high. The supply was low. This meant the cattle were worth more in the cities.

The Cattle Drives

Cattle ranchers needed to get their cattle to railroads. They were often hundreds of miles from the cattle ranches. Ranchers hired cowhands to take their cattle on cattle drives to the railheads. In a cattle drive, cowhands rode on horseback next to the herd of cattle to make them move. The cattle drives had to stay near rivers. This way the cattle had water to drink. The work was dirty, hard, and dangerous.

The cattle drives ended in the late 1880s for three reasons. First, there was the invention of barbed wire. This wire had sharp points on it. Settlers used barbed wire to make fences on their property. The fences blocked the cattle trails. Second, more railroads were built. Railheads were closer to the ranches. Ranchers did not need to send the cattle on long cattle drives. Third, ranchers in other states did not want Texas longhorns near their cattle. Longhorns had ticks, bugs that could cause disease in other cattle. Many states passed laws to keep out Texas cattle.

Before You Read

Find and underline each vocabulary word.

demand *noun*, the amount of something that people want to buy at a certain price

supply *noun*, the amount of something that people want to sell at a certain price

railhead *noun*, a town where railroad tracks begin or end

barbed wire *noun*, wire with sharp points on it

After You Read

REVIEW **Why did Texas cattle ranchers want to sell their animals in the East and North?** Highlight the sentence that tells about selling cattle in cities.

REVIEW **What led to the end of the big cattle drives?** Circle three reasons why cattle drives ended.

Name _____ Date _____

Summary: Conflicts on the Plains

War on the Plains

In the 1840s, settlers moved west to the Great Plains. They were looking for land and gold. The government built roads and railroads for the settlers. Many Indians lived on the Great Plains. The government tried to get them to sell their land. The government wanted the Indians to move to reservations.

The Plains Indians did not want to live and farm on the reservations. The reservations were small. The land was poor. Most of the Indians were not farmers. They were hunters. For years millions of buffalo lived on the Great Plains. The Indians hunted them for their meat and fur. The settlers killed many buffalo. New railroads, roads, and settlements hurt the buffalo habitat. By 1889, the buffalo were nearly extinct.

U.S. soldiers tried to make the Plains Indians give up their land. The Indians fought against the soldiers. Some famous battles were the Battle of the Little Bighorn, the Battle of Wounded Knee, and the Sand Creek Massacre. Finally the Indians were defeated and forced to move to the reservations.

Government Policy

Government officials wanted to make the Indians live like white settlers. Lawmakers wanted the Indians to assimilate. They tried to force the Indians to give up their culture and traditions. Indian children had to go to special schools. They were not allowed to have religious ceremonies. Indian children were not allowed to speak Indian languages. They could not wear Indian clothing.

The government wanted the Dawes Act to become farmers. In 1887, Congress passed the Dawes Act. This law broke reservation land into small pieces. The government gave some pieces to Indians who promised to farm them. It sold the rest of the land to settlers.

Before You Read

Find and underline each vocabulary word.

reservation *noun*, land the government reserved for Indians

habitat *noun*, the area where an animal or plant normally lives or grows

extinct *adjective*, when a certain type of plant or animal no longer exists

assimilate *verb*, to change a group's culture and traditions so that it blends with a larger group

After You Read

REVIEW **Why did Plains Indians need large areas of land?** Circle reasons why Indians did not want to live on reservations.

REVIEW **Why did the buffalo herds shrink?** Highlight the sentence that tells how settlers changed the habitat.

REVIEW **What did the Dawes Act do to reservation land?** Circle the sentence that tells what happened to reservation land.

Answers

Name _____ Date _____

Summary: Immigrants in America

Before You Read
Find and underline each vocabulary word.

persecution *noun*, unfair treatment or punishment

ethnic group *noun*, a group of people who share a culture or language

tenement *noun*, a poorly built apartment building

After You Read

REVIEW In what ways were Asian immigrants treated differently than immigrants from Europe? Underline two sentences that tell how immigrants from Asia were treated.

REVIEW What did immigrants do to help the United States grow? Highlight the sentence that tells how immigrants helped build the United States.

Arriving in America

Before 1880, most immigrants living in America came from countries in northern or western Europe. Between 1880 and 1924, about 25 million new immigrants came to the United States. Many came from countries in southern or eastern Europe such as Italy, Russia, Hungary, Greece, and Poland. Some immigrants came looking for jobs. Others were escaping persecution. Most immigrants found greater political freedom in the United States. Arriving immigrants had to pass through immigration stations, such as Ellis Island in New York Harbor and Angel Island in San Francisco Bay. Government officials asked immigrants about their plans. They were checked for diseases. Many immigrants from China came to the west coast. Asian immigrants faced more prejudice than European immigrants. More Chinese immigrants were turned away and sent back to China.

Living in a New Country

Immigrants often lived in large cities. Immigrants had their own languages, religions, and customs. They lived in neighborhoods with family or friends that belonged to their ethnic group. Life was hard for immigrants. Many lived in tenements. Many immigrants worked in dangerous factories. Businesses liked to hire immigrants because they worked many hours and were not paid a lot of money. Some Americans worried that immigrants would take their jobs. They did not want immigrants to speak other languages or follow other customs. Immigrants faced prejudice from some Americans. In 1921 and 1924, Congress limited the number of immigrants that could come to the United States.

Immigrants helped to make the United States one of the richest, fastest-growing countries in the world. Immigrants built railroads, dug mines, and worked in factories.

Name _____ Date _____

Summary: The Rise of Big Business

Before You Read
Find and underline each vocabulary word.

corporation *noun*, a business in which many people own shares, or parts, of the business.

competition *noun*, occurs when more than one business sells the same goods or service to customers.

monopoly *noun*, a company that has no competition.

labor union *noun*, an organization of workers that tries to improve pay and working conditions for its members.

strike *noun*, when workers refuse to work in order to force business owners to make changes

After You Read

REVIEW In what ways did inventions of the late 1800s save time? Underline the sentences that tell how inventions helped people.

REVIEW What is a monopoly? Circle the sentences that tell what no competition meant for consumers.

REVIEW Why did workers form labor unions? Highlight changes the unions wanted.

A Time of Invention

In the late 1800s, inventions changed people's lives. They could do more work in less time. E. Remington and Sons made the first typewriter. It saved office workers time. Elijah McCoy invented the oil cup. It dripped oil on machine parts. This helped the parts run longer. Alexander Graham Bell invented the telephone. People in different places could talk to each other. Thomas Edison invented light bulbs. Electric lights kept streets bright at night. Factories and shops could stay open longer.

Big Business

New machines and technologies helped businesses grow. Andrew Carnegie used a new invention to start his steel company. John D. Rockefeller started Standard Oil. The company became a corporation. It bought small companies. This got rid of competition. Standard Oil became a monopoly. It owned 90 percent of America's oil. No competition meant consumers had fewer choices. Monopolies could provide poor service or charge higher prices. After making large fortunes, Carnegie and Rockefeller gave millions of dollars to schools, libraries, churches, and hospitals.

Workers' Lives Change

Factories hired many people to run machines. Factory work was boring and dangerous. Workers did the same thing for ten or twelve hours a day. They often worked in unsafe conditions. Factory workers did not make much money. Some families needed more money to survive. They sent their children to work.

Factory workers formed labor unions. They had more power as a group. They wanted businesses to change. Unions wanted safer work. They wanted an eight-hour day and better pay. They did not want children to work. Unions used strikes. Businesses fought back. Some strikers were hurt or killed, but labor unions kept fighting for their rights.

Answers *continued*

Summary: Growing Cities

Before You Read
Find and underline each vocabulary word.

stockyard *noun*, a fenced area where large numbers of animals are kept until they are used for food or moved

skyscraper *noun*, a very tall building

rapid transit *noun*, a system of trains that people use to travel around cities

slum *noun*, a poor, crowded part of a city

settlement house *noun*, a community center for people in cities

After You Read
REVIEW **Why did so many people move to cities in the late 1800s and early 1900s?** Circle the sentence that tells what people were looking for in cities.

REVIEW **What kinds of help did immigrants find in settlement houses?** Underline the sentences that say why people went to Hull House.

Moving to Cities

Many people moved to cities in the late 1800s and early 1900s. Many immigrants lived in cities. People who lived on farms also moved to the city. Machines were used on many farms. Fewer workers were needed. (People moved to cities to find jobs.) Cities grew very fast. By 1910, almost half of all Americans lived in a city.

Chicago was a city that grew quickly. It was in a good place. Chicago is near Lake Michigan. Canals linked Chicago to the Mississippi and Illinois rivers. Railroads and boats brought natural resources to the city. Logs were shipped to factories. Machines cut the logs into lumber. Wheat and corn were also shipped to Chicago. Mills turned them into food. Cows and pigs were sent to stockyards. One stockyard could hold thousands of animals. Factories turned the animals into meat.

Changes in Cities

Cities changed as they got bigger. Thomas Edison and Nikola Tesla were inventors. They invented new ways to make electricity and send it through wires. New inventions needed electricity for power. Electric elevators were used in skyscrapers to carry people to different floors. Theater stages were lit with electric lights. Stores used electric signs to attract shoppers. Electricity powered the rapid transit system. Streetcars and subways moved people around the city quickly.

Growing cities had problems. Cities became crowded and noisy. There was not enough housing. People lived in slums. City people, especially immigrants, helped each other find housing and jobs. Reformers wanted city life to be better. In 1889, Jane Addams and Ellen Gates Starr started Hull House. This was a new settlement house in Chicago. People came to Hull House to learn English. They got medical care and looked for jobs. There were clubs for children. Reformers in other cities built settlement houses.

Summary: Time of Reform

Before You Read
Find and underline each vocabulary word.

progressives *noun*, reformers who believe the government should make laws to protect citizens' rights

muckraker *noun*, someone who "rakes up," or points out unpleasant truths

After You Read
REVIEW **What did the Pure Food and Drug Act and the Meat Inspection Act do to make food safer?** What did the Pure Food and Drug Act stop factories from doing? Circle the sentence that tells you the answer. What did the Meat Inspection Act make factories do? Circle the sentence that tells you the answer.

REVIEW **What is the NAACP and what is its purpose?** Circle the words that tell what NAACP means. Underline two sentences that say what the NAACP worked for.

The Progressives

In the early 1900s, adults and children worked in unsafe factories. Factories polluted cities. Dirty air and water made people sick. Progressives wanted to make factories and cities safer. They fought for laws to end child labor and protect factory workers.

Upton Sinclair was a muckraker. He wrote a book about the dangers of meat factories. In 1906, Congress passed two laws. One law was The Pure Food and Drug Act. (It stopped factories from using harmful chemicals in food.) The second law was The Meat Inspection Act. (It said factories had to be cleaner and safer.) President Theodore Roosevelt also wanted to protect the environment. He saved land for national parks and wilderness areas.

Working for Equal Rights

Women fought for the right to vote for many years. In 1920, Congress passed the Nineteenth Amendment. It gave women suffrage.

In the early 1900s, African Americans faced prejudice when they tried to get jobs or a places to live. Some states did not allow African Americans to vote. Some laws made African American children go to different schools. W.E.B. Du Bois wrote about African American life. He helped people see why laws should be changed. Booker T. Washington started a school to educate African Americans. In 1909, the (National Association for the Advancement of Colored People) (NAACP) was founded. "Colored People" was a term then used for African Americans. The NAACP worked for equality. It wanted African Americans to be treated fairly. Between 1910 and 1930, about 1.5 million African Americans moved to northern cities. This was called the Great Migration. African Americans wanted better lives. They found jobs in factories and businesses in the North.

Answers

Name _____ Date _____

Summary: World War I

Before You Read
Find and underline each vocabulary word.

alliance *noun*, an agreement between nations to work together and to defend each other

trench warfare *noun*, a type of fighting in which soldiers fought from long ditches

armistice *noun*, an agreement to stop fighting

isolationism *noun*, when a country stays out of other countries' affairs

After You Read

REVIEW **What were two major causes of World War I?** Highlight words that tell about things that led to the war.

REVIEW **What was trench warfare?** Highlight the sentence that tells about trench warfare.

REVIEW **What caused the shortage of workers in the United States during World War I?** Underline the words that say why factories lost workers.

War in Europe

In the early 1900s, nationalism was strong. Britain, France, Germany, and Italy wanted to be world powers. They raced to claim colonies. They made big armies. Countries formed alliances. Britain, France, and Russia made one alliance. They were called the Allies. Germany and Austria-Hungary made another alliance. They were called the Central Powers. Other countries joined in. The Allies and Central Powers declared war on each other. World War I began.

America Enters the War

Most Americans wanted the United States to stay out of the war. In 1917, Germany attacked American ships. Congress declared war on the Central Powers. The United States joined the Allies.

Many American men left to fight in the war. America's factories lost many workers. Many African Americans left the South to work in northern factories. Women also worked in factories.

Soldiers fought from long trenches. They tried to capture the enemy. Thousands of men were killed in trench warfare. This fighting lasted for four years. Soldiers used many new weapons. Machine guns, cannons, and tanks were used on the ground. Submarines sank ships. Airplanes were used in war for the first time.

America helped the Allies win the war. On November 11, 1918, the Allies and Central Powers signed an armistice. Leaders from each alliance met in Versailles, France. They signed a peace treaty. President Wilson wanted the treaty to include a new organization. It was called the League of Nations. The organization would work for peace. Many Americans felt they had done enough for other countries. There was a growing feeling of isolationism. The United States did not join the League of Nations.

Name _____ Date _____

Summary: New Territories

Before You Read
Find and underline each vocabulary word.

imperialism *noun*, when nations gain colonies to build empires

isthmus *noun*, a narrow strip of land with water on two sides

After You Read

REVIEW **How did Alaska and Hawaii become United States territories?** Circle the words that tell the answer.

REVIEW **Where did most of the fighting take place in the Spanish-American War?** Underline the name of the battle Roosevelt won.

The Nation Expands

In 1867, the United States was recovering from the Civil War. Russia offered to sell its colony of Alaska to the United States. William Seward was the Secretary of State. He convinced Congress to buy Alaska from Russia. Most Americans thought the idea was foolish. They changed their minds when gold was found near Alaska in 1896. Not many people found gold, but they found other valuable resources. Buying Alaska no longer seemed foolish.

In the late 1700s, Americans sailed to Hawaii. They grew pineapple and sugar cane on large plantations. By the late 1800s, Americans owned most of the land and businesses. Hawaiians were unhappy about the Americans' power. Queen Liliuokalani wanted her people to have the land. Americans in Hawaii revolted against her. They asked to join the United States. In 1898, Hawaii became a territory of the United States. Some people thought the United States had started a policy of imperialism.

The Spanish-American War

In the 1890s, Spain had colonies in Cuba and Puerto Rico. It also controlled Guam and the Philippine Islands. In 1895, Cubans revolted against Spain. American newspapers wrote shocking stories about Spain's cruelty to Cuba. The stories were not all true, but people believed them. In 1898, newspapers blamed Spain for blowing up an American ship in Cuba. The United States declared war on Spain.

Theodore Roosevelt led volunteers called the Rough Riders. With African American soldiers called Buffalo Soldiers, they won the battle of San Juan Hill. The U.S. Navy destroyed Spanish ships in Cuba. Spain gave Puerto Rico, the Philippines, and Guam to the United States. After the war, Theodore Roosevelt became President. He wanted to cut a canal across the isthmus of Panama. Panama was part of the nation of Colombia. Roosevelt helped Panama gain its independence. It took 10 years to build the Panama canal. It opened in 1914. Trade increased and shipping was faster between the east and west coasts.

Answers continued

Name _____ Date _____

Summary: The 1920s

Before You Read

Find and underline each vocabulary word.

assembly line *noun*, a line of workers or machines that puts a product together piece by piece

division of labor *noun*, a system in which workers perform different parts of a large task

credit *noun*, getting an item today, but paying for it later with small payments

After You Read

REVIEW **How did credit change the way people paid for goods?** How did people make payments? Underline the sentence that tells you.

REVIEW **In what way did the lives of American women change in the 1920s?** Circle the sentences that answer the question.

A Growing Economy

During the 1920s, the United States became one of the richest nations in history. The automobile industry grew very fast. Henry Ford changed the way factories made cars. He used assembly lines and division of labor. Ford's ideas made it faster and cheaper to make cars. As the auto industry grew, the steel, rubber, and oil industries also grew. Its success helped the nation's economy grow.

Americans believed the economy would keep growing. This changed the way they bought goods. Many people used credit to buy items. They made small payments. This was easier than making one big payment with cash. Credit allowed many people to own homes for the first time. Using credit also meant people owed money.

A Changing Society

The 1920s was an exciting time. In 1920, women won the right to vote. The 1920s were called the *Jazz Age*. Women changed the way they lived. They wore modern clothes. They took jobs in business. They played sports.

Many African Americans moved north to work in industrial cities. In New York City, African Americans formed new communities. One community was called Harlem. Many writers and artists lived in Harlem. Some African American musicians played jazz. This was a new kind of music. Millions of people heard jazz on the radio. They danced to jazz. The 1920s were called the *Jazz Age*.

During this time, many Mexicans came to the United States. They worked on large farms. Some worked in Texas. Other Mexicans worked in California.

Movies, like radio, became popular in the 1920s. People heard about new heroes on the radio. In 1927, they heard about Charles Lindbergh. He flew over the Atlantic Ocean alone. People from different parts of the country had more in common.

Name _____ Date _____

Summary: The Great Depression

Before You Read

Find and underline each vocabulary word.

stock market *noun*, a place where people can buy and sell shares of a company's stock

unemployment *noun*, the number of people without a job

depression *noun*, a period when many people can't find work, and many others have no money to keep businesses going

After You Read

REVIEW **What made unemployment go up during the Great Depression?** Underline two sentences that tell why many people lost their jobs.

REVIEW **What kinds of projects did the PWA hire people to work on?** Highlight the projects done by the PWA.

Hard Times for Americans

During most of the 1920s, the United States economy grew. Many people invested their money. They bought stocks in companies. A stock is a small part of a company. The value of stock goes up when a company does well. The value of stock goes down when a company does poorly. Then stockowners lose money.

By the end of the 1920s, the economy had started to slow down. In 1929, the value of many stocks quickly dropped. The American stock market crashed. Stockowners were frightened. Many stocks became worthless. Thousands of people lost all of their money.

The economy became even weaker. Factories did not need many workers. Businesses closed. Many people lost their jobs, so unemployment went up. Some families had to give up their homes. Each day, hungry people waited for free food at community kitchens.

Many farmers did not make enough money, so they went out of business. In the early 1930s, almost no rain fell in the Great Plains. Farmers' lives became even harder. The soil turned to dust. This area was called the Dust Bowl. This time of hardship is known as the Great Depression. It was the worst depression in United States history.

The New Deal

In 1932, Franklin D. Roosevelt became President. He wanted to stop the Depression. Roosevelt started new programs to help Americans. He called these programs the New Deal. Congress quickly passed the programs into law. Some programs gave food and shelter to people. The Public Works Administration (PWA) hired people to build dams and improve roads and parks. The New Deal did not end the depression, but it gave people new hope.

Answers

Name _____ Date _____

Summary: The Cold War

Before You Read
Find and underline each vocabulary word.

communism *noun,* a system in which the government controls production and owns the nation's natural and capital resources

capitalism *noun,* a system in which ordinary people and businesses control the production of goods and services

arms race *noun,* a contest between nations to build bigger and more powerful weapons

After You Read

REVIEW What was the Berlin Airlift just before the Cold War began? Circle the paragraph that tells how the United States and Britain helped people in West Berlin.

REVIEW What did Kennedy do to end the Cuban Missile Crisis? Underline the sentences that tell why President Kennedy sent warships to Cuba.

Superpowers at War

After World War II, the United States and the Soviet Union were the world's strongest nations. They were called superpowers. They had different ideas about economics and government. They fought a war of ideas called the Cold War. The Soviet Union was a communist country. In communism, the government controls production and resources. It decides where people live and work. The United States is a capitalist country. In capitalism, people and businesses control the production of goods. People decide where they live and work.

The Cold War began in Europe after World War II. The Soviet Union won control of Eastern Europe. It controlled half of Germany and half of Germany's capital, Berlin. The United States, Britain, and France controlled western Germany and West Berlin. In June 1948, the Soviet Union blocked roads and railroads that led to West Berlin. The United States, Great Britain, and France flew in supplies. This was called the Berlin Airlift.

Cold War Conflicts

After World War II, Korea was divided into North and South Korea. North Korea became communist. South Korea was a capitalist country. North Korean army invaded South Korea. The United Nations sent soldiers to help South Korea. China sent soldiers to help North Korea. The war ended in 1953. Neither side won. Korea is still divided.

The United States and the Soviet Union were in a nuclear arms race. In 1959, Cuba became a communist country and the Soviets secretly put missiles there. President Kennedy was afraid the Soviet Union would attack the United States. He sent warships to surround Cuba. He hoped a blockade would force the Soviet Union to remove its missiles. This conflict was called the Cuban Missile Crisis. For six days, nuclear war seemed possible. Then the Soviet Union removed the missiles.

Name _____ Date _____

Summary: World War II

Before You Read
Find and underline each vocabulary word.

dictator *noun,* a ruler who has total power over a country and its people

war bonds *noun,* a loan from the American people to the federal government

internment camp *noun,* a place where prisoners are held during wartime

atomic bomb *noun,* a powerful bomb that can destroy an entire city

concentration camp *noun,* a place where large numbers of people are held prisoner and forced to work

After You Read

REVIEW Why didn't the United States join the Allies in 1939? Circle the sentence that tells the answer.

REVIEW What action did the United States take after the attack on Pearl Harbor? Highlight the sentence about the United States going to war.

REVIEW What did the United States military do to force Japan to surrender? Highlight the names of the Japanese cities bombed by the United States.

The Road to War

After the Great Depression, millions of people were unemployed all around the world. They wanted strong leaders. In 1933, Adolf Hitler became the dictator of Germany. Hitler blamed Jews for Germany's problems. Nazi soldiers arrested many Jews and sent them to prison. Mussolini was Italy's dictator. Italy was Germany's ally. They were the Axis Powers. Poland, Britain, and France formed the Allied Powers. In 1939, Hitler invaded Poland. The Allies declared war on Germany. World War II began. At the beginning of the war most Americans did not want to fight in Europe again.

America Goes to War

In 1940, Japan joined the Axis. Japan wanted to expand its empire in Asia. In 1941, Japan destroyed U.S. Navy ships at Pearl Harbor. Thousands of Americans died. The United States declared war on Japan.

The United States joined the Allied Powers. The Axis Powers declared war on the United States. Many Americans joined the military. Americans supported the war. They bought war bonds. Women worked in factories. Americans collected metal to make war supplies.

Some Americans feared Japanese Americans would help Japan. The government forced thousands of Japanese Americans to live in internment camps.

Fighting the War

The war was fought in Europe, North Africa, and the Pacific. In May 1945, Germany surrendered. In August, Americans dropped atomic bombs on two Japanese cities, Hiroshima and Nagasaki. The bomb dropped on Hiroshima killed 100,000 people. Japan surrendered. World War II ended.

As the war ended, Allied troops found out that Nazis had forced millions of Jews and other people into concentration camps. Over 12 million people died in the camps. About six million of those people were Jews. This mass murder is known as the Holocaust.

Answers *continued*

Name _____ Date _____

Life in the 1950s

Post-War Prosperity

In 1952, General Dwight D. Eisenhower was elected President. He was a war hero who had led the Allied troops in Europe during World War II. Americans trusted him to bring peace and prosperity to the country. The United States economy grew quickly under Eisenhower. Many veterans returned home after the war. They wanted to have families and buy houses. So many new families were started that the United States had a baby boom.

Because of the baby boom, there were not enough houses for everyone. Builders started building huge housing developments. The government gave veterans loans to buy new houses. New families also bought cars and household items, such as washing machines and clothes driers.

Businesses grew and produced more products. So workers had more income. Families had more things to buy. They made budgets to plan for saving and spending.

Cultural Changes

In the 1950s, cars became very important. People living in the suburbs needed a car to drive everywhere. They drove to work, to shop, and to have fun. People drove to national parks. They drove to drive-in theaters to watch movies. They ate at drive-in burger restaurants and ice cream shops. Shopping centers outside of cities became very popular.

Cars made it easy for people to go to new places. Now television made it easy for people to see places without leaving their homes. On television, people could see far-away events as they happened. They watched soap operas and comedy shows.

In the 1950s, television and radio helped rock 'n' roll become popular. Teenagers loved rock 'n' roll and huge crowds cheered for singers like Chuck Berry and Elvis Presley. Some people said rock 'n' roll would not last. But rock 'n' roll continued to grow and changed into new kinds of music that people listen to today.

Find and underline each vocabulary word.

veteran *noun,* a person who has served in the military

baby boom *noun,* increase of babies born after World War II

budget *noun,* a plan for saving and spending income

REVIEW What did families use budgets for? Highlight the sentence that tells what people planned.

REVIEW In what new ways did people use their cars during the 1950s? Draw a box around the paragraph that tells you places people drove to.

Name _____ Date _____

Civil Rights

The Movement Begins

Nearly 100 years after the Civil War, the civil rights of African Americans were limited by state laws and discrimination. Some civil rights are the right to vote, the right to equal treatment, and the right to speak out.

In the early 1950s, segregation was legal. Many Americans believed it should not be. African Americans went to court to end segregation. In 1954, the Supreme Court ordered the desegregation of public schools.

An Alabama law said that African Americans had to sit at the back of the bus. In 1955 in Montgomery, Alabama, Rosa Parks refused to move to the back of a bus. She was arrested. Her church organized a protest. African Americans boycotted the buses until buses were desegregated. This was the Montgomery Bus Boycott. Martin Luther King Jr. helped lead the boycott. He believed in nonviolent protest. He wanted people to fight back using peaceful actions. In 1956, the Supreme Court said that segregation on buses was illegal.

Civil Rights Victories

In 1960, African Americans held sit-ins in 54 cities. They sat at lunch counters that only served food to white people. They would not leave until they were served. In 1963, Congress was discussing a bill to end segregation. Martin Luther King Jr. and other leaders organized a protest march in Washington D.C. to show support for the bill. The march on Washington got Americans to pay attention to the civil rights movement.

President Lyndon Johnson worked with Congress to pass the Civil Rights Act of 1964. It banned segregation in schools, at work, and in public places. The Voting Rights Act of 1965 guaranteed citizens of all races and ethnic backgrounds the right to vote.

In 1968, Martin Luther King Jr. was shot. People from all backgrounds continued the struggle for civil rights.

Find and underline each vocabulary word.

civil rights *noun,* the rights and freedoms that countries guarantee their citizens

desegregation *noun,* ending the separation of people by racial or ethnic group

nonviolent protest *noun,* a way of bringing change without using violence

REVIEW What was the goal of the Montgomery Bus Boycott? Underline the sentence that tells about the boycott.

REVIEW What did the march on Washington do to help the civil rights movement? Draw a box around the sentence that tells how the march on Washington affected people in America.

Answers

Name _____ Date _____

Summary: Challenges of the 1970s

Before You Read

Find and underline each vocabulary word.

resign *verb*, to give up your job

migrant worker *noun*, a person who moves from place to place to find work, mostly on farms

accord *noun*, an agreement.

The Nixon Years

Richard Nixon was elected President in 1968. He helped build better relations between the United States and the two largest Communist countries: China and the Soviet Union.

In 1973, Israel was attacked by Egypt and Syria. Oil-producing countries that supported Egypt and Syria wanted to punish the United States for helping Israel. They produced less oil, so oil prices went up. High oil prices made costs rise for making and shipping goods, so prices rose. This is called inflation.

In 1972, Nixon's campaign workers broke into the Democratic Party headquarters in the Watergate building to steal information. They were caught. Nixon said he did not know about the break-in. An investigation proved that he had lied and was trying to cover up the crime. Nixon had to resign in 1974. Vice President Gerald Ford became President.

After You Read

REVIEW What events caused inflation during the 1970s? Highlight the sentence that tells what started the war in the Middle East in 1973. Then circle the sentences that tell what action oil-producing countries took.

A Time of Change

In the 1970s many people struggled for equal rights. Women were paid less than men for doing the same job. They wanted equality. By the late 1980s, more women were legislators and 40 states had equal pay laws.

American Indians on reservations did not have good health care or education. Unemployment was high. They wanted more control of reservations. They wanted the government to honor treaties. Migrant workers formed unions and forced employers to improve conditions. Consumers pushed for product safety laws.

REVIEW What were two goals of the Indian rights movement? Circle two sentences that tell you the answer.

The Carter Years

In 1976 Jimmy Carter was elected President. Carter brought leaders from Israel and Egypt together to sign the Camp David Peace Accord. Carter tried to control inflation by raising taxes and lowering government spending. But oil prices continued to rise. In 1980, Carter lost the election to Ronald Reagan. Carter won the Nobel Peace Prize in 2002.

REVIEW What were President Jimmy Carter's successes? Highlight the sentence that tells what President Carter did to solve the problems in the Middle East.

Name _____ Date _____

Life in the 1960s

Before You Read

Find and underline each vocabulary word.

space race *noun*, a struggle between the United States and the Soviet Union to be the first country to send people into space

demonstration *noun*, a large gathering of people who want to tell the public and the government their opinion

cease-fire *noun*, an agreement to stop all fighting

Presidents Kennedy and Johnson

In 1960, John F. Kennedy was elected President. Kennedy wanted Americans to serve their country. He began the Peace Corps to send volunteers to countries that needed help.

While Kennedy was President, the United States got into the space race. The Soviet Union won the race. In 1957, a Soviet rocket sent Sputnik I into space. It was the first human-made object to circle Earth. In April 1961, a Soviet cosmonaut named Yuri Gagarin circled Earth in a space capsule. The next month, Alan Shepard became the first American to go into space. In February 1962, John Glenn circled Earth. In 1969, Neil Armstrong and Buzz Aldrin were the first humans to land on the moon.

Kennedy was assassinated in 1963. Vice President Lyndon Johnson became President. He created the Great Society programs to help Americans in need.

After You Read

REVIEW Who won the race to send a person into space? Underline the sentence that tells you about the first person to circle Earth.

The Vietnam War

Vietnam was split in two. North Vietnam was Communist. South Vietnam was capitalist. North Vietnam supported communists who wanted to overthrow the South Vietnamese government. The United States sent military advisors and supplies to help South Vietnam. Then they sent soldiers to fight.

Some Americans thought the United States should fight to stop communism. Many other Americans disagreed. They thought the United States should not interfere in a civil war. They held demonstrations to protest the war.

In 1969, Richard Nixon became President. He brought some soldiers home, but U.S. planes increased bombing in North Vietnam. They began bombing Cambodia. In 1973, North Vietnam, South Vietnam, and the United States agreed to a cease-fire. The American soldiers returned home. The North Vietnamese defeated the South Vietnamese in 1975. More than 55,000 U.S. soldiers and millions of Vietnamese people died in the war.

REVIEW Why did many people in the United States protest against the war in Vietnam? Draw a box around the sentence that tells you the answer.

Answers continued

Summary: The 1980s

Before You Read
Find and underline each vocabulary word.

deregulation *noun*, the process of removing rules about what businesses can and cannot do

deficit *noun*, shortage caused by a government spending more money than it collects in taxes

coalition *noun*, a group of allies that work together to achieve a goal

After You Read

REVIEW Why did President Reagan spend government money on the military? Underline the sentence that tells the answer.

REVIEW How did President Reagan help end the Cold War? Highlight the sentence that tells who Reagan met with to talk about the arms race. Then circle the sentence that tells what the two leaders did.

Reagan Becomes President

Ronald Reagan was elected President in 1980. Many Presidents before Reagan used government money to pay for programs to provide people with services such as health care, job training, and housing. Reagan spent less money on government programs.

Reagan believed a strong economy would help people more than government programs. He used deregulation to help businesses. At the end of his term, about 20 million more people had jobs than when he took office. Reagan spent a lot more government money on the military. He thought a strong military would keep America safe and end the Cold War. Increased spending caused the highest deficit America had ever had.

International Events

In the 1980s the Soviet Union was having serious trouble. Its economy could not provide enough goods, jobs, and housing for its people. Too much money was spent on the arms race with the United States.

Soviet leader Mikhail Gorbachev worked to end the Cold War. He wanted a better relationship with the United States. Reagan and Gorbachev first met in 1985 to talk about the arms race. In 1987, they signed a treaty that lowered the number of nuclear weapons each country had.

In 1988, George Bush was elected President. The Soviet Union was growing weaker. The Cold War was over. Many nations split from the Soviet Union to form independent countries.

In 1990, there was more trouble in the Middle East. Saddam Hussein, the leader of Iraq, invaded a neighboring country, Kuwait, to take over its oil fields. President Bush asked other countries in the United Nations to form a coalition to fight Iraq. The Persian Gulf War lasted about seven weeks. In 1991, the coalition forces won because they had better technology and highly trained soldiers. Iraq left Kuwait, but Hussein stayed in power.

Summary: Life in the 1990s

Before You Read
Find and underline each vocabulary word.

Internet *noun*, network that links computers around the world with each other

high-tech *adjective*, high-technology, uses the most recent knowledge and equipment

free-trade agreement *noun*, treaties among countries that trade with one another

After You Read

REVIEW In which places did President Clinton help settle conflicts? Circle the names of three places where President Clinton helped settle conflicts.

REVIEW What effect did computers have on the economy in the 1990s? Circle the sentence that answers the question.

REVIEW In what ways did better communication change life for people during the 1990s? Highlight the sentence that tells you the answer.

Clinton's Presidency

In 1992, Bill Clinton was elected President. He believed government money should be used to help people. There was not enough money because of the budget deficit from the Reagan years. The economy grew and more taxes were collected. Clinton put more money into social programs. By 1998, the United States had a budget surplus. The government had more money than it spent.

Clinton helped start peace processes in Northern Ireland and the Middle East. In the former country of Yugoslavia, different groups fought to form separate nations. The United States and other countries sent troops to stop the fighting there in 1999.

Clinton's second term was hurt by a scandal. He was impeached by the House of Representatives. The Senate found him not guilty.

A Changing Economy

During the 1990s, the United States had the longest period of economic growth in its history. Many people had more income to save, spend, or invest. Changes in computers and the development of high-tech businesses helped the economy grow. Computer programs were invented that people could use at home, at school, and at work. The Internet made it possible for people to get information, shop, and communicate quickly and easily.

New technology made the U.S. economy more productive. Jobs changed with the economy. More people did service jobs. Some companies moved factories overseas where they could make products at a lower cost. People with more education did better in the 1990s than people with less education.

A Connected World

Improved communication and transportation made trade between countries easier and less expensive. Nations are now more interdependent. Mexico, Canada, and the United States signed free-trade agreements in the 1990s.

Answers

CHAPTER 19, LESSON 1

Summary: Neighbors in North America

Canada

Canada is the United States' neighbor to the north. It has three territories and ten provinces. Its history is similar to American history. American Indians lived first in both countries. Europeans colonized both countries. In Canada, the colonists were mostly French. After a French-British war in 1754, Canada became a British colony. Many people in Canada speak both French and English. Both languages are now official languages there. In 1867, Canada gained its independence from Britain. Canada is a democracy. Like the United States, Canada is multicultural.

In 1992, Canada signed the North American Free Trade Agreement (NAFTA) with the United States and Mexico. NAFTA increased trade among the three nations. Canada is the United States' biggest trade partner. The two countries also work together to solve environmental problems that affect both countries.

Mexico

Mexico is the United States' neighbor to the south. It has 31 states and one federal district. The Maya and Aztecs lived in Mexico first, and they built large, beautiful cities. Spain colonized Mexico in 1521. In 1821, Mexico fought Spain for its independence and won. Mexico has a representative government that gives a lot of power to the President. Most Mexicans have a mixture of Spanish and Mexican Indian heritage. Spanish is the official language, but many people speak Indian languages. Mexican art, building styles, and food are common in the Southwest United States, which was once part of Mexico.

Many Mexicans work in maquiladoras, and many Mexicans come to the United States to work. This helps the U.S. economy. In 1992, Mexico signed NAFTA with the United States and Canada. Trade between the three countries increased. Today, Mexico's most important trading partner is the United States. After Canada, Mexico is the United States' second most important trading partner.

Before You Read
Find and underline each vocabulary word.

province *noun*, a political region of a country that is similar to a state

multicultural *adjective*, having many cultural traditions

maquiladora *noun*, a factory in Mexico near the U.S. border

After You Read
REVIEW Why is French one of the two official languages in Canada? Circle the sentence that tells the answer.

REVIEW How and when did Mexico gain its independence? Draw a box around the sentence that tells how and when Mexico gained its independence.

REVIEW What are some of Mexico's connections with the United States? Circle the sentences that tell about connections with Mexican culture, work, and trade.

CHAPTER 18, LESSON 4

Summary: Twenty-First Century Begins

The 2000 Election

On December 31, 1999, people all over the world celebrated the beginning of a new millennium. The new millennium really began on January 1, 2001. In a presidential election, the vote of individual citizens is called the popular vote. The candidate who wins the popular vote in a state wins all of that state's Electoral College votes. To win the election you have to win the electoral vote.

The 2000 presidential election was unusual because no one knew who won for weeks. The race was very close. Whoever won the vote in Florida would win the election. In Florida, Bush won the first count. Gore said the votes were not counted properly. Finally, the Supreme Court said that the Florida votes would not be recounted. Bush became President.

Attack on the Nation

On September 11, 2001, nearly three thousand people were killed by acts of terrorism in the United States. Terrorists hijacked four airplanes. They crashed two airplanes into the World Trade Center in New York, and one into the Pentagon in Washington, D.C. A fourth plane crashed in Pennsylvania. The terrorists were from a group called al-Qaeda. They were against the United States' involvement in the Middle East. After the attacks, Bush accused the country of Afghanistan of hiding the leader of al-Qaeda, Osama bin Laden, and his followers. In October, 2001, a coalition of nations led by the United States went to war in Afghanistan. They defeated the government but they did not find bin Laden.

In 2003, Bush said Saddam Hussein, the leader in Iraq, was a danger to his neighbors and to the United States. In March 2003, the United States went to war in Iraq. After defeating Hussein's army and capturing Hussein, the military stayed in Iraq while a new Iraqi government formed.

Before You Read
Find and underline each vocabulary word.

millennium *noun*, a period of 10 centuries, or 1,000 years

popular vote *noun*, the vote of individual citizens

Electoral College *noun*, representatives, called electors, from each state

terrorism *noun*, the use of violence against ordinary people to achieve a political goal

After You Read
REVIEW What is the difference between the popular vote and the electoral vote? Circle the words that tell what a popular vote is. Highlight the words that tell what the votes in the Electoral College are. Underline the words that explain how a presidential election is won.

REVIEW How did the United States respond to the terrorist attacks of September 11, 2001? Circle the sentences that tell you the answer.

Answers *continued*

Name _____ Date _____

Summary: Citizenship and Democracy

Before You Read

Find and underline each vocabulary word.

naturalization *noun*, the process of learning the laws of the country and the rights and duties of citizens

register *verb*, to sign up

responsibility *noun*, a duty that people are expected to fulfill

volunteer *noun*, a person who helps other people without pay

After You Read

REVIEW At what age can citizens register to vote? Circle the sentence that tells the answer.

REVIEW In what ways can learning about issues prepare young people to be good citizens? Circle the sentences that tell why education is important for young people.

Citizenship

In many countries throughout history, most people have had no say in their government. In a democracy, all people help shape the government. The United States is a democracy that gives its citizens many rights. The Bill of Rights in the Constitution lists some rights, such as the right to speak freely, the right to practice any religion, and the right to a fair trial in court. One of the most important rights is the right to vote. When citizens vote, they help choose their government leaders. At age 18, citizens can register to vote.

Our government protects these rights. The government also protects the rights of all people to be treated fairly in housing and jobs, so that no one can discriminate against them because of religion or race. People who come to the United States from other countries can become citizens through the process of naturalization.

Citizens' Responsibilities

Our government gives citizens freedom and many rights. But citizens have responsibilities to the United States, too. Citizens must obey the law. This helps to keep our communities safe. Citizens must pay taxes. Taxes help the government pay for police, roads, and many other important services. Citizens are responsible for voting. Citizens must take turns being on a jury. Men over 18 years old have the responsibility of registering for the military. Young people have responsibilities, too. They must go to school. Education helps young people make good choices and decisions. This helps them become good citizens.

Our government works hard to make the United States a good place to live. But people need to help our democracy stay strong. Some ways to help are by learning about what is happening in the community, voting, and volunteering. Volunteers help communities in many ways. A strong democracy like the United States depends on its citizens to participate.

Name _____ Date _____

Summary: United States Today

Before You Read

Find and underline each vocabulary word.

refugee *noun*, a person who escapes war or other danger and seeks safety in another country

heritage *noun*, something that is passed down from one generation to the next

motto *noun*, a short statement that explains an ideal or goal

After You Read

REVIEW Why did immigration to the United States change after 1965? Circle the sentence that tells the answer.

REVIEW What do all U.S. citizens share? Draw a box around the sentence that tells the answer.

A Nation of Immigrants

Millions of immigrants come to the United States. Some come for a better life, and some come for religious or political freedom. Until 1965, most immigrants came from Europe or Mexico. In 1965, Congress changed the immigration laws. Now immigrants come from many nations. Spanish-speaking immigrants come from Central and South America and the Caribbean. Refugees from wars in El Salvador and Nicaragua came.

People also come from Africa and the West Indies. Today about one-fourth of America's immigrants are Asians from India, China, the Philippines, and other countries. Immigrants often live in communities where other people from their country live. They influence the culture and government of the places where they live.

Many People, One Nation

Many immigrants to the United States find the freedom they need to start successful careers. The United States has a diverse population, with many different ethnic groups. People bring music, food, language, art, and customs from their countries. Each person brings knowledge, skills, and talents. These things improve the United States. Ethnic diversity is one of the greatest strengths of the United States.

All people in the United States share a heritage of democracy. All United States citizens share the Constitution and the Bill of Rights. The Constitution and the Bill of Rights explain the rights of U.S. citizens. Our democratic heritage unites us into one nation. You can see the Latin motto "E Pluribus Unum" on American money. These Latin words mean "out of many, one." These words remind us that the United States became one nation by joining together 13 colonies. Today 50 states and many ethnic groups are joined together into one nation.

Answers

Name _____ Date _____

Support for Language Development

1. Write in the letters for the pictures that go with the definitions below.

capital resource   human resource   scarcity

opportunity cost   conservation

b the skills and knowledge of the people doing the work

e the protection and wise use of natural resources

c not having as much of something as people want

a a tool, machine, or building people use to produce goods and services

d the thing you give up when you decide to do or have something else

2. Read the section of the lesson called "Other Important Resources." Then decide if the following words are capital, human, or natural resources. Write the words in the correct column.

peanuts   oven

tractor   soil

factory workers   water

sunshine   farmers

Capital	Human	Natural
tractor oven	factory workers farmers	peanuts sunshine soil water

---

Name _____ Date _____

Support for Language Development

1. Write in the letters that go with the pictures below.

geography   landform   plateau

climate   equator

e the imaginary line around the middle of the Earth

a the study of the world and the people and things that live there

d the type of weather a place has over a long period of time

c a high, steep-sided area rising above the surrounding land

b a feature on the surface of the land

2. Read the section called "Landforms." Then write the names of bodies of water (rivers, lakes), mountains (ranges), and other features (plains, canyons) in the correct columns below.

Bodies of Water	Mountains	Plains/Canyons/Other
Pacific Ocean Mississippi River Atlantic Ocean	Coast Ranges Sierra Nevada Mountains Rocky Mountains Appalachian Mountains	Basin and Range area Bryce Canyon Interior Plains Atlantic Coastal Plain

Answers *continued*

Name _____ Date _____

Support for Language Development

1. Write the word that goes with the definition below.

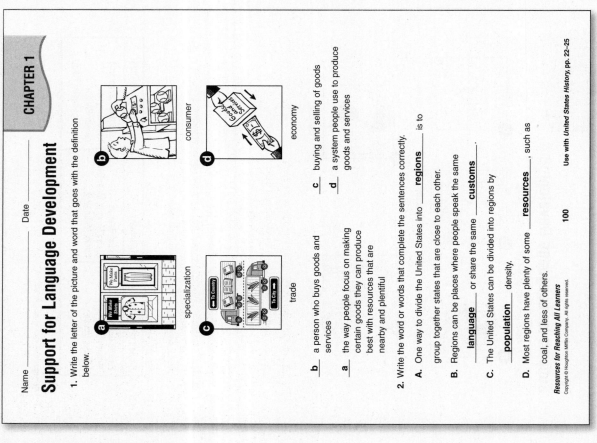

environment   erosion   pollution   ecosystem

pollution   Anything that makes the soil, air, or water dirty and unhealthy

environment   The surroundings in which people, plants, and animals live

ecosystem   A community of plants and animals along with the surrounding soil, air, and water

erosion   The process by which water and wind wear away the land

2. Read the section called "Changing the Land." Write the correct word or words to complete each sentence below.

Changing the ___**Land**___

___**Natural**___ ___**forces**___ , such as wind and moving ___**water**___ , constantly shape and reshape the land.

___**Human**___ ___**activities**___ , such as digging mines and building ___**highways**___ , also change the land.

Name _____ Date _____

Support for Language Development

1. Write the letter of the picture and word that goes with the definition below.

specialization   trade   consumer   economy

b   a person who buys goods and services

a   the way people focus on making certain goods they can produce best with resources that are nearby and plentiful

c   buying and selling of goods

d   a system people use to produce goods and services

2. Write the word or words that complete the sentences correctly.

A. One way to divide the United States into ___**regions**___ is to group together states that are close to each other.

B. Regions can be places where people speak the same ___**language**___ or share the same ___**customs**___ .

C. The United States can be divided into regions by ___**population**___ density.

D. Most regions have plenty of some ___**resources**___ , such as coal, and less of others.

Answers

Name _____ Date _____

Support for Language Development

1. Write the vocabulary word on the line next to its meaning.

surplus	potlatch	clan

potlatch — large feast that lasts for several days

clan — group of related families

surplus — extra

2. Write the word or words that complete the sentence correctly.

A. The Northwest is close to the **Pacific** Ocean.

B. Two key resources of the Tlingit were **salmon** and **forests** .

C. On special occasions Northwest Indians held a **potlatch** .

D. American Indians dried **surplus** salmon, so they had food all year long.

Name _____ Date _____

Support for Language Development

1. Write the letter of the picture and word that goes with the definition below.

a — pueblo

b — agriculture

c — civilization

d — glacier

c a group of people living together with organized systems of government, religion, and culture

b farming, or growing plants

a the Spanish word for town

d a huge, thick sheet of slowly moving ice

2. Read the sentences below. Which happened first? Write "1" in front of the first event. Write "2" in front of the second event. Write "3" in front of the third event. Write "4" in front of the fourth event.

2 A. Ice Age ended.

1 B. Ancient people crossed the land bridge between Asia and Alaska.

4 C. Aztecs built Tenochtitlán.

3 D. Agriculture began in Central Mexico.

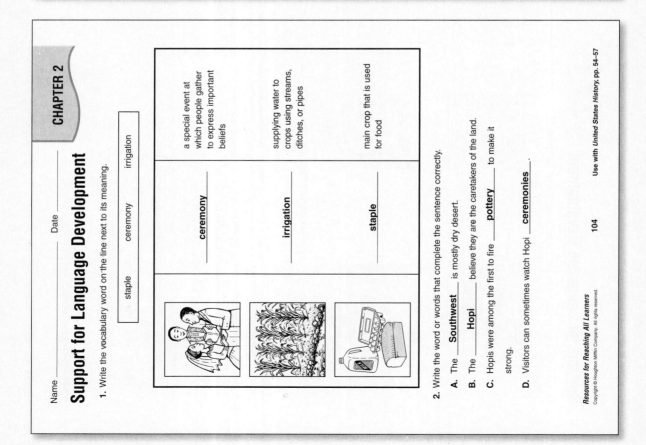

Name _____ Date _____

CHAPTER 2

Support for Language Development

1. Write the vocabulary word on the line next to its meaning.

| staple | ceremony | irrigation |

	ceremony	a special event at which people gather to express important beliefs
	irrigation	supplying water to crops using streams, ditches, or pipes
	staple	main crop that is used for food

2. Write the word or words that complete the sentence correctly.

A. The **Southwest** is mostly dry desert.

B. The **Hopi** believe they are the caretakers of the land.

C. Hopis were among the first to fire **pottery** to make it strong.

D. Visitors can sometimes watch Hopi **ceremonies** .

Name _____ Date _____

CHAPTER 2

Support for Language Development

1. Write the vocabulary word on the line next to its meaning.

| lodge | nomad | travois |

	lodge	a house made of bark, earth, and grass
	travois	similar to a sled, used by nomads to carry their possessions
	nomad	a person who moves around and does not live in one place

2. Read the sentences below. Which happened first? Write "1" in front of the first event. Write "2" in front of the second event. Write "3" in front of the third event.

3 A. Comanche Indians spread across the Great Plains.

2 B. Plains Indians began to ride and raise horses.

1 C. Spanish introduced horses into North America.

Answers

Name _____ Date _____

Support for Language Development

1. Write the vocabulary word on the line next to its meaning.

merchant	kingdom	caravan

	caravan	A group of people and animals who travel together
	kingdom	A place ruled by a king or queen
	merchant	Someone who buys and sells goods to earn money

2. Read "Trade with China." Write the word or words that complete the sentence correctly.

A. Before 1500 most people in Europe, Africa, and Asia did not know that the **Americas** existed.

B. **Marco** **Polo** spent 16 years working for the ruler of China.

C. **Zheng** **He** brought a giraffe from Africa back to China.

Resources for Reaching All Learners
Copyright © Houghton Mifflin Company. All rights reserved.

107   Use with *United States History*, pp. 84–87

Name _____ Date _____

Support for Language Development

1. Write the letter of the picture and word that goes with the definition below.

wampum   barter   longhouse

b exchange of goods without using money

c a large house made of wooden poles and bark

a carefully shaped and cut seashells strung like beads

2. Write the word that completes the sentence correctly.

A. The Eastern Woodlands were rich in natural **resources** .

B. In the warm south, people built houses with no **walls** .

C. In the cold north, people lived in **longhouses** .

3. Read the section called "Farming and Building" in your text. In the box labeled "Compare," tell how the northern and southern regions were alike. In the box labeled "Contrast," tell how the regions were different.

Compare	Contrast
Corn , **beans** , and **squash** were the staple crops for most woodland Indians	In **warm** southern climates, people built houses without walls. Farther north, people needed protection from the **cold** .

Resources for Reaching All Learners
Copyright © Houghton Mifflin Company. All rights reserved.

106   Use with *United States History*, pp. 68–71

Answers *continued*

Name _____ Date _____

Support for Language Development

1. Write the letters of the pictures and words that go with the definitions below.

a
MARIA'S RESTAURANT

SALES	$500.00
Cost of labor	$200.00
Cost of food	$200.00
PROFIT	$100.00

profit

b

astrolabe

c

slavery

d

navigation

e

technology

__e__ the use of scientific knowledge and tools to do things better and more rapidly

__d__ the science of planning and controlling the direction of a ship

__b__ a navigation tool that measures the height of the sun or a star against the horizon

__a__ money left after all expenses have been paid

__c__ a cruel system in which people are bought and sold and made to work without pay

2. Read the section of the lesson called "The Renaissance." Then write the word or words that complete the sentence correctly.

A. Europeans learned about the compass and gunpower from the __Chinese__.

B. The __printing__ __press__ meant ideas could spread faster.

C. New __navigation__ tools meant new sea routes could be explored.

Resources for Reaching All Learners
Copyright © Houghton Mifflin Company. All rights reserved.

108   Use with *United States History*, pp. 90–93

Name _____ Date _____

Support for Language Development

1. Write the word on the line next to the definition.

settlement   circumnavigate   epidemic

__settlement__   a small community of people living in a new place

__epidemic__   an outbreak of a disease that spreads quickly and affects many people

__circumnavigate__   to sail completely around something

2. Read the chart in your textbook showing the Columbian Exchange. Then write the words in the box under the correct heading.

corn   bananas
pigs   beans
horses   diseases
potatoes   chocolate

From Americas	From Europe
corn	bananas
beans	horses
potatoes	pigs
chocolate	diseases

Resources for Reaching All Learners
Copyright © Houghton Mifflin Company. All rights reserved.

109   Use with *United States History*, pp. 96–101

Answers

Name _____ Date _____

Support for Language Development

1. Write the letter of the picture and word that goes with the definition below.

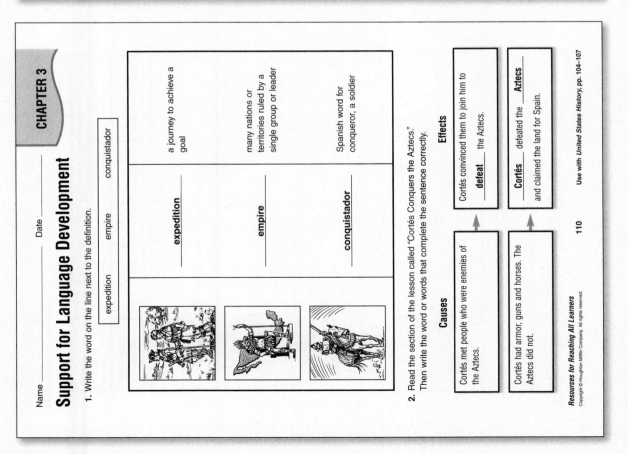

a _____ mission

b _____ colony

c _____ hacienda

b a territory ruled by another country

a a religious community where priests taught Christianity

c a large farm or ranch, often with its own church and village

2. Read "New Settlements." Match the Spanish explorer or priest to the description.

Pedro Menéndez de Avilés	started a settlement at Santa Fe, New Mexico, in 1598.
Junípero Serra	founded missions on the coast of California in 1769.
Don Juan de Oñate	started St. Augustine in Florida in 1565.

Name _____ Date _____

Support for Language Development

1. Write the word on the line next to the definition.

expedition	empire	conquistador

	expedition	a journey to achieve a goal
	empire	many nations or territories ruled by a single group or leader
	conquistador	Spanish word for conqueror, a soldier

2. Read the section of the lesson called "Cortés Conquers the Aztecs." Then write the word or words that complete the sentence correctly.

Causes

Cortés met people who were enemies of the Aztecs.

Cortés had armor, guns and horses. The Aztecs did not.

Effects

Cortés convinced them to join him to **defeat** the Aztecs.

Cortés defeated the **Aztecs** and claimed the land for Spain.

Answers *continued*

Name _____ Date _____

Support for Language Development

1. Write the letter of the picture and the word that go with the definition below.

indentured servant

invest

cash crop

stock

charter

a someone who agreed to work for a number of years in exchange for the cost of the voyage to North America

d a piece of ownership of a company

e a document giving permission to a person or group to do something

b to put money into something to earn more money

c a crop that people grow and sell to earn money

2. Read the section of the lesson called "The Jamestown Colony" and fill in the missing words.

Cause		Effect
The water wasn't good for drinking. Insects carried diseases.	→	The settlers died from __hunger__ and __disease__.

Name _____ Date _____

Support for Language Development

1. Write the vocabulary word on the line next to its meaning.

armada   claim   invasion

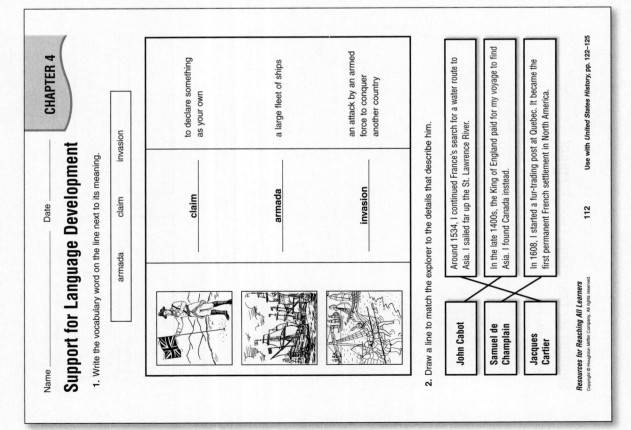

	claim	to declare something as your own
	armada	a large fleet of ships
	invasion	an attack by an armed force to conquer another country

2. Draw a line to match the explorer to the details that describe him.

John Cabot	Around 1534, I continued France's search for a water route to Asia. I sailed far up the St. Lawrence River.
Samuel de Champlain	In the late 1400s, the King of England paid for my voyage to find Asia. I found Canada instead.
Jacques Cartier	In 1608, I started a fur-trading post at Quebec. It became the first permanent French settlement in North America.

Answers

Name _____ Date _____

Support for Language Development

1. Write the vocabulary word on the line next to its meaning.

missionary	diversity	tolerance

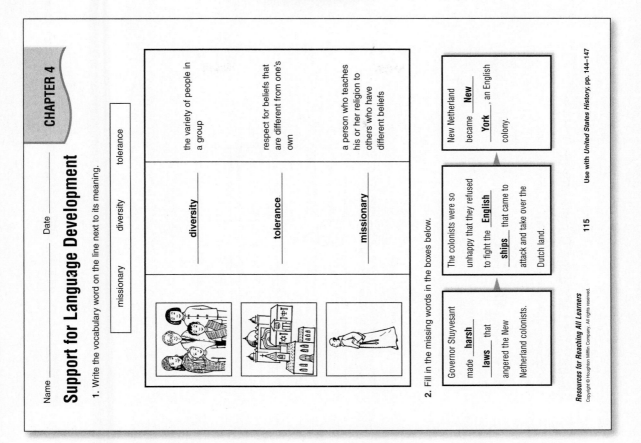

diversity	the variety of people in a group
tolerance	respect for beliefs that are different from one's own
missionary	a person who teaches his or her religion to others who have different beliefs

2. Fill in the missing words in the boxes below.

Governor Stuyvesant made **harsh** **laws** that angered the New Netherland colonists.

The colonists were so unhappy that they refused to fight the **English** **ships** that came to attack and take over the Dutch land.

New Netherland became **New** **York**, an English colony.

Name _____ Date _____

Support for Language Development

1. Write the vocabulary word on the line next to its meaning.

compact	pilgrim	cape

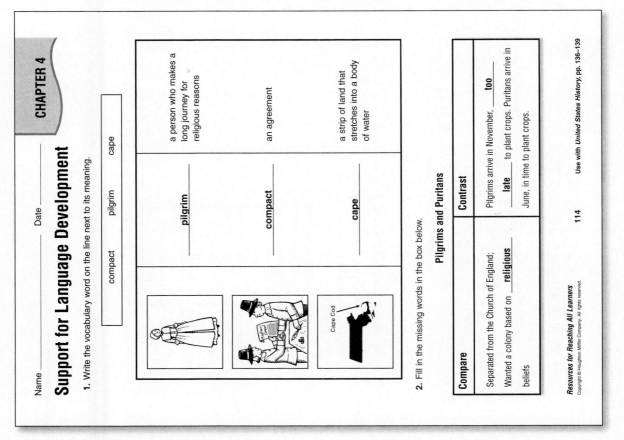

pilgrim	a person who makes a long journey for religious reasons
compact	an agreement
cape	a strip of land that stretches into a body of water

Cape Cod

2. Fill in the missing words in the box below.

Pilgrims and Puritans

Compare	Contrast
Separated from the Church of England; Wanted a colony based on **religious** beliefs	Pilgrims arrive in November, **too** **late** to plant crops. Puritans arrive in June, in time to plant crops.

Answers *continued*

Name _____ Date _____

Support for Language Development

1. Write the letter of the picture and word that goes with the definition below.

a town meeting **b** banish **c** dissenter **d** self-government

a   A gathering where colonists held elections and voted on the laws for their towns

d   When the people who live in a place make laws for themselves

c   A person who does not agree with the beliefs of his or her leaders

b   To force someone to leave

2. Read about the following dissenters in your textbook. Then draw a line to connect the phrase on the left with the name on the right.

I was the leader of the Wampanoag nation.	Roger Williams
I believed government and religion should be separate.	Anne Hutchinson
I held meetings where men and women could discuss religion.	Thomas Hooker
I wanted to let all men, even those who did not belong to the church, to vote.	Metacomet

Reaching All Learners
117   **Use with *United States History*, pp. 166–169**

Name _____ Date _____

Support for Language Development

1. Write the letter of the picture and word that goes with the definition below.

a growing season   **b** tidewater   **c** fall line   **d** backcountry

b   The water in rivers and streams that rises and falls every day with the ocean's tides

a   The time of year when it is warm enough to grow crops

d   The land "in back of" the area where most colonists settled

c   When rivers from higher land flow to lower lands, and often form waterfalls

2. Read about the thirteen colonies in your textbook. Then draw lines to match the colonies on the left to the sentences on the right.

In the Southern colonies	it was hard to find good farmland.
In New England	the tidewater region provided rich farmland.
In the Middle colonies	glaciers dropped fertile soil in the area.

Reaching All Learners
116   **Use with *United States History*, pp. 160–163**

Answers

Name _____ Date _____

Support for Language Development

1. Write the vocabulary word on the line next to its meaning.

representative	proprietor	treaty

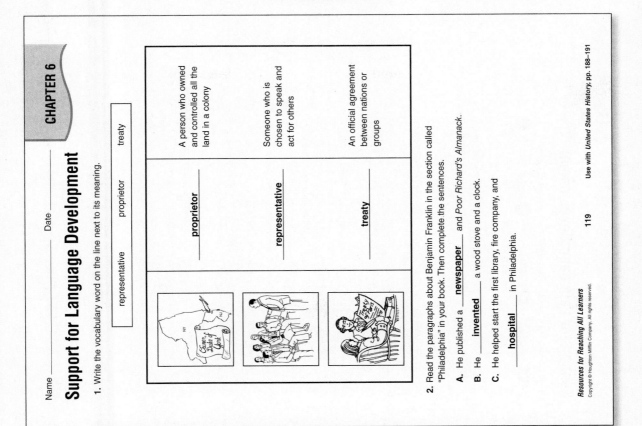

proprietor	A person who owned and controlled all the land in a colony
representative	Someone who is chosen to speak and act for others
treaty	An official agreement between nations or groups

2. Read the paragraphs about Benjamin Franklin in the section called "Philadelphia" in your book. Then complete the sentences.

A. He published a **newspaper** and *Poor Richard's Almanack*.

B. He **invented** a wood stove and a clock.

C. He helped start the first library, fire company, and **hospital** in Philadelphia.

Name _____ Date _____

Support for Language Development

1. Write the letter of the picture and word that goes with the definition below.

slave trade   export   industry

Middle Passage   import

c All the businesses that make one product or provide one service

b A product sent to another country and sold

e A product brought into one country from another country

d The trip from Africa to the West Indies

a The business of buying and selling human beings

2. Read the section of the lesson called "Using the Sea." Write the correct words to complete the sentences below.

Because farming was difficult in New England, some colonists looked for other ways to earn a **living** .

Boston became a center for the **shipbuilding** industry.

Many people made their living by catching and selling **fish** .

By the 1700s, **whaling** was an important industry.

Answers *continued*

Name _____ Date _____

Support for Language Development

1. Write the letter of the picture and word that goes with the definition below.

a — free enterprise

b — artisan

c — laborer

d — apprentice

b Someone who is skilled at making something by hand

d Someone who studies with a master to learn a skill or business

a A system in which people may start any business that they believe will succeed

c A person who does hard physical work

2. Read the section in your textbook called "A Mix of People." Then write the correct word or words to complete the sentences below.

A. The people of the Middle Colonies came from many __lands__.

B. Colonial proprietors believed in __religious__ __tolerance__.

C. Religious tolerance and __inexpensive__ land attracted many people.

Name _____ Date _____

Support for Language Development

1. Write the letter of the word that goes with the definition below.

a plantation   **b** legislature   **c** refuge   **d** debtor

c A safe place

b A group of people with the power to make and change laws

a A large farm on which crops are raised by workers who live on the farm

d A person who owes money

2. Read the section in your textbook called "New Colonies in the South." Then write the correct words to complete the sentences below.

A. 1632: Calvert hopes to make Maryland a __refuge__ for Catholics.

B. 1633: King Charles I forms Carolina to keep __France__ and __Spain__ out of the area.

C. 1729: King George II divides __Carolina__ into North Carolina and South Carolina.

D. 1732: King George II gives land to Oglethorpe. He wants Georgia to be a place for poor people and __debtors__.

3. Read the section in your textbook called "Governing the Colony." Then number the sentences in the order they happened.

3 A. The legislature makes the Anglican Church the official church.

2 B. The House of Burgesses becomes the first elected legislature in the colonies.

1 C. Colonists want a voice in the laws of Virginia.

Answers

Name _____ Date _____

Support for Language Development

1. Write the letter of the picture that goes with the definition below.

a   b   c   d

proclamation   ally   congress   rebellion

a An official public statement

d A fight against a government

c A group of representatives who meet to discuss a subject

b A person or group that joins with another to work toward a goal

2. Fill in the blanks in the boxes on the left.

Causes

The British wanted to settle in the Ohio River Valley and to trade with the **American Indians** who lived there.

Britain and France ended the war and signed the **Treaty of Paris**.

British soldiers stayed in the Ohio River Valley.

Effects

Britain declared war on France.

France gave Britain control of Canada and most of the land east of the Mississippi River.

Pontiac led American Indians in a war against the British.

Use with *United States History*, pp. 228–231

Name _____ Date _____

Support for Language Development

1. Write the vocabulary word on the line next to its meaning.

overseer   spiritual   indigo

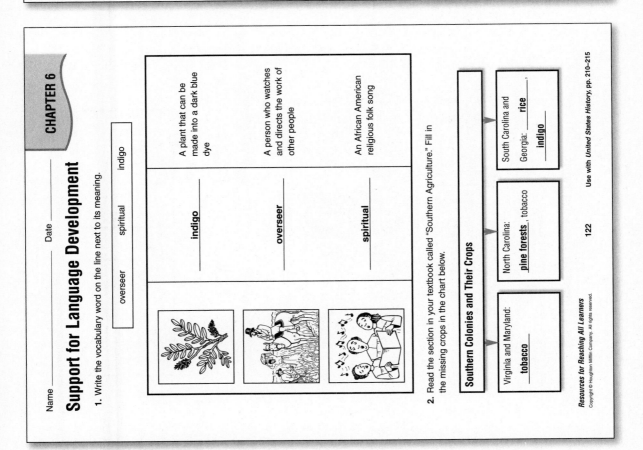

indigo	A plant that can be made into a dark blue dye
overseer	A person who watches and directs the work of other people
spiritual	An African American religious folk song

2. Read the section in your textbook called "Southern Agriculture." Fill in the missing crops in the chart below.

Southern Colonies and Their Crops

Virginia and Maryland: **tobacco**

North Carolina: **pine forests**, tobacco

South Carolina and Georgia: **rice**, **indigo**

Use with *United States History*, pp. 210–215

Use with *United States History*

Answers *continued*

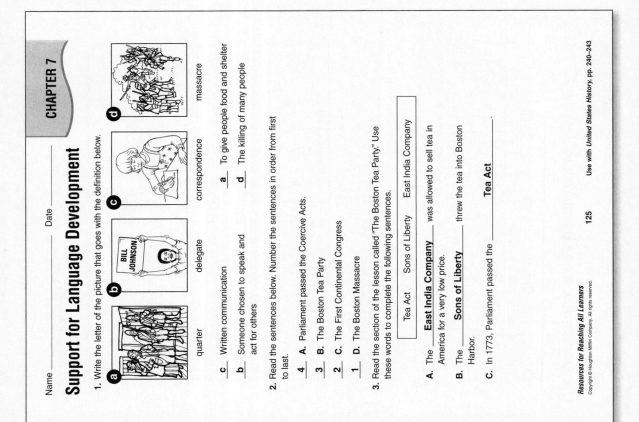

Name _____ Date _____

Support for Language Development

1. Write the letter of the picture that goes with the definition below.

quarter   delegate   correspondence

c Written communication
b Someone chosen to speak and act for others

a To give people food and shelter
d The killing of many people

2. Read the sentences below. Number the sentences in order from first to last.

4 A. Parliament passed the Coercive Acts.
3 B. The Boston Tea Party
2 C. The First Continental Congress
1 D. The Boston Massacre

3. Read the section of the lesson called "The Boston Tea Party." Use these words to complete the following sentences.

Tea Act   Sons of Liberty   East India Company

A. The **East India Company** was allowed to sell tea in America for a very low price.

B. The **Sons of Liberty** threw the tea into Boston Harbor.

C. In 1773, Parliament passed the **Tea Act** .

Name _____ Date _____

Support for Language Development

1. Write the vocabulary words in the correct space.

tax   boycott   protest   liberty   repeal   smuggling

a. **liberty**   b. **tax**   c. **smuggling**
d. **repeal**   e. **protest**   f. **boycott**

2. Read the sentences. Write the letters and numbers for the problems and solutions.

A. British government passed the Townshend Acts.
B. The government passed the Stamp Act.

1. The Daughters of Liberty boycott all British goods.
2. Merchants agreed to boycott British goods.

Problem		Solution
A	→	1
B	→	2

Answers

Name _____ Date _____

Support for Language Development

1. Write the letter of the picture and word that goes with the definition below.

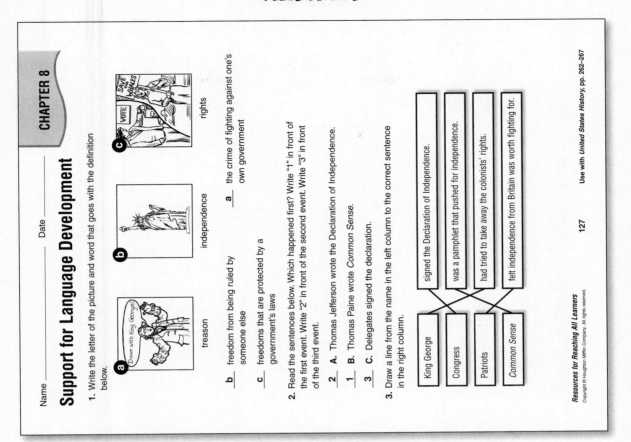

a treason

b independence

c rights

a the crime of fighting against one's own government

b freedom from being ruled by someone else

c freedoms that are protected by a government's laws

2. Read the sentences below. Which happened first? Write "1" in front of the first event. Write "2" in front of the second event. Write "3" in front of the third event.

2 A. Thomas Jefferson wrote the Declaration of Independence.

1 B. Thomas Paine wrote *Common Sense*.

3 C. Delegates signed the declaration.

3. Draw a line from the name in the left column to the correct sentence in the right column.

King George	signed the Declaration of Independence.
Congress	was a pamphlet that pushed for independence.
Patriots	had tried to take away the colonists' rights.
Common Sense	felt independence from Britain was worth fighting for.

Name _____ Date _____

Support for Language Development

1. Write the letter of the picture that goes with the definition below.

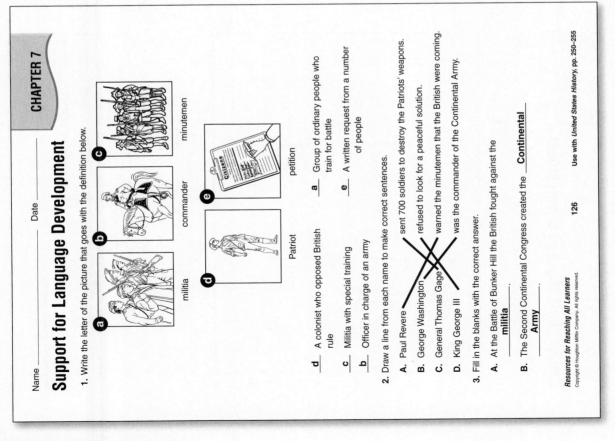

a militia

b commander

c minutemen

d Patriot

e petition

d A colonist who opposed British rule

c Militia with special training

b Officer in charge of an army

a Group of ordinary people who train for battle

e A written request from a number of people

2. Draw a line from each name to make correct sentences.

A. Paul Revere — sent 700 soldiers to destroy the Patriots' weapons.

B. George Washington — refused to look for a peaceful solution.

C. General Thomas Gage — warned the minutemen that the British were coming.

D. King George III — was the commander of the Continental Army.

3. Fill in the blanks with the correct answer.

A. At the Battle of Bunker Hill the British fought against the **militia**.

B. The Second Continental Congress created the **Continental Army**.

Support for Language Development

Name _____ Date _____

1. Write the letter for the picture and word that goes with each definition.

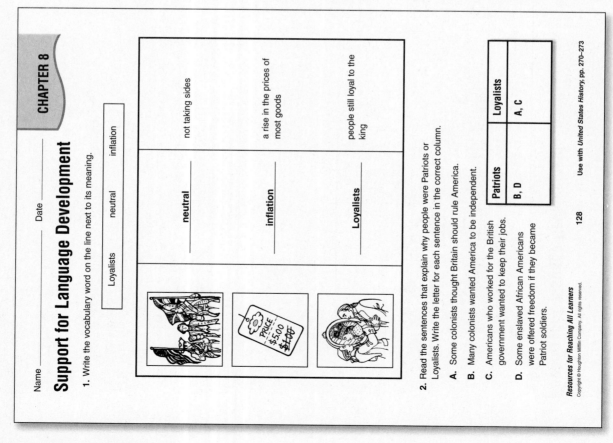

retreat   mercenary   victory

c   the defeat of an enemy

a   to move away from the enemy

b   a soldier who is paid to fight for a foreign country

2. Read the following sentences. In the effects box, write the number of the sentence that matches the cause.

1. The men of the Continental Army became good soldiers because of their training.

2. Washington's army had to retreat.

3. The Americans took almost 1,000 prisoners and were overjoyed at the victory.

Causes	Effects
A. The Americans attacked the German mercenaries in Trenton.	3
B. Friedrich von Steuben taught the Americans to march and use their weapons properly.	1
C. The British defeated the Continental Army in the Battle of Long Island in New York.	2

Support for Language Development

Name _____ Date _____

1. Write the vocabulary word on the line next to its meaning.

Loyalists   neutral   inflation

neutral   not taking sides

inflation   a rise in the prices of most goods

Loyalists   people still loyal to the king

2. Read the sentences that explain why people were Patriots or Loyalists. Write the letter for each sentence in the correct column.

A. Some colonists thought Britain should rule America.

B. Many colonists wanted America to be independent.

C. Americans who worked for the British government wanted to keep their jobs.

D. Some enslaved African Americans were offered freedom if they became Patriot soldiers.

Patriots	Loyalists
B, D	A, C

Answers

Name _____ Date _____

Support for Language Development

1. Write the letter of the picture that goes with the definition below.

a — constitution   b — citizen   c — territory   d — ordinance

d A law

b An official member of a city, state, or nation

c Land ruled by a nation that has no representatives in its government

a A written plan for government

2. Read the section of the lesson called "Problems for the New Nation." Then write the word or words that complete each sentence correctly.

A. By 1786, it was clear that the Articles of Confederation could not make the **states** work together.

B. Congress still owed money for the **War of Independence**.

C. Congress could not raise the money because it was not allowed to collect **taxes**.

3. Read the section of the lesson called "The Articles of Confederation." Then circle whether each question is true or false.

A. The Articles of Confederation made Congress the national government. True /(False)

B. The articles created a strong national government. True /(False)

C. The Articles gave most of the power to the state governments. (True)/ False

D. Congress could not declare war. True /(False)

Name _____ Date _____

Support for Language Development

1. Write the vocabulary word on the line next to its meaning.

strategy   traitor   surrender

Word	Meaning
surrender	to give up
strategy	a plan of action
traitor	someone who is not loyal

2. Which happened first? Write "1" in front of the first event. Write "2" in front of the second event. Write "3" in front of the third event. Write "4" in front of the fourth event.

2 A. Greene's strategy to wear out the British forced Cornwallis to retreat.

1 B. The British decided to change their strategy by invading the South.

4 C. The United States and Britain signed the Treaty of Paris.

3 D. Washington's army and the French navy trapped the British at Yorktown.

Benedict Arnold

Answers *continued*

Name _____ Date _____

Support for Language Development

1. Write the letter of the word that goes with the definition below.

a unconstitutional   **b** amendment   **c** checks and balances

d veto   **e** democracy

e   A government in which the people have the power to make political decisions

b   A change made to the Constitution

a   Determined by the Supreme Court to not agree with the Constitution

c   A system in which each branch of government can limit the power of the other two branches

d   When the President rejects laws made by Congress

2. Draw a line from the name of a part of the government on the left to the name for the branch of government. Then write what job it does.

A. President   Judicial Branch   **Decides what laws mean**

B. Supreme Court judge   Legislative Branch   **Makes the laws**

C. Senator   Executive Branch   **Carries out laws**

Resources for Reaching All Learners
Copyright © Houghton Mifflin Company. All rights reserved.

133   Use with *United States History*, pp. 312–317

Name _____ Date _____

Support for Language Development

1. Write the letter of the picture that goes with the definition below.

a   **b**   **c**

federal   ratify   republic

c   A government in which the citizens elect leaders to represent them

b   To officially accept

a   A system of government in which the states share power with a central government

2. Write the word or words that complete each compromise.

Problem	Solution
The Northern states wanted an end to the slave trade. The Southern states would not accept the new government on these terms.	Northern and Southern states agreed to end the **slave** **trade** by 1808.
Smaller states argued that bigger states would have more delegates. This would give bigger states more power.	Each state would have the **same** number of representatives in the Senate. In the House of Representatives, the number would depend on each state's **population**.

Resources for Reaching All Learners
Copyright © Houghton Mifflin Company. All rights reserved.

132   Use with *United States History*, pp. 302–307

Answers

Name _____ Date _____

Support for Language Development

1. Write the letter of the picture that goes with the definition below.

pioneer   frontier   flatboat   canal

c Large, rectangular boat partly covered by a roof

b The edge of a country or a settled region

d A waterway built for boat travel and shipping

a One of the first people to enter or settle a region

2. Read the section of the lesson called "Daniel Boone." Then read the sentences below. Write a number in front of each event to show what happened first, second, third, and fourth.

3 Daniel Boone helped clear a new road through the Cumberland Gap.

2 On the other side of Cumberland Gap, they found beautiful and rich land.

4 Boone guided families across the Appalachians into Kentucky.

1 Daniel Boone and several other men traveled to the other side of the Cumberland Gap.

3. Read the section of the lesson called "Making a Home." Then read the sentences below. Circle the main idea. Underline the details.

A. Settlers traveled to an unknown land and lived far from family and friends.

B. Pioneers cut down trees to create a clearing in the woods.

C. Frontier life was hard.

D. Settlers grew corn and other grains and raised farm animals.

Resources for Reaching All Learners   **135**   Use with *United States History*, pp. 344–347

Name _____ Date _____

Support for Language Development

1. Write the letter of the picture that goes with the definition below.

inauguration   Cabinet   political party   capital

d The city where the government meets

b A group chosen by the President to help run the executive branch and give advice

a The official ceremony to make someone president

c A group of people who share similar ideas about government

2. Read the sentences below. Write numbers on the lines below to show what happened first, second, and third.

2 A. Work began on the building of the new capital.

1 B. George Washington was elected President.

3 C. Washington retired as President.

Resources for Reaching All Learners   **134**   Use with *United States History*, pp. 320–323

Answers continued

Name _____ Date _____

Support for Language Development

1. Write the letter of the word that goes with the definition below.

a prosperity **b** nationalism **c** foreign policy

c A government's actions toward other nations

a Economic success and security

b Devotion to one's country

2. Read the sentences below. Write numbers on the lines below to show which event happened first, second, third, and fourth.

2 A. The British navy fired at Fort McHenry.

1 B. The U.S. declared war on Britain.

4 C. British forces attacked Americans in New Orleans.

3 D. The U.S. and Britain signed the Treaty of Ghent.

Name _____ Date _____

Support for Language Development

1. Write the letter of the picture that goes with the definition below.

corps   source   interpreter   manufacturers

d People who use machines to make goods

a A team of people who work together

c Someone who helps people who speak different languages understand each other

b The place where a river begins

2. Draw a line from the name on the left column to the correct sentence on the right column.

Left	Right
Sacagawea	sold Louisiana to the United States.
Thomas Jefferson	led the Corps of Discovery.
Zebulon Pike	wanted to help farmers.
Meriwether Lewis and William Clark	was an interpreter for the Corps of Discovery.
Napoleon Bonaparte	led a group to find the source of the Mississippi River.

Answers

Name _____ Date _____

Support for Language Development

1. Write the letter of the picture that goes with the definition below.

c mass production

b interchangeable parts

a textile

e entrepreneur

d productivity

e a person who takes risks to start a new business

c making many products at once

a cloth or fabric

d the amount of goods and services made by a worker in a certain amount of time

b parts made by a machine to be exactly the same size and shape

2. Read the sentences below. In the box on the right, write the letter of the sentence that explains the effect of each invention.

A. Factories and farmers could ship their goods to almost any city in the country by train.

B. Cotton was soon America's largest export.

C. The new ways of making goods increased the productivity of the United States.

Causes		Effects
cotton gin	→	B
interchangeable parts	→	C
steam locomotives	→	A

Resources for Reaching All Learners
Copyright © Houghton Mifflin Company. All rights reserved.

139   Use with *United States History*, pp. 378–383

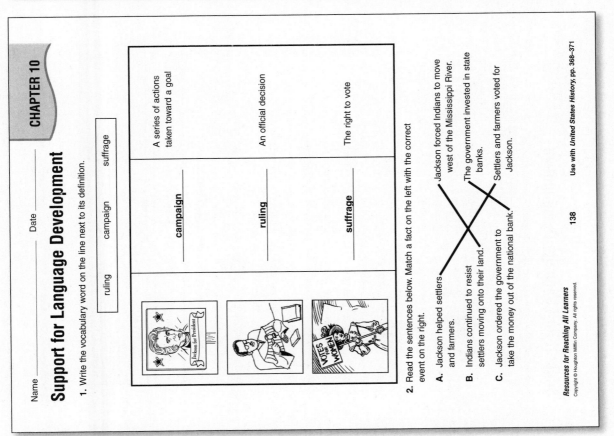

Name _____ Date _____

Support for Language Development

1. Write the vocabulary word on the line next to its definition.

ruling   campaign   suffrage

campaign — A series of actions taken toward a goal

ruling — An official decision

suffrage — The right to vote

2. Read the sentences below. Match a fact on the left with the correct event on the right.

A. Jackson helped settlers and farmers.

B. Indians continued to resist settlers moving onto their land.

C. Jackson ordered the government to take the money out of the national bank.

Jackson forced Indians to move west of the Mississippi River.

The government invested in state banks.

Settlers and farmers voted for Jackson.

Resources for Reaching All Learners
Copyright © Houghton Mifflin Company. All rights reserved.

138   Use with *United States History*, pp. 368–371

Answers *continued*

Name _____ Date _____

Support for Language Development

1. Write the letter of the word that goes with the definition below.

a annexation **b** manifest destiny **c** front **d** cession

d something that is given up

b the belief that the United States should spread across North America, from the Atlantic Ocean to the Pacific Ocean

a joining two countries or pieces of land together

c where the fighting takes place in a war

2. Read the sentences below. Number them from 1 to 5 in the order that they happened.

5 James Polk became President, and Congress voted to annex the Republic of Texas.

2 Santa Anna led a large army to San Antonio to stop the rebellion.

4 To gain his freedom, Santa Anna agreed to give Texas its independence.

1 Tejanos and Texans rebelled against Mexico and fought for their independence.

3 Sam Houston led an attack on Santa Anna's army and captured Santa Anna.

Name _____ Date _____

Support for Language Development

1. Write the letter of the picture that goes with the definition below.

a **b** **c**

famine   injustice   reform

b the abuse of a person's rights

a a widespread shortage of food

c an action that makes something better

2. Fill in the blanks with the correct answer.

A. The Irish potato crop failed in 1846. It caused a **famine**, and many people left Ireland to go to the United States.

B. Thousands of Germans left Europe because of war and crop **failures**.

C. Many women who worked for **reform** realized they also faced **injustice** as women.

D. The **temperance** movement wanted people to control or cut back the drinking of alcohol.

3. Draw a line to match the reform movement with its goal.

Antislavery Movement — Wanted to give women the same rights as men

Temperance Movement — Wanted to stop the practice of slavery

Women's Rights Movement — Wanted people to control or cut back the drinking of alcohol

Answers

Name _____ Date _____

Support for Language Development

1. Write the letter of the word that goes with the definition below.

a tariff   **b** states' rights   **c** sectionalism

c Loyalty to one part of the country

a A tax on imported goods

b The idea that states, not the federal government, should make decisions about matters that affect them

2. Read the section of the lesson called "Resistance to Slavery." Then write the word or words that best complete each sentence.

A. After Nat Turner's rebellion, **southern** states passed laws to **control** both enslaved and free blacks.

B. Slavery became a source of deep **conflict** between the North and South.

C. Many Southerners thought that slavery was too **important** to their **economy** to give up.

Name _____ Date _____

Support for Language Development

1. Write the letter of the picture that goes with the definition below.

wagon train   forty-niner   gold rush   boomtown

c many people hurrying to the same area to look for gold over a short time

b gold miner who went to California in 1849 during the gold rush

a a line of covered wagons that moved together

d a town whose population grows very quickly

2. Draw a line to connect the first part of the sentence in the left column with the best answer in the right column.

In 1843, a group of about 1,000 traveled on the Oregon Trail to find — good, inexpensive land.

In 1847, the Mormons traveled on the Mormon Trail to find — a place where they could practice their religion.

In 1849, forty-niners rushed to California — to dig for gold.

3. Fill in the blanks with the correct words from "After the Gold Rush."

A. Miners and farmers killed large numbers of California **Indians** and took over their land.

B. American newcomers forced many **California** property owners off their land.

C. **Cities** such as San Francisco grew.

D. By 1850, California had enough people to become a **state**.

Answers *continued*

Name _____ Date _____

Support for Language Development

1. Write the letter of the picture and word that goes with the definition below.

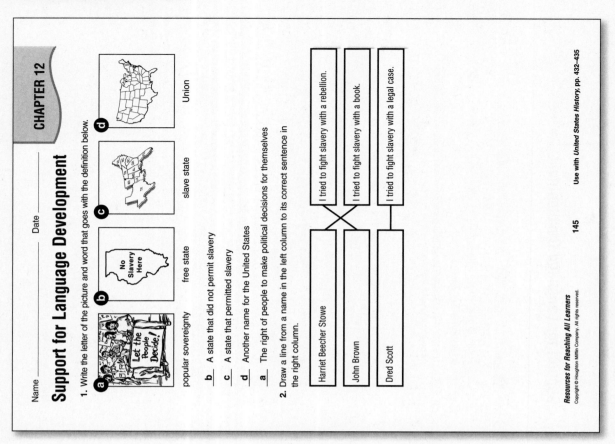

a	b	c	d
popular sovereignty	free state	slave state	Union

b A state that did not permit slavery

c A state that permitted slavery

d Another name for the United States

a The right of people to make political decisions for themselves

2. Draw a line from a name in the left column to its correct sentence in the right column.

Harriet Beecher Stowe — I tried to fight slavery with a rebellion.

John Brown — I tried to fight slavery with a book.

Dred Scott — I tried to fight slavery with a legal case.

145   Use with *United States History*, pp. 432–435

Name _____ Date _____

Support for Language Development

1. Write the letter of the word that goes with the definition below.

a discrimination   **b** Underground Railroad   **c** abolitionist

c Someone who joined the movement to end slavery

b A series of escape routes and hiding places used to bring people out of slavery

a The unfair treatment of particular groups

2. Write the name of the person being described in the boxes on the right.

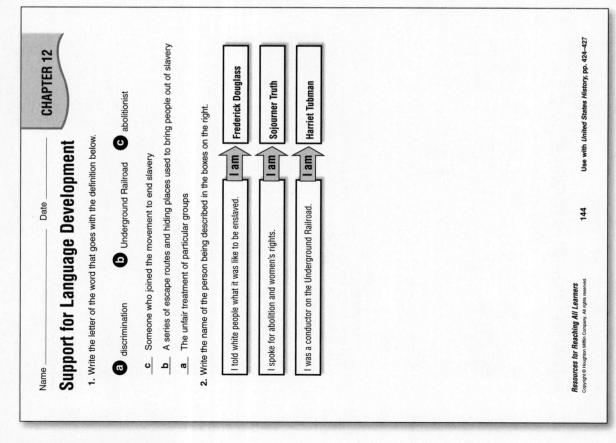

I told white people what it was like to be enslaved. **I am** Frederick Douglass

I spoke for abolition and women's rights. **I am** Sojourner Truth

I was a conductor on the Underground Railroad. **I am** Harriet Tubman

144   Use with *United States History*, pp. 424–427

Answers

Name _____ Date _____

Support for Language Development

1. Write the letter of the picture and word that goes with the definition below.

border states   casualties   draft   emancipation

d   the freeing of enslaved people

b   soldiers who are killed or wounded in war

c   the way an army forces people to be soldiers

a   slave states that stayed in the Union

2. Read the sentences below. Which happened first? Write "1" in front of the first event. Write "2" in front of the second event. Write "3" in front of the third event. Write "4" in front of the fourth event.

3   **A.**   Emancipation Proclamation

2   **B.**   Battle of Antietam

4   **C.**   Battle near Gettysburg, Pennsylvania

1   **D.**   Formation of the Confederacy

3. Read the section in the lesson called "North Against South." In the box labeled "Compare," write how the Union and the Confederacy were alike. In the box labeled "Contrast," write how they were different.

Compare	Contrast
Both the North and the South thought they could **win** quickly.	The **North** had more people and more factories for making weapons and supplies than the **South** .

Name _____ Date _____

Support for Language Development

1. Write the letter of the word that goes with the definition below.

a Confederacy   **b** civil war   **c** secession

c   When part of a country breaks away from the rest

b   A war between two groups of regions within a nation

a   The states that separated from the Union

2. Circle the word that best completes each sentence.

A. The (Republican Party) / Democratic Party opposed slavery.

B. In 1861, eleven northern / (Southern) states left the Union and formed a separate government.

C. Stephen Douglas / (Abraham Lincoln) said slavery was evil, but did not think the government could outlaw it.

D. Southerners / (Northerners) wanted to end slavery.

Answers *continued*

Name _____ Date _____

Support for Language Development

1. Write the letter of the word that goes with the definition below.

a telegraph   **b** total war   **c** desert

b   The strategy of destroying an enemy's resources

c   To leave the army without permission

a   A machine that sends electric signals over wires

2. Read the section of the lesson called "Grant and Lee." In the box labeled "Cause," tell which army was getting stronger. In the box labeled "Effect," fill in the word that tells what happened.

Causes

The **Union** suffered terrible losses, but Grant kept attacking.

Effect

Lee **surrendered** to Grant at Appomattox.

Name _____ Date _____

Support for Language Development

1. Write the vocabulary word on the line next to its meaning.

home front   civilian   camp

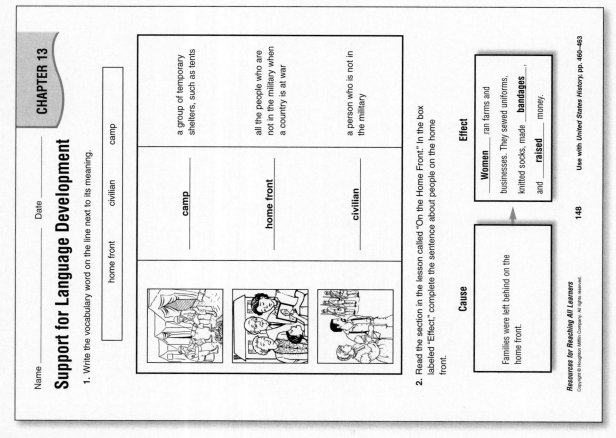

camp — a group of temporary shelters, such as tents

home front — all the people who are not in the military when a country is at war

civilian — a person who is not in the military

2. Read the section in the lesson called "On the Home Front." In the box labeled "Effect," complete the sentence about people on the home front.

Cause

Families were left behind on the home front.

Effect

Women ran farms and businesses. They sewed uniforms, knitted socks, made **bandages**, and **raised** money.

Answers

Name _____ Date _____

Support for Language Development

1. Write the vocabulary word on the line next to its meaning.

sharecropping	Jim Crow	segregation

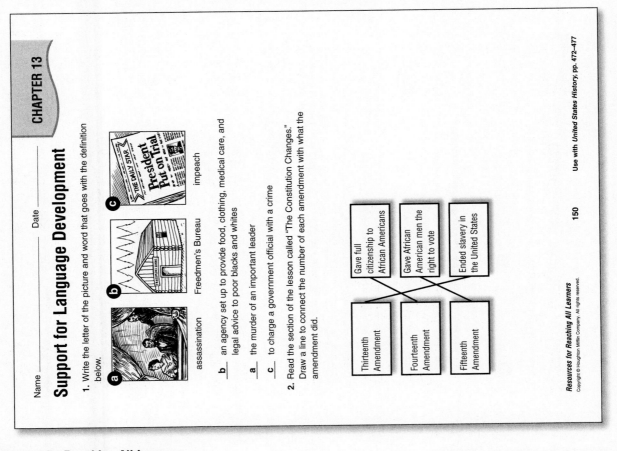

Jim Crow	laws that segregated African Americans from other Americans
segregation	forced separation of races of people
sharecropping	system where farmers used land and gave landowners a share of the crop

2. Read the section of the lesson called "Responses to Reconstruction." Then write the word or words that complete the sentences correctly.

A. **Reconstruction** angered some people in the South.

B. Some people wanted to stop **African** **Americans** from taking part in government.

C. The **Ku** **Klux** **Klan** threatened, beat, and even killed African Americans to keep them from voting.

Name _____ Date _____

Support for Language Development

1. Write the letter of the picture and word that goes with the definition below.

a b c

THE DAILY STAR
President Put on Trial

assassination   Freedmen's Bureau   impeach

b an agency set up to provide food, clothing, medical care, and legal advice to poor blacks and whites

a the murder of an important leader

c to charge a government official with a crime

2. Read the section of the lesson called "The Constitution Changes." Draw a line to connect the number of each amendment with what the amendment did.

Thirteenth Amendment	Gave full citizenship to African Americans
Fourteenth Amendment	Gave African American men the right to vote
Fifteenth Amendment	Ended slavery in the United States

Answers *continued*

Name _____ Date _____

Support for Language Development

1. Write the letter of the word that goes with the definition below.

a prejudice   **b** transcontinental

b From one edge of a continent to the other

a A negative opinion of a group of people, not based on fact

2. Read the section of the lesson called "The Telegraph Helps Communication." For each sentence, circle whether it is true or false.

Using horses, stagecoaches, or steamboats were quick ways to send messages across the country.   True   ~~False~~

The telegraph carried messages from the East Coast to the West Coast in just a few minutes.   ~~True~~   False

3. Read the sentences. Write the letters in the boxes to show what happened first, second, third, and fourth.

A. The transcontinental railway was completed.

B. Congress provided land and money to build the transcontinental railroad.

C. Former soldiers, African Americans, and immigrants laid the tracks.

D. Western farmers made money by shipping cattle and wheat to the East.

| B | first | C | second | A | third | D | fourth |

Name _____ Date _____

Support for Language Development

1. Write the letter of the picture and word that goes with the definition below.

a drought   **b** Exodusters   **c** homestead

a A long period with little or no rain

b African Americans who moved to the Great Plains

c A settler's home and land

2. Read the sentences below. The sentences with letters are problems. The sentences with numbers are solutions. Match each problem with a solution. Write the letters and numbers in the boxes below.

A. There were not many people on the Great Plains to do farm work.

B. The land was dry. There were frequent droughts.

C. There wasn't a lot of wood on the Great Plains.

1. Homesteaders used sod to build homes.

2. Homesteaders dug wells and used windmills to pump water.

3. Homesteaders invented new farm machines.

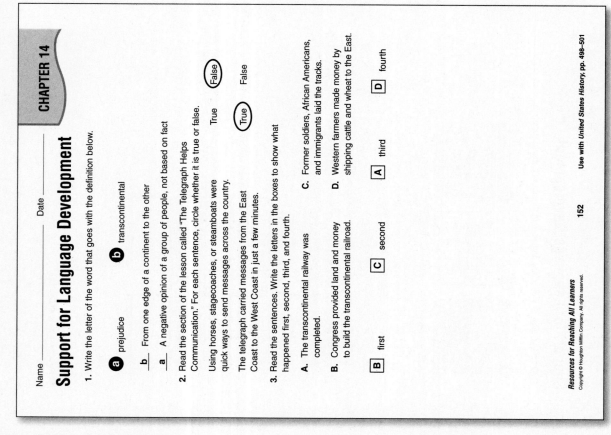

Answers

Name _____ Date _____

Support for Language Development

1. Write the letter of the word that goes with the definition below.

a assimilate   **b** extinct   **c** habitat   **d** reservation

b — When a certain type of plant or animal no longer exists

c — The area where an animal or plant normally lives or grows

d — Land the government reserved for Indians

a — To take in a group and change its culture and traditions

2. Read "War on the Plains" in the lesson. Fill in the missing words below.

Plains Indians fought **soldiers** who tried to force them onto **reservations** .

3. Read the "Government Policy" section. Then complete the sentences.

The government tried to force American Indians to change.

- The government made Indian **religious** **practices** illegal.
- They were not allowed to speak **Indian** **languages** .
- They were not allowed to wear **traditional** **clothing** .

Name _____ Date _____

Support for Language Development

1. Write the letter of the word that goes with the definition below.

a barbed wire   **b** demand   **c** railhead   **d** supply

d — The amount of something that people want to sell at a certain price

a — Wire with sharp points on it

b — The amount of something that people want to buy at a certain price

c — A town where railroad tracks begin or end

2. Supply and demand affect how much things are worth. Read "Demand and Supply for Cattle" in the lesson. Write how the supply and demand affected the price of cattle.

Cause: There were many longhorn cattle in Texas. Not many people wanted to buy them.

Effect: Cattle sold in Texas for only about $4 each.

Cause: There were many people in the North and East that wanted to buy beef and leather. There were not many longhorn cattle.

Effect: Cattle sold in those regions for about $40 each.

3. Read "The End of the Drives" in the lesson. Complete the sentence.

Cattle drives ended because of the invention of **barbed** **wire** , the growth of **railroads** , and because too many cattle grazed on **crowded** **ranges** .

Answers *continued*

Name _____ Date _____

Support for Language Development

1. Write in the letter of the picture and word that goes with each definition.

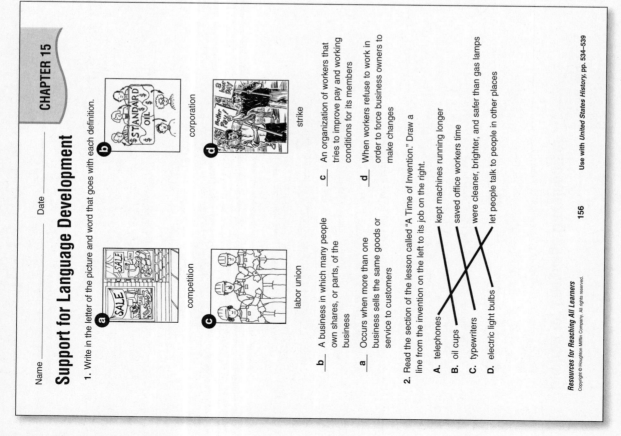

a — SALE / SALE
competition

b — STANDARD OIL
corporation

c — labor union

d — Better Pay!
strike

b A business in which many people own shares, or parts, of the business

a Occurs when more than one business sells the same goods or service to customers

c An organization of workers that tries to improve pay and working conditions for its members

d When workers refuse to work in order to force business owners to make changes

2. Read the section of the lesson called "A Time of Invention." Draw a line from the invention on the left to its job on the right.

A. telephones — kept machines running longer

B. oil cups — saved office workers time

C. typewriters — were cleaner, brighter, and safer than gas lamps

D. electric light bulbs — let people talk to people in other places

---

Name _____ Date _____

Support for Language Development

1. Write the letter of the word that goes with the definition below.

a persecution   **b** ethnic group   **c** tenement

a Unfair treatment or punishment

c A poorly built apartment building

b A group of people who share a culture or language

2. Read the section in the lesson called "Arriving in America." Write the word or words that complete each sentence correctly.

A. Some immigrants came to the United States to escape
persecution .

B. Other immigrants were looking for **work** .

C. Most immigrants found **political freedom** in America.

3. Read the section of the lesson called "Laws Against Immigration." Then read the main idea below. Complete the details with two other jobs that immigrants had in the United States.

Immigrants helped the United States become one of the richest and fastest-growing countries in the world.

Immigrants built thousands of miles of **railroads**

Immigrants dug deep **coal mines**

Immigrants worked in **factories**

Answers

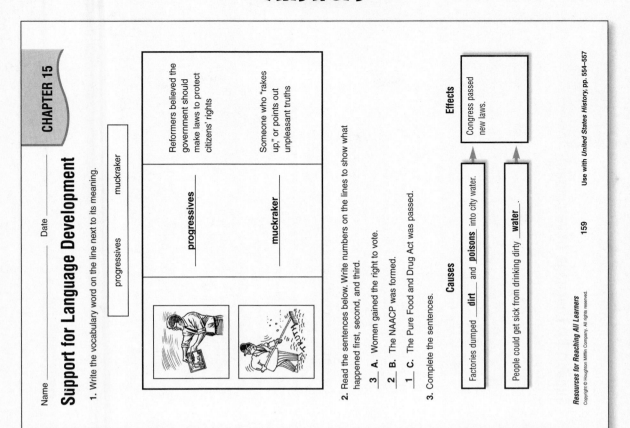

Name _____ Date _____

Support for Language Development

1. Write the vocabulary word on the line next to its meaning.

progressives   muckraker

progressives — Reformers believed the government should make laws to protect citizens' rights

muckraker — Someone who "rakes up," or points out unpleasant truths

2. Read the sentences below. Write numbers on the lines to show what happened first, second, and third.

___3___ **A.** Women gained the right to vote.

___2___ **B.** The NAACP was formed.

___1___ **C.** The Pure Food and Drug Act was passed.

3. Complete the sentences.

Causes	Effects
Factories dumped **dirt** and **poisons** into city water.	Congress passed new laws.
People could get sick from drinking dirty **water**.	

159   Use with *United States History*, pp. 554–557

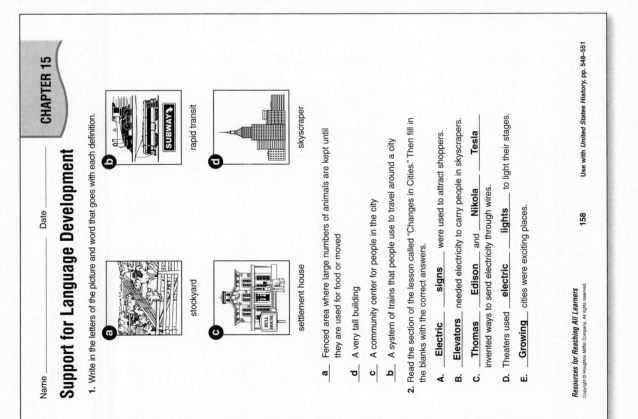

Name _____ Date _____

Support for Language Development

1. Write in the letters of the picture and word that goes with each definition.

stockyard

rapid transit

settlement house

skyscraper

___a___ Fenced area where large numbers of animals are kept until they are used for food or moved

___d___ A very tall building

___c___ A community center for people in the city

___b___ A system of trains that people use to travel around a city

2. Read the section of the lesson called "Changes in Cities." Then fill in the blanks with the correct answers.

A. **Electric** **signs** were used to attract shoppers.

B. **Elevators** needed electricity to carry people in skyscrapers.

C. **Thomas** **Edison** and **Nikola** **Tesla** invented ways to send electricity through wires.

D. Theaters used **electric** **lights** to light their stages.

E. **Growing** cities were exciting places.

158   Use with *United States History*, pp. 548–551

Answers continued

Name _____ Date _____

Support for Language Development

1. Write the letter of the word that goes with the definition below.

a alliance   **b** trench warfare   **c** armistice   **d** isolationism

__c__   An agreement to stop fighting

__b__   A type of fighting in which soldiers crouch down in trenches and fire their weapons from there

__d__   When a country stays out of other countries' affairs

__a__   An agreement between nations to work together and to defend each other

2. Read the section of the lesson called "America Enters the War." Then read the sentences below. Write a T if the sentence is true and an F if the sentence is false.

__F__   The United States entered the war because Austria-Hungary attacked Serbia.

__T__   The United States joined the war after Germany began attacking American ships.

__F__   The United States joined the Central Powers to make the world safe for democracy.

3. Read the sentences below. Number the events in the order they happened.

__4__   **A.** The United States joined the Allies.

__2__   **B.** Austria-Hungary declared war on Serbia.

__1__   **C.** Nations made alliances.

__3__   **D.** The Allies and the Central Powers declared war on one another.

__5__   **E.** The Allies won the war.

Name _____ Date _____

Support for Language Development

1. Write the letter of the word that goes with the definition below.

a imperialism   **b** isthmus

__a__   When nations gain colonies to build empires

__b__   A narrow strip of land with water on two sides

2. Read the section of the lesson called "Building the Panama Canal." Then complete the sentences below.

The United States built the Panama Canal at the **isthmus** of Panama.

→ **Ships** no longer had to travel around South America.

→ Ships sailing from the east or west coasts of the United States saved thousands of miles. So, trade **increased**.

Answers

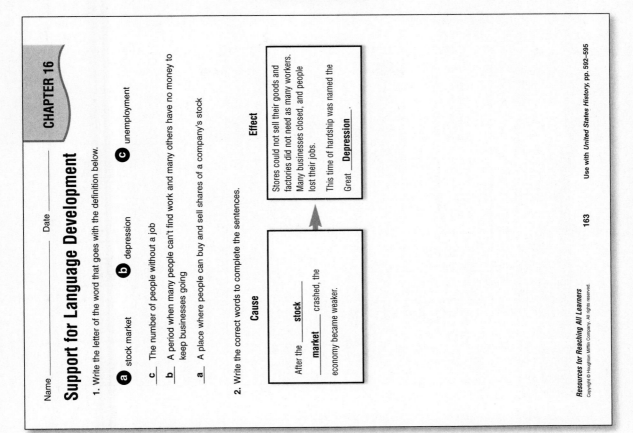

Name _____ Date _____

Support for Language Development

1. Write the letter of the word that goes with the definition below.

a stock market   **b** depression   **c** unemployment

c The number of people without a job

b A period when many people can't find work and many others have no money to keep businesses going

a A place where people can buy and sell shares of a company's stock

2. Write the correct words to complete the sentences.

Cause

After the **stock** **market** crashed, the economy became weaker.

Effect

Stores could not sell their goods and factories did not need as many workers. Many businesses closed, and people lost their jobs.

This time of hardship was named the Great **Depression**.

Resources for Reaching All Learners
Copyright © Houghton Mifflin Company. All rights reserved.

163   Use with *United States History*, pp. 592–595

Name _____ Date _____

Support for Language Development

1. Write the vocabulary word on the line next to its meaning.

assembly line   credit   division of labor

credit : Getting an item today, but paying for it later with small payments

assembly line : A line of workers or machines that puts a product together piece by piece

division of labor : When workers perform different parts of a large task

2. Read the section of the lesson called "Consumer Goods and Credit." Then write the correct word to complete the sentence.

Causes

The economy boomed during the 1920s. Americans believed it would keep growing.

Effects

Many people used **credit** to buy refrigerators and washing machines.

Others **invested** their money in things such as land and paintings.

Resources for Reaching All Learners
Copyright © Houghton Mifflin Company. All rights reserved.

162   Use with *United States History*, pp. 586–589

Answers *continued*

CHAPTER 17

Name _____ Date _____

Support for Language Development

1. Write the vocabulary word on the line next to its meaning.

> communism   capitalism   arms race

arms race	a contest between nations to build bigger and more powerful weapons
communism	a system in which the government controls production and owns the nation's natural and capital resources
capitalism	a system in which ordinary people and businesses control the production of goods and services

2. The United States and the Soviet Union had several conflicts during the Cold War. Reread "Cold War Conflicts" and write the names of two other conflicts in the boxes.

After World War II, the United States and the Soviet Union fought a war of ideas called the Cold War.

| Berlin Airlift | Korean War | Cuban Missile Crisis |

Resources for Reaching All Learners 165 Use with *United States History*, pp. 612–615
Copyright © Houghton Mifflin Company. All rights reserved.

CHAPTER 16

Name _____ Date _____

Support for Language Development

1. Write the letter of the word and picture next to the correct definition.

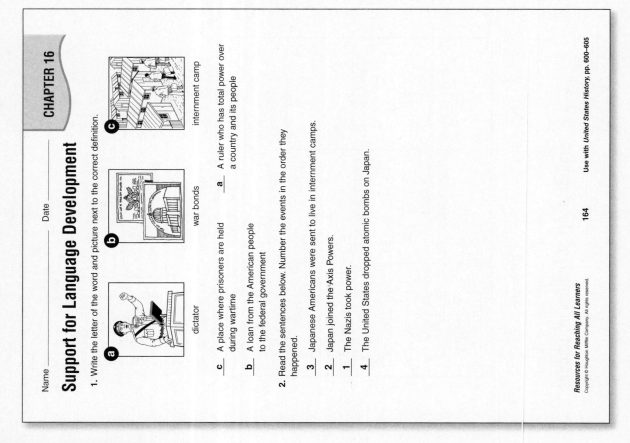

dictator   war bonds   internment camp

a A ruler who has total power over a country and its people

c A place where prisoners are held during wartime

b A loan from the American people to the federal government

2. Read the sentences below. Number the events in the order they happened.

3 Japanese Americans were sent to live in internment camps.

2 Japan joined the Axis Powers.

1 The Nazis took power.

4 The United States dropped atomic bombs on Japan.

Resources for Reaching All Learners 164 Use with *United States History*, pp. 600–605
Copyright © Houghton Mifflin Company. All rights reserved.

Resources for Reaching All Learners
Copyright © Houghton Mifflin Company. All rights reserved.

248

Use with *United States History*

Answers

Name _____ Date _____

Support for Language Development

1. Write the letter of the word that goes with the definition below.

a veteran   **b** baby boom   **c** budget

__b__ Increase of babies born after World War II

__c__ A plan for saving and spending income

__a__ A person who has served in the military

2. Read the sentences below. Then write a letter for each problem (the cause) in the boxes on the left. Write a number for the sentence that tells the effect (what happened because of the cause) in the boxes on the right.

A. Businesses grew and workers had more income.

B. People bought cars in record numbers.

1. People drove to national parks, movies, and restaurants.

2. Families could make more choices about what to buy.

Causes   **Effects**

A → 2

B → 1

Name _____ Date _____

Support for Language Development

1. Write the vocabulary word on the line next to its meaning.

civil rights   desegregation   nonviolent protest

nonviolent protest	a way of bringing change without using violence
civil rights	the rights and freedoms that countries guarantee their citizens
desegregation	ending the separation of people by racial or ethnic group

2. Reread the section of the lesson called "Civil Rights Victories." In the boxes, write the names of two more Acts that were passed to recognize equal rights.

1	1954: desegregation of all public schools
2	1956: desegregation of buses
3	Civil Rights Act of 1964
4	Voting Rights Act of 1965

CHAPTER 18

Name _____ Date _____

Support for Language Development

1. Write the letter of the word that goes with the definition below.

a accord   **b** resign   **c** migrant worker

b To give up your job

c A person who moves from place to place to find work, mostly on farms

a An agreement

2. Read the section called "The Carter Years" in your textbook. In the box labeled "Solution," tell what President Carter did to help solve the conflict in the Middle East.

Problem

Israel and Egypt had been enemies for 30 years.

Solution

In 1978, President Carter helped the leaders sign a __peace__ __agreement__

CHAPTER 17

Name _____ Date _____

Support for Language Development

1. Write the vocabulary word on the line next to its meaning.

space race   demonstration   cease-fire

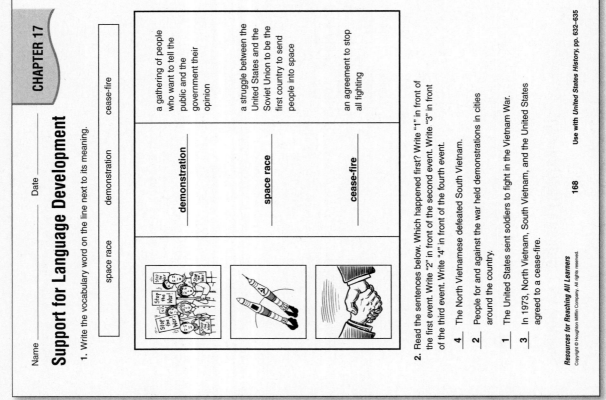

demonstration — a gathering of people who want to tell the public and the government their opinion

space race — a struggle between the United States and the Soviet Union to be the first country to send people into space

cease-fire — an agreement to stop all fighting

2. Read the sentences below. Which happened first? Write "1" in front of the first event. Write "2" in front of the second event. Write "3" in front of the third event. Write "4" in front of the fourth event.

4 The North Vietnamese defeated South Vietnam.

2 People for and against the war held demonstrations in cities around the country.

1 The United States sent soldiers to fight in the Vietnam War.

3 In 1973, North Vietnam, South Vietnam, and the United States agreed to a cease-fire.

Answers

Name _____ Date _____

Support for Language Development

1. Write the letter of the picture and word that goes with each definition below.

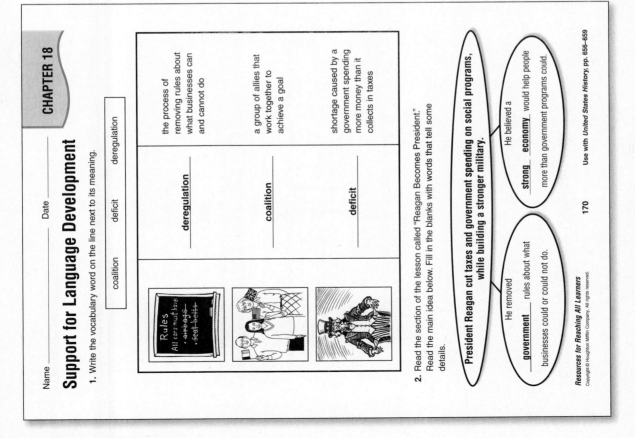

a

b

c
Internet

c links computers around the world with each other

b treaties among countries that trade with one another — free-trade agreement

a uses the most recent knowledge and equipment — high-tech

2. Read the sentences below. Which one happened first? Write "1" in front of the first event. Write "2" in front of the second event. Write "3" in front of the third event.

2 A. By 1998, the United States had a budget surplus.

3 B. Clinton was impeached by the House of Representatives.

1 C. There was a budget deficit from the Reagan years.

3. Write the word or words that complete the sentence correctly.

A. During the Clinton presidency the economy **grew** .

B. In the 1990s, more people in the United States found work in **service** **jobs** than in manufacturing or farming.

C. Trade between nations increased as new technology improved **communication** and **transportation** .

D. In the 1990s free-trade agreements were signed by the United States, **Mexico** , and **Canada** .

171   Use with *United States History*, pp. 664–669

Name _____ Date _____

Support for Language Development

1. Write the vocabulary word on the line next to its meaning.

coalition	deficit	deregulation

Rules All cars must have: · airbags · seat belts	**deregulation**	the process of removing rules about what businesses can and cannot do
	coalition	a group of allies that work together to achieve a goal
	deficit	shortage caused by a government spending more money than it collects in taxes

2. Read the section of the lesson called "Reagan Becomes President." Read the main idea below. Fill in the blanks with words that tell some details.

President Reagan cut taxes and government spending on social programs, while building a stronger military.

He believed a **strong** **economy** would help people more than government programs could.

He removed **government** rules about what businesses could or could not do.

170   Use with *United States History*, pp. 656–659

Answers *continued*

Name _____ Date _____

Support for Language Development

1. Write the letter of the word that goes with the definition below.

a multicultural **b** province **c** maquiladora

___b___ A political region of a country that is similar to a state

___a___ Having many cultural traditions

___c___ A factory in Mexico near the U.S. Border

2. Choose the best words to complete the sentence.

Canada	Mexico
With many immigrants, Canada is a **multicultural** society.	Most **Mexicans** are mestizos, people of both Spanish and Mexican Indian ancestry.

Name _____ Date _____

Support for Language Development

1. Write the letter of the word that goes with the definition below.

a popular vote **b** millennium **c** terrorism **d** Electoral College

___d___ Representatives, called electors, from each state

___a___ The vote of individual citizens

___c___ The use of violence against ordinary people to achieve a political goal

___b___ A period of 10 centuries, or 1,000 years

2. Read the section of the lesson called "The 2000 Election." In the box labeled "Cause" tell who decided that the votes would not be counted again.

Causes

The **Supreme Court** decided that the votes in Florida would not be counted again.

Effects

Bush won the first count, so he won Florida's electoral votes and became President.

3. Read the sentences below. Which happened first? Write "1" in front of the first event. Write "2" in front of the second event. Write "3" in front of the third event. Write "4" in front of the fourth event.

___1___ A. Bush becomes President of the United States.

___4___ B. United States goes to war in Iraq.

___2___ C. Terrorist attacks on New York and Washington, D.C.

___3___ D. United States goes to war in Afghanistan.

Answers

Name _____ Date _____

Support for Language Development

1. Write the letter of the picture that goes with the definition below.

naturalization   register   responsibility   volunteer

a the process of learning the laws of the country and the rights and duties of citizens

d a person who helps other people without being paid

c a duty that people are expected to fulfill

b to sign up

2. Fill in the blanks with the correct word.

A. Immigrants can become citizens after they go through a legal process called **naturalization**.

B. At age 18, citizens can **register** to vote.

C. Organizations in every community depend on the time and talent of **volunteers**.

D. Citizens have a **responsibility** to serve on juries in law courts.

3. Read the sections in the lesson called "Voting and Other Rights" and "Citizens' Responsibilities." Then read the phrases below. Write the letter that is in front of the phrase in the column under "Rights" or "Responsibilities."

A. obeying the law
B. speaking freely
C. paying taxes
D. practicing religion

Rights	Responsibilities
B	A
D	C

Name _____ Date _____

Support for Language Development

1. Write the letter of the word that goes with the definition below.

a heritage   **b** refugee   **c** motto

b A person who escapes war or other danger and seeks safety in another country

a Something that is passed down from one generation to the next

c A short statement that expresses an ideal or a goal

2. Fill in the blank with the correct word.

Everyone in the United States lives under the Constitution and the Bill of Rights.

The Constitution and the Bill of Rights are the democratic **heritage** of all people in the United States.
